Lecture Notes in Computer Science 12574

More information about this subseries at http://www.springer.com/series/7411

Francine Krief · Hasnaâ Aniss ·
Léo Mendiboure · Serge Chaumette ·
Marion Berbineau (Eds.)

Communication Technologies for Vehicles

15th International Workshop
Nets4Cars/Nets4Trains/Nets4Aircraft 2020
Bordeaux, France, November 16–17, 2020
Proceedings

 Springer

Editors
Francine Krief 🆔
LaBRI Lab
Bordeaux INP
Talence, France

Léo Mendiboure 🆔
COSYS-ERENA
Université Gustave Eiffel
Pessac, France

Marion Berbineau 🆔
COSYS-LEOST
Université Gustave Eiffel
Villeneuve d'Ascq, France

Hasnaâ Aniss 🆔
COSYS-ERENA
Université Gustave Eiffel
Pessac, France

Serge Chaumette 🆔
LaBRI Lab
Bordeaux INP
Talence, France

ISSN 0302-9743   ISSN 1611-3349   (electronic)
Lecture Notes in Computer Science
ISBN 978-3-030-66029-1   ISBN 978-3-030-66030-7   (eBook)
https://doi.org/10.1007/978-3-030-66030-7

LNCS Sublibrary: SL5 – Computer Communication Networks and Telecommunications

This Springer imprint is published by the registered company Springer Nature Switzerland AG
The registered company address is: Gewerbestrasse 11, 6330 Cham, Switzerland

Preface

The Communication Technologies for Vehicles Workshop series provides an international forum on the latest technologies and research in the field of intra- and inter-vehicles communications. This workshop is organized annually to present original research results in areas related to the physical layer, communication protocols and standards, mobility and traffic models, experimental and field operational testing, and performance analysis.

First launched by Tsutomu Tsuboi, Alexey Vinel, and Frei Liu in Saint Petersburg, Russia (2009), the workshop has been held in Newcastle upon Tyne, UK (2010), Oberpfaffenhofen, Germany (2011), Vilnius, Lithuania (2012), Villeneuve-d'Ascq, France (2013), Offenburg, Germany (2014 Spring), Saint Petersburg, Russia (2014 Fall), Sousse, Tunisia (2015), San Sebastiàn, Spain (2016), Toulouse, France (2017), Madrid, Spain (2018), and Colmar, France (2019). These proceedings gather the papers presented at the 15th edition of the workshop, which took place in Bordeaux, France, in November 2020. The workshop was supported by the University of Bordeaux, the Gustave Eiffel University, and the Informatics Research Bordeaux Laboratory (LaBRI), France.

The call for papers resulted in 22 submissions. Each of them was assigned to the Technical Program Committee members and 18 submissions were accepted for publication. Each paper had three reviewers. The order of the papers in these proceedings corresponds to the workshop program.

This year the keynote speakers were:

- Léo Mendiboure, "The Blockchain: a decentralized solution for security and privacy protection in vehicular networks," University of Bordeaux, France
- Divitha Seetharamdoo, "Integration of Antennas for communication systems in complex platforms," Gustave Eiffel University, France
- Grégoire Danoy, "UAV swarms: From theoretical mobility models to proof of concept," University of Luxembourg, Luxembourg

We extend a sincere thank you to all the authors who submitted the results of their recent works and to all the members of the Technical Program Committee.

November 2020

Francine Krief
Hasnaâ Aniss
Léo Mendiboure
Serge Chaumette
Marion Berbineau

Organization

Organizing Committee

Hasnaâ Aniss   Gustave Eiffel University, France
Marion Berbineau   Gustave Eiffel University, France
Serge Chaumette   University of Bordeaux, France
Auriane Dantès   CNRS, France
Katel Guérin   University of Bordeaux, France
Abdelmename Hedhli   Gustave Eiffel University, France
Francine Krief   Bordeaux INP, France
Léo Mendiboure   University of Bordeaux, France

Steering Committee

Marion Berbineau   Gustave Eiffel University, France
Benoît Hilt   University of Upper Alsace, France
Juan Moreno   Metro Madrid, Spain
  Garcia-Loygorri
Alain Pirovano   National School of Civil Aviation, France
Alexey Vinel   Halmstad University, Sweden

TCP Co-chairs (Nets4Cars)

Toufik Ahmed   Bordeaux INP, France
Antonio Freitas   Clermont Auvergne University, France
Farzin Godarzi   Federal Highway Research Institute, Germany
Nadir Hakem   University of Quebec in Abitibi-Temiscamingue,
                                  Canada
Mohamed Kassab   Higher Institute of Computer Science and Mathematics
                                  of Monastir, Tunisia
Houda Labiod   Telecom ParisTech, France
Mohamed Mosbah   Bordeaux INP, France
Alexey Vinel   Halmstad University, Sweden

TCP Co-chairs (Nets4Trains)

Hervé Bonneville   Mitsubishi Electric R&D Centre Europe, France
Iyad Dayoub   University Polytechnic Hauts-de-France, France
Jaizki Mendizabla   Centre of Studies and Technical Investigations
                                  of Gipuzkoa, Spain
Juan Moreno   Metro Madrid, Spain
  Garcia-Loygorri

Stephan Sand	German Aerospace Center, Germany
José Soler	Technical University of Denmark, Denmark
Iñaki Val	IKERLAN, Spain

TCP Co-chairs (Nets4Aircraft)

Serge Chaumette	University of Bordeaux, France
Alain Pirovano	National School of Civil Aviation, France
Damien Roque	French Aeronautics and Space Institute, France

Contents

Road

Simulation of Cyberattacks in ITS-G5 Systems 3
  Jean Cassou-Mounat, Houda Labiod, and Rida Khatoun

Towards an Extensible Security Monitoring Architecture
for Vehicular Networks 15
  Amir Teshome Wonjiga and Marc Lacoste

Anomaly Detection on Roads Using C-ITS Messages 25
  Juliet Chebet Moso, Ramzi Boutahala, Brice Leblanc, Hacène Fouchal,
  Cyril de Runz, Stephane Cormier, and John Wandeto

Leveraging GPS Data for Vehicle Maneuver Detection 39
  Abdallah Aymen, Jemili Imen, Mabrouk Sabra, and Mohamed Mosbah

Analysis and Comparison of IEEE 802.11p and IEEE 802.11bd 55
  Badreddine Yacine Yacheur, Toufik Ahmed, and Mohamed Mosbah

An Investigation of the Bits Corruption in the IEEE 802.11p 66
  Sébastien Bindel, Dorine Tabary, Soumia Bourebia, Frédéric Drouhin,
  and Benoît Hilt

Measurements of Communication Channel in Different Scenarios
with the Channel Characterization Tool System 78
  Nerea Fernández-Berrueta, Iker Moya, Javier Añorga, Mario Monterde,
  Jaione Arrizabalaga, and Jon Goya

Survey on Decision-Making Algorithms for Network Selection
in Heterogeneous Architectures 89
  Ali Mamadou Mamadou, Mouna Karoui, Gerard Chalhoub,
  and Antonio Freitas

Radio Access Technologies Selection in Vehicular Networks:
State-of-the-Art and Perspectives for Autonomous Connected Vehicles 99
  Sidoine Juicielle Kambiré, Hasnaâ Aniss, Francine Krief,
  Sassi Maaloul, and Marion Berbineau

Toward the Integration of V2V Based Clusters in a Global Infrastructure
Network for Vehicles. 113
  Sabrine Belmekki, Martine Wahl, Patrick Sondi, Dominique Gruyer,
  and Charles Tatkeu

Train

Integration of Antennas for Communication System
on Complex Platforms.. 125
  Naveen Kumar, Ozuem Chukwuka, and Divitha Seetharamdoo

5G for Remote Driving of Trains 137
  Yamen Alsaba, Marion Berbineau, Iyad Dayoub, Emilie Masson,
  Gemma Morral Adell, and Eric Robert

Sensing the Health of the Catenary-Pantograph Contact on Railway
Vehicles with Radio Receivers: Early Results................. 148
  Juan Moreno, Julián Martín Jarillo, and Sonsoles García-Albertos

Freight Telematics Systems: An Intelligent Wagon 157
  Roberto C. Ramirez, Iker Moya, Imanol Puy, Unai Alvarado, Iñigo Adin,
  and Jaizki Mendizabal

NEWNECTAR: A New gEneration of Adaptable Wireless Sensor NEtwork
for Way Side objeCTs in rAilway enviRonments 166
  Dereje Mechal Molla, Hakim Badis, Laurent George,
  and Marion Berbineau

Air

Allowing People to Communicate After a Disaster Using FANETs 181
  Frédéric Guinand, François Guérin, and Pawel Łubniewski

Remote ID and Vehicle-to-Vehicle Communications for Unmanned
Aircraft System Traffic Management 194
  Ethan Murrell, Zach Walker, Eric King, and Kamesh Namuduri

A Unified Smart Mobility System Integrating Terrestrial, Aerial and Marine
Intelligent Vehicles 203
  Chahrazed Ksouri, Imen Jemili, Mohamed Mosbah,
  and Abdelfettah Belghith

Author Index 215

Road

Simulation of Cyberattacks in ITS-G5 Systems

Jean Cassou-Mounat[1]($\boxtimes$), Houda Labiod[2]($\boxtimes$), and Rida Khatoun[2]

[1] Transpolis, 01500 Saint-Maurice-de-Rémens, France
jean.cassou-mounat@transpolis.fr
[2] Telecom Paris, Institut Polytechnique de Paris, LTCI, 91120 Palaiseau, France
{houda.labiod,rida.khatoun}@telecom-paris.fr

Abstract. Connected vehicles bring new challenges for communication technologies. Vehicles become capable of performing actions depending on wireless V2X communications (ex: automatic emergency braking, crossing paths with other vehicles, handling platooning situations). Despite being essential in the case of industrial deployments, cybersecurity also acts as a scientific lock to secure the system from its conception. Facing with the increasing number of cyberattacks, but also with the increasing of the attack surface of vehicles, the securing of V2X communications is necessary. However, all existing attacks cannot always be tested with proper hardware. The simulation software approach allows us to free ourselves from this constraint. In this paper, we investigate the security vulnerabilities of ITS-G5 (European DSRC) communications in the presence of outside attackers. We considered 4 attacks: jamming, replay, falsification and network congestion. We used VENTOS platform to execute the different scenarios and demonstrated with it that these attacks have a real impact on vehicle's driving.

Keywords: C-ITS · ITS-G5 · IEEE 802.11p · DSRC · Cybersecurity · Simulation · Jamming attack · Replay attack · Falsification attack · Congestion attack

1 Introduction

Cooperative Intelligent Transport Systems (C-ITS), refer to the cooperation between multiple subsystems including road users, base stations, roadside infrastructure operators, traffic signals, etc. This cooperation aims to provide more safety on the roads. The ultimate goal of next-generation vehicle-to-everything (V2X) communication systems is enabling accident-free and safer driving, efficient road capacity, cooperative automated driving and other use cases using roadway efficiently. To achieve this goal, the communication system will need to enable a diverse set of use cases, each with a specific set of requirements. As the first vehicles equipped with V2X technology begin to appear on the market, cyber-attacks are hovering over this technology. History has previously shown that attacks on production vehicles could result in dramatic consequences for the vehicle's occupants [1]. Therefore, early identification of vulnerabilities is essential in order to reduce risks. Communication technologies, in the form of V2X communication, will play a key role. We find different communication modes: 1) vehicle-to-vehicle (V2V); 2)

© Springer Nature Switzerland AG 2020
F. Krief et al. (Eds.): Nets4Cars/Nets4Trains/Nets4Aircraft 2020, LNCS 12574, pp. 3–14, 2020.
https://doi.org/10.1007/978-3-030-66030-7_1

vehicle-to-infrastructure (V2I), e.g., communication with roadside units (RSUs), traffic lights, or, in the case of a cellular network, a base station; 3) vehicle-to-pedestrian; and 4) vehicle-to-network (V2N), where the vehicle connects to an entity within the network, e.g., a back-end server or a traffic information system.

Several V2X technologies exist today. Among them, there are two major ones: ITS-G5 (short range) and LTE-V2X (both short and long range). ITS-G5 is an access technology designed by ETSI for V2X communications and based on IEEE 802.11p physical layer [2]. As VW has shown, along with the Golf 8 and ID.3, ITS-G5 technology is the most advanced V2X communication [3]; therefore, we focus on it in this article. QoS management as well as security management are taken into account in the ITS-G5 stack, as shown in Fig. 1. The Decentralized Congestion Control (DCC) is an example of mechanism that is used to mitigate network congestion at the MAC layer [4].

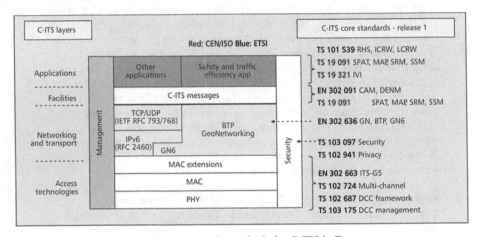

Fig. 1. Protocol stack standards for C-ITS in Europe

The Public Key Infrastructure (PKI) system is a key paradigm used to secure V2X communications and enable trust in the whole ecosystem related to C-ITS systems. This ITS-specific PKI infrastructure brings authenticity and integrity for V2X messages [5]. The European Telecommunication Standard Institute (ETSI) has indeed defined numerous security requirements depending on the content of the exchanged messages and the provided ITS use cases (day 1, day 2 and day 3): authentication, confidentiality, integrity, non-repudiation, privacy, availability. However, C-ITS systems are very complex and are subject of a huge number of various attacks and their main purpose is to reduce these attacks' surfaces. Moreover, all existing attacks cannot always be tested with real proper hardware equipment.

In order to carry studies of cyber-attacks on C-ITS systems, numerous simulation tools have emerged. However, few of them incorporate security. In the same way, the attacking tools developed for V2X are rare. Among these few solutions, the simulation software VENTOS [6] interests us particularly because of its stack developed to study security attacks in collaborative driving situations. Our paper aims to investigate the effectiveness of using such a C-ITS simulation tool considering cyberattacks and more specifically analyzing four types of attacks: jamming attack, replay attack, falsification attack and congestion attack.

Other articles found in the literature also used VENTOS in their study [7, 8]. However, their analysis focuses more on comparisons between technologies or on pure CACC.

The remainder of this paper is organized as follows. Section 2 briefly describes related works on cyberattack taxonomies and C-ITS simulation tools and platforms. Section 3 details our simulation study for each attack use case. Finally, Sect. 4 concludes this paper and gives some perspectives.

2 Related Work

Cybersecurity in connected vehicles has been a major subject for years. This topic appears more and more critical with the increase of on-board connectivity and remote control, thus increasing the exposure area. Therefore, many articles regarding ITS-G5, simulation and security need to be considered. This section intends to depict the state of the art on cyber-attacks simulations in ITS-G5 systems.

2.1 Cyber-Attack Taxonomy

Since the birth of this type of communication at the beginning of the 2000s in the US, the security threats in DSRC/WAVE[1] have been highlighted [9–11]. As shown in Fig. 2, most of the attack classes found in more basic communication systems are also present here: spoofing, tampering, repudiation, information disclosure, denial of service and elevation of privilege. For example, DoS attacks aims to paralyze the communication between the network and the user. It can be of two types: message flooding or jamming signal. Regarding the first type, an attack could consist in the generation of a huge amount of messages on the control channel (CCH), or on the service channel (SCH). In that way, On-board Units (OBUs) and Roadside Units (RSUs) could not process the data. From another side, a jamming attack would create interference on the physical layer. Another example, in the spoofing family is GPS spoofing, which is also a threat for V2X. In this attack, attackers could broadcast false radio signals thanks to a GPS satellite simulator in order to make the vehicle believe that it is somewhere else. Many known attacks have been widely analyzed. The most famous one is the Jeep Cherokee's vulnerability that led two cybersecurity researchers to remotely hack a driving vehicle [1]. This attack raised awareness regarding the possibility of a remote attack. Indeed, many researches had been carried out on the CAN bus [12] to alleviate this weakness.

To help us to choose some relevant attacks to study, we used a threat analysis defined in [14]. In this article, authors sorted attacks by motivation, difficulty, likelihood, impact and risk, in order to emphasize the major ones. As all kind of attacks cannot be analyzed in one article, we chose jamming, replay, falsification and congestion attacks. The ease of a jamming attack added to it's a quite high impact makes it a likely scenario. The difficulty of replay and falsification attacks reduces the risk but make their impact higher. However, to the best of our knowledge, no paper deals with the threats related to congestion despite the strong impact on quality of communication.

---

[1] Wireless Access in Vehicular Environments - US access layer, equivalent to the European ITS-G5.

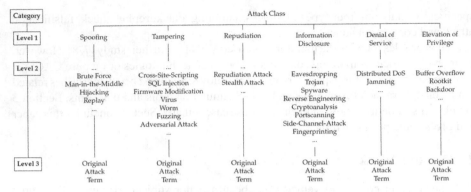

Fig. 2. Classification attack [13]

2.2 C-ITS Simulation Tools and Platforms

To analyze the selected four types of attacks, we opted for the use of a simulation tool. The use of simulation software to study vulnerabilities in C-ITS communication protocols is fairly recent. The first simulation software that embeds C-ITS layers appears in early 2010. There are a number of vehicle traffic simulators available (cf. Fig. 3). Some of them fit into a strict analysis of the road network, while others go beyond this by adding a DSRC communication layer. Most of them are based on the SUMO software. Specific software layers are added as needed.

Software	VEINS	VANETZA	ARTERY	VENTOS	ITETRIS	TATA ELXSI & SPIRENT
Type	Public OpenSource	Public OpenSource	Public OpenSource	Public OpenSource	Public	Private
Traffic software	SUMO	/	SUMO	SUMO	SUMO	Proprietary software
V2X Layer	Proprietary software	/	VEINS	VEINS	Proprietary software	Proprietary software
Target	Research	Research	Research	Research	Research	Benchmarking and validation

Fig. 3. C-ITS simulation tools and platforms

We utilized VENTOS (for VEhicular NeTwork Open Simulator) to study some of the discussed attacks on a V2X vehicle system. VENTOS is an integrated simulator devoted to study the vehicle traffic, collaborative driving and vehicle-infrastructure interaction. It made up of many different features: Adaptive Cruise Control (ACC), Cooperative Adaptive Cruise Control (CACC), platoon management protocol, Traffic Signal Control, etc. VENTOS is based on three modules. Its modular structure is illustrated in

Fig. 4. Veins [15] deals with the wireless communication, including multi-channel operation, noise and interference effects [16]. It also includes WAVE higher layer model for
sending Basic Safety Messages (BSM) or Cooperative Awareness Messages (CAM).
OMNET++ is a modular simulation infrastructure allowing to interface software and
to launch calculations. Finally, SUMO is a traffic simulator. It is used in particular for
simulations in an urban environment. VENTOS developers made the decision to have
particularly developed lower layers. They have chosen to set layer 3 (transport layer)
aside in its operation, thus simplifying the architecture into a simple PHY-MAC-APPLI
trio. As in a TCP-IP protocol, messages are encapsulated.

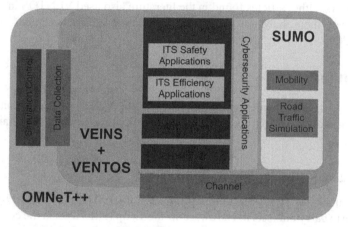

Fig. 4. Modular structure of VENTOS [15]

In VENTOS, several factors influence the decoding of a packet: the location of transmitter and receiver, the characteristics of the antenna, multi-path transmission, blocking
obstacle and interference from other transmitting nodes. In order to have a more realistic
radio layer, the software bases its channel description through a framework (MiXiM)
that models radio signals and provides a mathematical toolbox to work on them. The
Signal-to-Interference-plus-Noise-Ratio (SINR) is then calculated, in order to feed a Bit
Error Rate (BER) model according to the type of studied modulation (BPSK, QPSK,
QAM, etc.). The BER of the header and the payload data are calculated separately, then
applied to the length of the packet to calculate the Packet Error Rate (PER). The packet
is then transmitted to the MAC layer.

The PHY layer also includes a modeling of the transmit/receive antennas. Due to the
complexity of the latter, a wide range of configurations is proposed. In the simulations
carried out in our work, the choice was made to use a monopole antenna positioned
on the roof of the car. The behavior of the MAC layer in VENTOS can be specified in
the form of a state machine. Transitions between states are triggered after the end of a
counting, as in backoff algorithms. Because of its position between the PHY layer and
the APPLI layer, packets can arrive from the upper layer whatever the state of the MAC
layer, thus implying a duplication of the state machine. The software also highlights
the development of important features of MAC layers as carrier detection, collision

avoidance (CSMA/CA) and message acknowledgements according to the protocol used. As mentioned above, VENTOS includes a higher layer model of the DSRC/WAVE stack. It enables channel hopping (switching between CCH and SCH) according to the standard. It further includes Wave Short Message (WSM) handling, and periodic beaconing for sending WAVE service announcements (BSMs and/or CAMs). In order to study security attacks in collaborative driving, VENTOS provides a module to create adversary vehicles. The tool mentioned above fulfils then the expected criteria for our analysis. Its precise definition of PHY and MAC layer makes it a perceptive tool for our analysis. However, the limit on the upper layers will be one of the limits of our analysis, as no simulator can combine the criteria of cybersecurity and the accurate definition of the higher layers. Other articles found in the literature also used VENTOS in their study [7, 8]. However, their analysis focuses more on comparisons between technologies or on pure CACC.

3   Simulation Study

In this section, we give details on the implementation of the 4 attacks scenarios using VENTOS. An analysis of each scenario is made highlighting the main results and learned lessons.

3.1   Simulation Set-Up

We used the tracks of Transpolis company as a test track. This was nursed by the hope of being able to carry out tests in Hardware-in-the-Loop (HIL) tests in the coming years. With the help of OpenStreetMap (OSM) and SUMO format converter, it was possible to represent the tracks of the proving ground, as shown in Fig. 5.

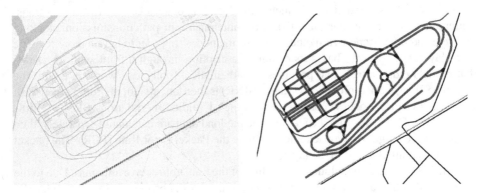

Fig. 5. Track modelling with OSM (left) and SUMO (right)

3.2   Jamming Attack Case

The jamming attack is a Denial of Service (DoS) attack. A jammer is defined as an entity deliberately attempting to disrupt the physical transmission and reception of wireless communications. Because it does not take into account the upper layers, interferences cannot be prevented by security mechanisms such as authentication, digital certificates or encryption. It focuses on the disruption of physical communication in the lower layers. Several types of jammer are identified [17]. The constant jammer emits a permanent radio signal that interferes with legitimate communication, violating the underlying MAC protocol. The random jammer is characterized by periods of interference and silence that can be unpredictable. The interferer can thus follow a random variable sample, following different distributions. Finally, the intelligent jammer, also called "Protocol Aware Jammer", is capable of interpreting and analyzing current transmissions. It can therefore target specific types of messages.

The jamming used in our study is a constant one. This jammer is placed statically in the center of the tracks. In order to have a wide spectrum of data, the simulations were repeated several times. The tests were done with 10 vehicles operating in platooning.

The interest of the jamming attack here is to perceive the impact of this type of attack on a paired ADAS-V2X system. In order to have a better visualization of the impacts, it is necessary to compare the speeds with and without jammer. The vehicles are accelerating at the beginning of the road from 0 to 30 km/h in 10 s.

Looking at Fig. 6, we can see that the first vehicle has very slight impact but that the latter is increasing at each vehicle, with a maximum impact for vehicle 10. In order to better understand the curves, it is important to notice that the upper part of each curve represents the test without a jammer while the lower part does represent the test with a jammer. With regard to acceleration, a maximum difference is noted after 25 s, which then fades with time. Once the vehicle exceeds the jammer's transmission limit, the messages are no longer received.

3.3 Replay Attack Case

A replay attack is performed when a compromised vehicle captures the packets that it receives in order to reject them at another time to resemble those sent by the vehicle. The data inside the packet may be outdated and no longer correspond to the original. If we take the example of a platoon, the security vulnerability analysis is assessed according to the fluctuation in speed of the platoon members over time. The attackers hear the platoon communication and store the transmitted packets. X seconds later, the packets stored are replayed to attack the stability of the platoon.

As for the jamming attack, the tests were done with 10 vehicles operating in platooning (Fig. 7).

The simulation software acts inside the communication channel by retrieving the data sent and by replaying it. The attack is launched after 20 s with a resending time of 10 s. The graph shows then that impact on the vehicle happens at 30 s. It receives then the message that it should have received 10 s sooner. The acceleration given to the vehicle thus matches the speed ramp: an acceleration and then a deceleration. This attack could have had a major impact if the ramp had been steeper, or in more complex use cases.

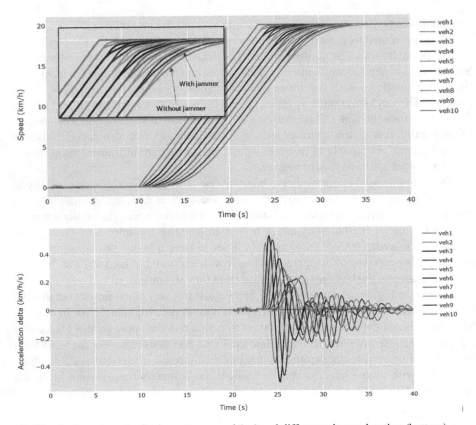

Fig. 6. Jamming attack - impact on speed (up) and difference in acceleration (bottom)

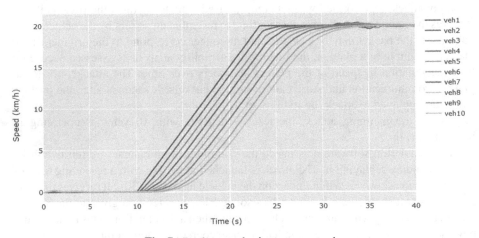

Fig. 7. Replay attack - impact on speed

3.4 Falsification Attack Case

The falsification attack allows an attacker to modify a received packet in order to create disorder in the vehicle network. These attacks have a clear impact on vehicles through the modification or reuse of non-compliant packets. Here, the attacker is playing on the acceleration parameter. When the vehicle decelerates, the opponent manipulates the packet in order to make it look like acceleration (and vice versa) (Fig. 8).

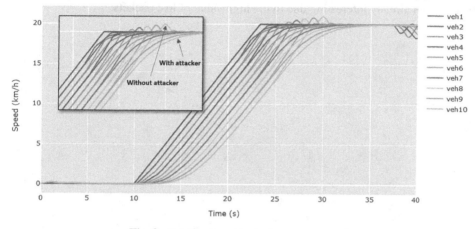

Fig. 8. Falsification attack - impact on speed

In the same way as for replay attack, VENTOS interfere between communications to modify the packet. Acceleration increases from 3 to 5 m/s after 20 s of simulation. The impact in speed is high because the attacker chooses the value to send to the vehicle. Due to the accordion effect, the impact is also higher for the last vehicle than for the first one.

3.5 Congestion Attack Case

As only few vehicles embed V2X communications, it is quite hard to imagine the impact that the presence of many vehicles in a small area could have on the quality of communication. This scenario allows us to challenge the availability of the network. To achieve this objective, we need to simulate an increasing traffic on the roads near the RSUs. To do this, it was chosen to create a traffic jam on Transpolis boulevards in order to see the effects of this concentration of vehicles on the V2X communication system, until saturation.

We started the simulation with two vehicles in order to have V2V (between OBUs) and V2I (between OBUs and RSUs) communications. The output data of interest are the physical layer data as well as the transmission/reception quality information. The objective is to be able to observe the evolution of the following parameters: number of lost packets, transmission time and propagation delay. During the simulations, it soon becomes clear that the increase in traffic implies a constant growth in the number of lost packets. The area of testing has a radio range of 300 meters implying an approximate area of 28 ha. Granted resources allowed us to simulate from 2 to 500 vehicles, which equals to one vehicle for 7.10^{-6} vehicle per square meter to 2.10^{-3} vehicle per square meter. However, these values are low estimates of what we can sometimes find in real-life situations.

Figure 9 displays the results regarding the number of lost packets. The curve climbs rapidly to 11% of lost packets and then seems to slow down. Further tests with a higher computing power could be done in order to evaluate the rest of the curve. However, the results seem already interesting due to the high value of lost packets.

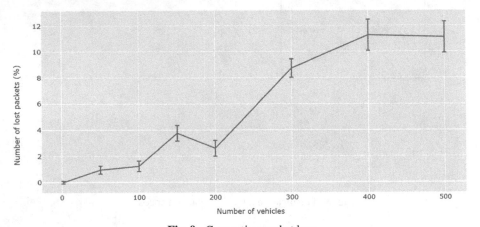

Fig. 9. Congestion packet loss

4   Difficulties and Limitations

Despite offering an interesting test platform, the software that has been used faces some limitations. As future work, we are planning to make evolve this simulation platform by creating a patch to improve compatibility with ITS-G5 standards and by considering the infrastructure in the calculation of the transmission quality. Meanwhile, another solution could be to develop cyberattack modules for simulation software that already embeds ITS-G5.

The quality of the data could also be improved. In this paper, evaluation metrics only consider speed and acceleration of the vehicles (regarding jamming, replay and falsification attacks). It would have been interesting to analyze other metrics that could reflect the state of the transmission channel (throughput, latency, packet delivery ratio, transmission delay, etc.).

Finally, one of the material limits that can have such simulation tools is that they do not allow to take into account all the complexity of V2X attacks. For example, the V2X ITS stack is not open and we cannot change modules related to radio communication and networking. Replay and falsification attacks are much easier when you have direct access to the communication channel.

5 Conclusion

We have presented in this paper, a way to analyze the impact of cyberattacks in C-ITS systems. In order to obtain reliable results, we have used real tracks with dedicated vehicle simulation software. We analyzed the impact of three common cyberattacks and a congestion scenario on C-ITS systems and road traffic. These attacks cover real threats on V2X communications. However, other attacks may be relevant to investigate in further analysis.

Our results show that cyberattacks could have a major impact for road safety. As future work, we are planning to do hardware-in-the-loop (HIL) tests. This type of tests would permit to mix real equipments with simulated ones.

References

1. Hackers Remotely Kill a Jeep on the Highway—With Me in It. Wired (2015). https://www.wired.com/2015/07/hackers-remotely-kill-jeep-highway/
2. ETSI. EN 302 663 V1.2.0, Access layer specification for intelligent transport systems operating in the 5GHz frequency band (2012). https://www.etsi.org/deliver/etsi_en/302600_302699/302663/01.02.00_20/en_302663v010200a.pdf
3. EuroNCAP Advanced Rewards - V2X Communication - Volkswagen Local Hazard Warning 2020 (2020). https://www.euroncap.com/fr/notations-et-r%C3%A9compenses/r%C3%A9compenses-euro-ncap-advanced/2020-volkswagen-local-hazard-warning
4. ETSI. TS 102 687 V1.2.1, Decentralized Congestion Control mechanisms for Intelligent Transport Systems operating in the 5 GHz range; Access layer part (2018). https://www.etsi.org/deliver/etsi_ts/102900_102999/102941/01.01.01_60/ts_102941v010101p.pdf
5. ETSI. TS 102 941 V1.1.1, Security, Trust and Privacy management (2012). https://www.etsi.org/deliver/etsi_ts/102900_102999/102941/01.01.01_60/ts_102941v010101p.pdf
6. Amoozadeh, M., Deng, H., Chuah, C.-N., Zhang, H.M., Ghosal, D.: Platoon management with cooperative adaptive cruise control enabled by VANET. Veh. Commun. 2(2), 110–123 (2015)
7. Ucar, S., Ergen, S.C., Ozkasap, O.: Security vulnerabilities of ieee 802.11p and visible light communication based platoon. In: 2016 IEEE Vehicular Networking Conference (VNC), pp. 1–4 (2016)
8. Amoozadeh, M., et al.: Security vulnerabilities of connected vehicle streams and their impact on cooperative driving. IEEE Commun. Mag. 53(6), 126–132 (2015)
9. Blum, J., Eskandarian, A.: The threat of intelligent collisions. IT Prof. 6(1), 24–29 (2004)
10. Raya, M., Hubaux, J.-P.: The security of vehicular ad hoc networks. In: Proceedings of the 3rd ACM Workshop on Security of Ad Hoc and Sensor Networks, SASN 2005, pp. 11–21. Association for Computing Machinery, New York (2005)
11. Shao, Y., Ge, Y., Yu, R., Wang, J.: A survey of vehicle to everything (V2X) testing. Sensors 19(01), 334 (2019)
12. Smith, C.: The car hacker's handbook: a guide for the penetration tester. No Starch Press, San Francisco (2012)
13. Sommer, F., Dürrwang, J., Kriesten, R.: Survey and classification of auto-motive security attacks. Information (Switzerland), Information 10(04), 148 (2019)
14. Kunz, S., Ravi, T.: Threats to security in DSRC/WAVE. In: Kunz, T., Ravi, S.S. (eds.) ADHOC-NOW 2006. LNCS 4104, pp. 266–279. Springer, Berlin (2006). https://doi.org/10.1007/11814764_22

15. Sommer, C., et al.: Veins – the open source vehicular network simulation framework. In: Virdis, A., Kirsche, M., (eds.) Recent Advances in Network Simulations. Springer, Cham (2019). https://doi.org/10.1007/978-3-030-12842-5_6
16. Eckhoff, D., Sommer, C.: A Multi-Channel IEEE 1609.4 and 802.11p EDCA Model for the Veins Framework, p. 2 (2012)
17. Serageldin, A., Alturkostani, H., Krings, A.: On the reliability of DSRC safety applications: a case of jamming. In: 2013 International Conference on Connected Vehicles and Expo (ICCVE), pp. 501–506 (2013)

Towards an Extensible Security Monitoring Architecture for Vehicular Networks

Amir Teshome Wonjiga[1]([⊠]) and Marc Lacoste[2]([⊠])

[1] University of Rennes 1, Rennes, France
`amir-teshome.wonjiga@inria.fr`
[2] Orange Labs, Department of Security, Chatillon, France
`marc.lacoste@orange.com`

Abstract. Extensibility for security monitoring in 5G vehicular networks remains largely unexplored despite strong requirements for interoperability, to support multiple properties (e.g., security, privacy, trust, sustainability) and to reach trade-offs. We discuss ITS security monitoring challenges and propose an extensible monitoring architecture to meet them. We design and implement a sample security monitoring probe for CAM and DENM and demonstrate on simulations the probe capabilities on a cooperative collision detection use case.

Keywords: Extensible security monitoring · ITS · CAM · DENM

1 Introduction

With the deployment of 5G, Intelligent Transport Systems (ITS) are turning into a reality. Technologies like Software-Defined Networking (SDN), Network Function Virtualization (NFV), and Multi-Access Edge Computing (MEC) are building blocks to meet the expected 5G requirements, notably for security [6,9]. To address multiple threats, security monitoring remains a major challenge [5].

The complexity and heterogeneity of 5G networks prevent a single sub-system from addressing all dimensions of the security monitoring challenge. The monitoring system is rather foreseen as composed of separate modules with complementary tasks. Additional dimensions include: the range of security properties to guarantee, such as privacy and trust [10], or sustainability to handle long in-field lifetimes of vehicles; and trade-offs between security and efficiency [8]. The security monitoring architecture should therefore be *extensible*.

Prior monitoring architectures addressed some of those challenges [15,18,20]. However, *extensibility* did not get the required amount of attention [16] – despite being identified as a key principle, e.g., in the ETSI Zero-touch network and Service Management architecture (ZSM) [4].

In this work-in-progress paper: (1) we propose an extensible ITS security monitoring architecture that supports multiple probes and security properties;

© Springer Nature Switzerland AG 2020
F. Krief et al. (Eds.): Nets4Cars/Nets4Trains/Nets4Aircraft 2020, LNCS 12574, pp. 15–24, 2020.
https://doi.org/10.1007/978-3-030-66030-7_2

(2) we present the design and implementation of a sample probe for several vehicular messaging protocols, taking as examples *Cooperative Awareness (CAM)* and *Decentralized Environmental Notification (DENM)*; (3) we demonstrate the probe detection capabilities on a collision detection use case.

In what follows, we introduce extensible security monitoring for vehicular networks (Sect. 2), and review related work (Sect. 3). We present the use case (Sect. 4), and the monitoring architecture and probe design (Sect. 5). We finally report on implementation and evaluation results (Sect. 6).

2   Extensible Security Monitoring

ITS feature Vehicle-to-Everything (V2X) communication. This includes high vehicle mobility, volatile network topology, low latency, security threats, and wide heterogeneity. It results in the following challenges for security monitoring.

Heterogeneity and Interoperability. The technology stack is overly complex, with *multiple domains* (e.g., User Equipment, Mobile Network Operator, Edge, and Cloud in a typical 5G architecture), and *multiple slices* for different services managed by *multiple stakeholders*. Security monitoring can therefore be performed at various levels and granularities.

Standardization provides a common ground for *interoperability* between different service providers to ensure correct system operation [24]. However, *heterogeneity* remains the main barrier for security monitoring, e.g., supporting more protocols may mean adding more functionalities in monitoring probes. A monolithic monitoring architecture will therefore become rapidly obsolete as technologies evolve.

Supporting Multiple Non-Functional Properties. Cyber-attacks may have critical consequences for vehicular networks, e.g., impacting safety, as loss of human lives is at stake. While *confidentiality, integrity,* and *availability* are essential, other properties (e.g., *privacy, trust*) should also be monitored. For instance, [12] identifies *Safety, Privacy, Efficiency, and Cyber-security (SPEC)* as the key properties to meet for fully automated (unmanned) networks of vehicles.

Accordingly, different types of monitoring probes are required. For instance: Intrusion Detection Systems (IDS) to monitor vulnerabilities and pro-actively prevent security breaches; trust management systems to ensure trust between participants; or distributed ledgers to guarantee decentralized integrity. Such probes can be easily integrated into an extensible architecture for monitoring.

Sustainability. Compared to other electronic devices, a vehicle has a long in-field life-time, which can reach decades. Monitoring requirements could therefore change substantially from the time the vehicle is produced to its end of service.

Enabling Trade-offs between Properties. Different security and efficiency properties need also to be reconciled. Vehicle security requirements may be dynamically adjusted depending on external or internal events: an electric vehicle may prioritize longer battery life than security monitoring tasks when the battery level is below some threshold. An adaptable monitoring architecture would enable to support such smart decisions.

Extensible Security Monitoring. The previous challenges can be met through an architecture not tied to a specific security property, vulnerability, or mechanism. The concept of *extensibility* should be seen in a broad sense (see Fig. 1) including: the supported use cases and applications, the security properties addressed, the types of implemented mechanisms and of connectivity technologies used, and the ability to dynamically add or replace those elements while maintaining acceptable trade-offs between efficiency and security. Thus, the extensibility feature requires not only addressing existing security monitoring issues, but also preparing the architecture for unforeseen challenges.

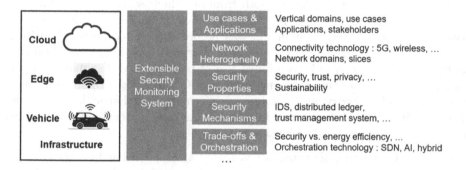

Fig. 1. Extensible security monitoring

Such an extensible architecture cannot be addressed as a single system. Rather it should follow a modular (i.e., component-based) design approach: individual functional or logical components address a specific dimension, with a standard way to exchange information and aggregate outputs.

3   Related Work

Extensible security monitoring in vehicular networks has been explored in the following directions:

5G Network Security Monitoring. Security monitoring systems in previous mobile networks are dependent on the physical hardware, usually proprietary, highly segmented, and uncoordinated – thus, unable to address the on-demand dimension of 5G networks. Most proposed architectures are based on SDN, NFV, and network slicing for security [11]. E.g. on integration of security management and orchestration within the life-cycle of 5G slices to customize security of tenants by deploying fine-grained policies [7]; or the definition of a Software Defined Monitoring (SDM) architecture to overcome limitations of legacy monitoring in current backhaul networks, with a mapping to both SDN and NFV reference models [13]. Unfortunately, those works remain mostly at the concept level, and need further efforts to reach a level of detail required by implementers. Moreover, most of them focus on scalability, but barely address extensibility.

Security Monitoring Probes for Vehicular Networks. Probes can be categorized according to different criteria. For instance: the probe location (in-vehicle, edge, cloud), the class of monitoring algorithm (machine learning based, rule/signature based, ...), the actions taken (active, passive), etc.

Researchers have also explored several specific security properties. For security, the in-vehicle context-aware intrusion detection system (CAID) integrates a physical model of the vehicle to enhance the IDS with context awareness [20]. CAID leverages machine learning to build a reference model, taking inputs from physical sensors. Driving anomaly detection [25] was also investigated based on large-scale vehicle data, collected both from at vehicle-sensor level and at fleet level. It uses a state graph to represent the correlation between the data. For trust, an event-oriented trust model was proposed to detect semantic attacks against DENM [18]. A trust probability is assigned to messages based on content and other criteria. The combined use of permissioned distributed ledgers (blockchains) and content-centric networking (CCN) was also explored for source reliability, and integrity and validity of information exchange between vehicles [15]. However, such security frameworks lack the extensibility to support multiple security properties for vehicular networks.

Security Monitoring Extensibility. Ray et al. [16] discussed some challenges in extensible security architecture design, best practices, limitations, and trade-offs to address future requirements. However, this work did not propose such an architecture. More generally, despite compelling motivations, the extensibility area for security monitoring remains largely unexplored.

4   A Sample Use Case

CAM and DENM. To support vehicular safety and traffic efficiency applications, prominent examples of notifications standardized at ETSI are *CAM* [2] and *DENM* [3]. They provide continuous status information about surrounding vehicles and asynchronous notification of events respectively.

CAMs are single-hop messages periodically sent by ITS nodes to neighboring nodes. They contain status data (e.g., location, speed, direction). Frequency may be adjusted according to the ITS application type. DENMs provide a multi-hop notification service about the road status. Typical event information includes event type (e.g., traffic jam, car breakdown), position, or expiration time [2,3].

Anticipated Cooperative Collision Avoidance (ACCA) [1,14]. Such messages are typically used to anticipate events to reduce the probability of collisions in situations when sensors have limited or no visibility (e.g., a few hundred meters, curved roads, see Fig. 2).

ACCA enables to detect and localize such events to trigger appropriate reactions. By cooperatively sharing the current status and detected events, vehicles can avoid accidents.

Several properties should be guaranteed on exchanged information such as *security* (e.g., no network vulnerabilities), *privacy* (minimal disclosure of private data, e.g., vehicle location, driver attributes), or *trustworthiness* (e.g., no fake positions). Such goals

Fig. 2. ACCA use case

may be met using our extensible monitoring architecture.

5 Extensible Security Monitoring Architecture

5.1 Architecture Overview

Figure 3 shows the components of the proposed security monitoring architecture, *extensibility* being a key design requirement.

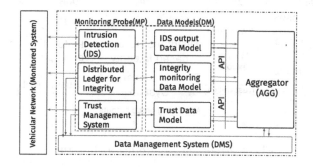

Fig. 3. Extensible security monitoring architecture

Monitoring Probes (MPs): perform security monitoring tasks. Each probe has with its own monitoring objective. Probes are implemented using off-the-shelf tools or custom-designed software. The probe output is added to a *Data Management System (DMS)*, used by the *Aggregator (AGG)* component. An IDS is typically used to monitor vulnerabilities of vehicular networks. IDS results (i.e., logs, alerts) are added to the *DMS*.

Data Model (DM): helps the *AGG* to interpret *MP* outputs. At least one model per probe is required. *DMs* should be described in a standard format (e.g., XML, JSON) to automate interactions with the *AGG*. For an IDS, the *DM* typically includes a reference to a Common Vulnerabilities and Exposures (CVE) database, and descriptions of alert/log formats.

Data Management System (DMS): stores the output of *MPs*, as information interface to the *AGG*. The implementation may be distributed to avoid single points of failure. The *DMS* should support different types of probes, e.g., relational database and separate tables for each probe output.

Aggregator (AGG): combines the outputs from different MPs stored in the *DMS*, for visualization or correlation purposes. The *AGG* also exposes a standard API to get the *DM* of each probe.

5.2 Integrating Probes in the Architecture

In terms of property, we focused on the case of security monitoring using a custom-designed probe for CAM/DENM (CD). Figure 4 shows how the probe fits in the overall monitoring architecture.

Policies are implemented as *DM* components correlated by the *AGG*. The same message flows can thus be used by other probes, like distributed ledger based integrity monitoring [21] or trust management systems [22], to monitor multiple properties, and handle trade-offs.

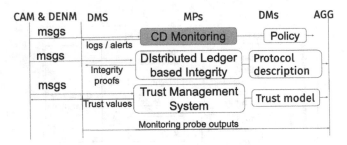

Fig. 4. Probes in monitoring architecture

Extensibility is simply supported by adding new *DM* components, for a single property with different monitoring probes, or for different properties, with the corresponding data models. The *AGG* handles trade-offs and orchestration.

5.3 A CAM/DENM Monitoring Probe

The high-level architecture of the probe is shown in Fig. 5, with its mapping into the standard 5G architecture, inspired from [14]. The probe consists of two components located at the *Edge* and *Cloud* 5G domains.

Edge Component: deployed in RSUs, and collects CAMs/DENMs from vehicles. When a vehicle enters the RSU coverage area, it is registered under that RSU and receives regular updates for subscribed services.

The Edge Component receives incoming messages from vehicle through a specific *Edge Interface*. In practice, this is mirrored traffic for monitoring purposes.

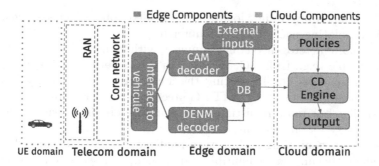

Fig. 5. CAM/DENM monitoring probe

This traffic is decoded using a *CAM decoder/DENM decoder* based on message type. The result is stored in a *Database (DB)*. The content of the database is then periodically transmitted to the central *Cloud Component*.

Cloud Component: a centralized component deployed in the Cloud domain. It collects *DBs* from RSUs and performs monitoring tasks. Cloud-based monitoring leverages the higher computing power of the Cloud compared to edge nodes, enabling more comprehensive analysis such as deep packet inspection. Also, it allows easily collecting *DBs* from RSUs. This provides a complete view of message exchanges between a vehicle and multiple RSUs, otherwise made more difficult with distributed computations between RSUs.

The Cloud Component contains a *CD Engine*. It takes *policies* as input, functionally equivalent to rules in a rule-based IDS. The policy provides information about what to look for in incoming packets – ranging from simple threshold values (e.g., *speed* < 70 km/h) to more complex models to detect semantic attacks [18]. The *CD Engine* performs actual monitoring of traffic coming from the Edge Component *DB*. Traffic violating the provided policy is returned through the *Output* interface.

6 Implementation and Evaluation

Implementation. We used *Artery* for vehicular network simulation, including the Simulation of Urban MObility (SUMO) module for traffic simulation [17]. Interface to vehicles is implemented using the standard SUMO protocol called Traffic Control Interface (TraCI).

In Artery, vehicular applications, called *Services*, are attached to each node. In our use case, vehicles and RSUs are attached with services to send and receive CAMs & DENMs. The RSU can also forward messages for all nodes in its area of coverage. Incoming messages to the RSU are mirrored to the monitoring probe where they are decoded, stored in the DB and periodically transmitted to the Cloud Component. The *Engine* is implemented in Java. *Policies* are provided in XML. The Engine gets the policy, the decoded CAM/DENM from the DB, and verifies if incoming traffic violates the provided policy. Alerts are generated when policy-violating packets are encountered.

We assume a heterogeneous environment with multiple connectivity technologies available (e.g., LTE, 5G, ITS-G5). In this experiment, Artery was used to get preliminary results illustrating the architecture functionality. However, this simulator is more targeted at ITS-G5 technology. To be closer to a cellular context, similar but more realistic results could be obtained using ArteryLTE instead of Artery for simulations.

The security monitoring architecture implementation is considered in a 5G context where the impact of multiple requirements on security are magnified. Though, the architecture remains mostly agnostic to the communication technology, such as the core network architecture. Therefore the approach should also be applicable to LTE.

Setup. For our evaluation, we consider the ACCA use case with two cars Car_0 and Car_1, and a RSU located between the two cars. Car_0 is stopped (vehicle breakdown), sending CAMs/DENMs to the RSU. Car_1 moves towards Car_0, on the same lane, sending CAM messages. The RSU runs services to receive both CAM and DENM. Upon message receipt, the $CAM/DENM$ *decoders* extract the required information from packets and stores the output in a DB. From CAM are extracted speed, position, date/time, and direction. From DENM, additional information is also collected on the detected event such as event code and expiration date.

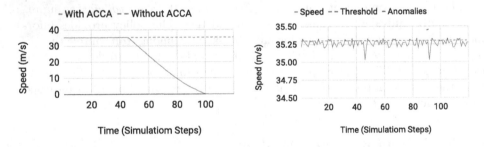

Fig. 6. Speed with and w/o ACCA   **Fig. 7.** Detection of speed anomalies

Evaluation. We evaluated the functionality of our probe using ACCA use case simulations. Figure 6 shows the speed of Car_1 *with* and *without* the ACCA application. Car_1 starts to slow down as soon as it starts receiving DENMs. To show the probe detection abilities, we configured a speed policy with a threshold value of $35.3 m/s$. Figure 7 shows the alerts raised when Car_1 speed increases above the threshold.

7   Conclusion and Outlook

We discussed the need for an *extensible* security monitoring architecture for vehicular networks. We proposed an architecture supporting different monitoring probes and correlation of their results. We presented a custom-designed security monitoring probe for CAM/DENM, and showed its functionality on a collision detection use case and for a predefined monitoring objective. Evaluating the monitoring architecture, specifically showing the extensibility in practice using multiple probes, is left for future work. The main challenge to evaluate the architecture would be to have a good enough *Data Model* and a practical *Aggregator*. For the monitoring probes, existing tools can be plugged and used.

Extensible security monitoring architectures have significant potential for future ITS systems. First regarding *convergence of multiple verticals*, for instance through integrated architectures for vehicular networks, drones, and satellites that may flexibly incorporate and coordinate components for applications such as rescue missions [19]. Second, in terms of *convergence of approaches for security automation*, such as between virtualization (SDN/NFV) and AI for threat detection, prevention, and containment. And third, *blending security, privacy, and trust* in Beyond 5G (B5G)/6G systems [23]. Trust models, policies, and mechanisms are still to be defined, with a trust architecture centered around trust domain interoperability. An extensible monitoring architecture will greatly help monitoring to be agnostic to those abstractions and to facilitate interoperability.

Acknowledgments. This work is partly funded by the EIT Digital Doctoral School (BDExp program). We thank Jean-Philippe Wary for his many insightful comments.

References

1. 5G-Croco Project, https://5gcroco.eu/
2. ETSI EN 102 637–2: ITS; Vehicular Communications; Basic Set of Applications; Part 2: Specification of Cooperative Awareness Basic Service
3. ETSI EN 102 637–3: ITS; Vehicular Communications; Basic Set of Applications; Part 3: Specifications of Decentralized Environmental Notification Basic Service
4. ETSI GS ZSM 002: Zero-touch network and Service Management (ZSM); Reference Architecture. V1.1.1 (2019)
5. INSPIRE-5GPlus: 5G Security: Current Status and Future Trends. D2.1 (2019)
6. Arfaoui, G., et al.: Security and resilience in 5G: current challenges and future directions. In: IEEE Trustcom/BigDataSE/ICESS, pp. 1010–1015 (2017)
7. Blanc, G., et al.: Towards a 5G security architecture: articulating software-defined security and security as a service. In: ARES, pp. 1–8 (2018)
8. Boos, P., Lacoste, M.: Networks of trusted execution environments for data protection in cooperative vehicular systems. In: Laouiti, A., Qayyum, A., Mohamad Saad, M.N. (eds.) Vehicular Ad-hoc Networks for Smart Cities. AISC, vol. 1144, pp. 99–109. Springer, Singapore (2020). https://doi.org/10.1007/978-981-15-3750-9_8

9. Jaballah, W.B., Conti, M., Lal, C.: Security and design requirements for software-defined VANETs. Comput. Netw. **169**, 107099 (2020)
10. Kang, J., et al.: Blockchain for secure and efficient data sharing in vehicular edge computing and networks. IEEE Internet Things J. **6**(3), 4460–4670 (2018)
11. Khan, R., et al.: A survey on security and privacy of 5G technologies: potential solutions, recent advancements, and future directions. IEEE Commun. Surv. Tutorials **22**(1), 196–248 (2019)
12. Le Lann, G.: Cyberphysical Constructs and Concepts for Fully Automated Networked Vehicles. Research Report RR-9297, INRIA Paris-Rocquencourt (2019)
13. Liyanage, M., et al.: Software defined monitoring (SDM) for 5G mobile backhaul networks. In: IEEE LANMAN, pp. 1–6 (2017)
14. García Olmos, A., Vázquez-Gallego, F., Sedar, R., Samoladas, V., Mira, F., Alonso-Zarate, J.: An automotive cooperative collision avoidance service based on mobile edge computing. In: Palattella, M.R., Scanzio, S., Coleri Ergen, S. (eds.) ADHOC-NOW 2019. LNCS, vol. 11803, pp. 601–607. Springer, Cham (2019). https://doi.org/10.1007/978-3-030-31831-4_43
15. Ortega, V., et al.: Trusted 5G vehicular networks: blockchains and content-centric networking. IEEE Veh. Technol. Mag. **13**(2), 121–127 (2018)
16. Ray, S., et al.: Extensibility in automotive security: current practice and challenges. In: 54th ACM/EDAC/IEEE DAC, pp. 1–6 (2017)
17. Riebl, R., Obermaier, C., Günther, H.-J.: Artery: large scale simulation environment for ITS applications. In: Virdis, A., Kirsche, M. (eds.) Recent Advances in Network Simulation. EICC, pp. 365–406. Springer, Cham (2019). https://doi.org/10.1007/978-3-030-12842-5_12
18. Sairam, A.S., Garg, A.: Detecting semantic attacks in intelligent transport system. In: 4th IEEE ICITE, pp. 185–189 (2019)
19. Shi, W., et al.: Drone assisted vehicular networks: architecture, challenges and opportunities. IEEE Netw. **32**(3), 130–137 (2018)
20. Wasicek, A., et al.: Context-aware intrusion detection in automotive control systems. In: Proceedings 5th ESCAR USA Conference, pp. 21–22 (2017)
21. Wonjiga, A.T., Peisert, S., Rilling, L., Morin, C.: Blockchain as a trusted component in cloud SLA verification. In: 12th IEEE/ACM UCC, pp. 93–100 (2019)
22. Yang, Z., et al.: Blockchain-based decentralized trust management in vehicular networks. IEEE Internet Things J. **6**(2), 1495–1505 (2019)
23. Ylianttila, M., et al.: 6G white paper: research challenges for trust, security and privacy. arXiv preprint arXiv:2004.11665 (2020)
24. Zeadally, S., et al.: Vehicular communications for ITS: standardization and challenges. IEEE Commun. Stan. Mag. **4**(1), 11–17 (2020)
25. Zhang, M., et al.: SafeDrive: online driving anomaly detection from large-scale vehicle data. IEEE Trans. Ind. Inform. **13**(4), 2087–2096 (2017)

Anomaly Detection on Roads Using C-ITS Messages

Juliet Chebet Moso[1,3], Ramzi Boutahala[1], Brice Leblanc[1],
Hacène Fouchal[1(✉)], Cyril de Runz[2], Stephane Cormier[1],
and John Wandeto[3]

[1] CReSTIC EA 3804, 51097, Université de Reims Champagne-Ardenne,
Reims, France
Hacene.Fouchal@univ-reims.fr
[2] BDTLN, LIFAT, University of Tours, Tours, France
[3] Dedan Kimathi University of Technology, Nyeri, Kenya

Abstract. Cooperative Intelligent Transport Network is one of the most challenging issue in networking and computer science. In this area, huge amount of data are exchanged. Smart analysis of this collected data could be achieved for many purposes: traffic prediction, driver profile detection, anomaly detection, etc. Anomaly detection is an important issue for road operators. An anomaly on roads could be caused by various reasons: potholes, obstacles, weather conditions, etc. An early detection of such anomalies will reduce incident risks such as traffic jams, accidents. The aim of this paper is to collect message exchanges between vehicles and analyze trajectories. This analysis becomes difficult since a privacy principle is applied in the case of C-ITS. Indeed, each message sent is generated with an identifier of the sender. This identifier is kept only over a specified time interval thus one vehicle will have multiple identifiers. We first have to solve Trajectory-User Linking problem by chaining anonymous trajectories to potential vehicles by considering similarity in movement patterns. After that we apply various methods to check variations of trajectories from normal ones. When we observe some differences, we can raise an alarm about a potential anomaly. In order to check the validity of this work, we generated a large amount of messages exchanges by many vehicles using the Omnet simulator together with the Artery, Sumo plug-in. We applied various variations on some obtained trajectories. Finally, we ran our detection algorithm on the obtained trajectories using different parameters (angles, speed, acceleration) and obtained very interesting results in terms of detection rate.

Keywords: Trajectory-User Linking · Moving objects · Similarity measure · Anomaly detection · Data analysis

1 Introduction

C-ITS eco-system generates a very huge amount of data. The collection of mobility data is done by online or offline means through devices attached/carried

F. Krief et al. (Eds.): Nets4Cars/Nets4Trains/Nets4Aircraft 2020, LNCS 12574, pp. 25–38, 2020.
https://doi.org/10.1007/978-3-030-66030-7_3

by the moving objects, road side units among other techniques. Usually, such data includes details that explain the movement of vehicles. Each trajectory of a moving entity is considered a multi-attribute, time-ordered sequence of locations traversed by the entity.

Trajectory mining is a process which entails the analysis of movement traces with the main goal being the extraction of spatial, spatial-temporal and behavioral patterns [1]. The main techniques used for this analysis perform classification, clustering, point of interest detection and anomaly detection. We can look at trajectory data mining as a three phased process which includes [2]: data preprocessing, data management (indexing and data storage) and pattern mining. The key drivers can be "economic (logistical optimization, customer behavior analysis, targeted advertising), scientific (animal behavior analysis, healthcare), administrative (urban planning, criminal investigation), or private" [3]. However, there remains a challenge on how to obtain knowledge and information from these data which can assist in mobility improvement [4].

The paths of moving objects on road networks are affected by the environmental and traffic conditions. To gain a better understanding of the movement patterns one needs to incorporate the environmental information in the analysis [5]. Further, to characterize the behavioral and lifestyle aspects of an entity, an analysis of daily trajectories is imperative. Trajectory pattern mining comes in handy in public security systems, recommender systems and path planning in emergency evacuations [6].

To obtain meaningful information from trajectories, the raw points need to be enriched with semantic attributes, which is basically a daunting process. To solve this issue, semantic annotations can be done by experts or users can add semantic labels to their trajectories. We can also label trajectories with points of interest (POIs) using their location information [2,7]. Working with semantically enriched trajectories enhances querying and pattern identification [8] which simplifies behaviour analysis of the moving object. Trip recommender systems, life experience sharing and context-aware computing are some of the applications which benefit from semantic trajectory analysis [2].

The advances in battery technology and availability of low cost storage devices have facilitated the capture of highly sampled trajectory data over an extended period of time. With the increased data, it is now possible to discover more interesting patterns during pattern mining. Nevertheless, the analysis of raw un-simplified trajectories can be virtually impossible and computationally resource intensive. This can be alleviated by the use of compression and pruning techniques during pattern mining [6].

When reporting their locations to a central repository, moving objects can have various strategies such as time-based, distance-based, and prediction-based strategies. Communication with a central server may also be interrupted for a while and restored later. This results in segmented trajectories with gaps due to missing readings and also variation in trajectory lengths. Also, for privacy reasons, the device identification(ID) numbers which uniquely identify a trajectory may be changed periodically. In order to reconstruct the movement of a vehicle over a long period of time, the device IDs from the consecutive trips must be identified through a linking process and the missing gaps filled.

We propose to solve the Trajectory-User Linking (TUL) problem by chaining anonymous trajectories to potential vehicles by considering similarity in movement patterns. This will be performed as a pre-processing step for the characterization and semantic analysis of moving objects though behavior analysis. Occurrence of obstacles on the road causes the vehicles passing the affected section to exhibit an avoidance behavior which can be viewed as a drift. We investigate the avoidance behavior through observation of movement variations on the obtained trajectories. When some threshold is reached, an anomaly is possible and is detected.

We make the following contributions: (a) we present a detailed state of the art on trajectory linking, trajectory mining, anomaly detection, and identify the open research issues; (b) we investigate trajectory linking problem using a real dataset of messages generated in Cooperative Intelligent Transportation System (C-ITS); (c) we perform anomaly detection based on concept drift on C-ITS messages.

The rest of this paper is structured as follows: Sect. 2 presents the state of the art investigation on Trajectory-User Linking, trajectory mining and anomaly detection. Section 3 presents the problem statement, methodology and description of the dataset. Section 4 presents the experiments and results, and Sect. 5 presents the conclusion and future work.

2   Related Works

This section introduces works on Trajectory-User Linking, trajectory mining and anomaly detection.

2.1   Trajectory-User Linking (TUL)

A recent area of research in location-based social network applications (LBSNs) is Trajectory-User Linking [9]. It is driven by the huge volume of data generated in these applications. To preserve privacy in LBSNs user identifiers are removed from the data during anonymization. Conversely, the ability to link the trajectories to the real users through analysis of check-in data and phone signals can be very useful in recommender and criminal identification systems. Due to the abundance of user classes and the sparsity of data, solving TUL is a challenging task. In [9], a semi-supervised learning model based on Recurrent Neural Networks (RNN), called TULER (TUL via Embedding and RNN) is proposed. TULER learns the semantic mobility patterns of spatio-temporal data by correlating trajectories to the users who generated them. It identifies the dependencies inherent in check-in data and infers hidden user patterns.

Additionally, TULVAE (TUL via Variational AutoEncoder), a semi-supervised learning technique is presented in [10]. TULVAE applies a neural generative architecture with stochastic latent variables in the analysis of geo-tagged social media data. It considers the fact that human trajectories exhibit a hierarchical semantic structure with high-dimensionality and data sparsity. Through processing vast quantities of unlabeled data, TULVAE tackles the data sparsity issue, thus generating useful knowledge and distinct mobility patterns.

The proliferation of location based services has resulted in the availability of heterogeneous mobility data from the various service providers. There is also a growing need for a better understanding of user behaviour across multiple services. To deal with the data heterogeneity issue, DPLink an end-to-end deep learning based framework for performing user identity linkage is proposed in [11]. It extracts representative features from the trajectory using a feature extractor, a location encoder and a trajectory encoder. The decision to link two trajectories as the same user is made using a comparator. The low-quality problem of mobility data is handled by a multi-modal embedding network and a co-attention mechanism in DPLink.

2.2 Trajectory Mining

Moving objects can be categorized into various classes based on their trajectories through trajectory classification. The aim of classification is to identify modes of transport, vessel types or user classes based on trajectory patterns [12]. The classification process is a three step process [2]: (i) Trajectory segmentation, (ii) Feature extraction from the segments, and (iii) Building of the classification model. The process requires as input a sequence of spatio-temporal points.

Clustering is one of the classification techniques applicable to trajectories where the clusters formed should have a low inter-class similarity and a high intra-class similarity. The output of clustering, especially in relation to behavior prediction can be applied in destination prediction, urban planning, market research and location recommendation [13]. The open research issues include: finding appropriate features for trajectory representation, similarity measures and development of algorithms for spatial data clustering [14]. The key challenge is how to identify relevant class distinguishing features and how to select the most discriminate features to be used in building the classification model [15]. One of the frequently used discriminant features is the distance between two trajectories which is computed using a distance measure or metric.

In evaluating user similarity, several literature studies focus on the geometric or sequential features of trajectories. Trajectory similarity is measured based on the co-location frequency (feature-based representations), which is the number of times two moving objects appear spatially close to one another. Other measures include subsequence similarity metrics such as the length of the Longest common subsequence (LCSS) [16], Edit Distance on Real Sequences (EDR) [17], Common Visit Time Interval (CVTI) [18], Maximal Semantic Trajectory Pattern (MSTP) [19], Multidimensional Similarity Measure (MSM) [20], and Stops and Moves Similarity Measure (SMSM) [21].

By defining distance and matching thresholds, LCSS reduces the effect of noisy data. When distance in LCSS is less than a given threshold in all dimensions, two points match. However, LCSS ignores gaps in sequences, resulting in the same similarity value for different pairs of trajectories for some problems.

EDR uses an edit distance to calculate the similarity between elements where all dimensions are taken into account for a match to occur. Penalties are assigned based on the length of the gaps between two matched sub-sequences resulting in more precise results than LCSS. The semantic dimension of stops is integrated by CVTI with the temporal dimension. It does not allow heterogeneous data to be modeled and calculated together, such as stops and moves.

During similarity analysis of semantic trajectories, MSTP considers the frequency at which stops are visited. It does not consider moves between stops and multiple data dimensions. The similarity rating in MSM is based on the matching scores of all pairs with at least one matching dimension. It allows definition of different similarity weights for every dimension and may assign a high score to trajectories with similarity only in a small portion of their length. SMSM considers both stops and moves within the trajectory and, by assigning weights, performs partial dimension matching and partial stop ordering. However, for users, calculating weights can be difficult.

LCSS and EDR require all elements to match across all dimensions when looking at the applicability of similarity measures based on trajectory dimensions, whereas MSM considers matching pairs in a single dimension. In situations where the trajectory contains outliers LCSS, EDR, MSM and SMSM which are robust to noise are applicable. MSM and SMSM are good options when dealing with semantic trajectories, though LCSS and EDR can be extended for semantic trajectory mining. The best measure is MSM when considering apps that use GPS trajectories annotated with stops only or trajectories extracted from social media, as it manages sparse data. MSM is useful when one wants to find users who visited the same place at similar times irrespective of the order of visits. When extracting the most similar paths or most popular routes between stops, SMSM is applicable.

2.3   Anomaly Detection

Anomalies can be defined as "patterns in data that do not conform to a well-defined notion of normal behavior" [22]. These patterns can also be referred to as outliers or exceptions, and represent new, rare or unknown data which may be of interest in a specific domain. In the presence of labeled data, anomaly detection can be done using supervised learning techniques where it is considered a binary classification problem with data instances being either normal or abnormal. However, this is rarely the case due to the limitation in availability of labeled data and the fact that the anomalous events are quite rare. Due to availability of massive amounts of unlabeled data, most anomaly detection approaches adopt unsupervised learning techniques.

Anomalies can be viewed in two ways: (i) erroneous data generated due to device failure or system faults, and (ii) unusual data representing rare/exceptional activities/events which are anomalous but actually happened [23]. Some of the anomalies linked to road networks include: vehicle collisions, vehicle breakdowns, debris on the road, pot holes, and vehicle(s) stopped in the middle of the road. Most of these can be attributed to driving behavior and the status of the road. The main aim of traffic management is to reduce the number of anomalies and improve traffic flow. It is desirable to know the locations, time and frequency of occurrence of these anomalies for efficient traffic management.

Anomaly detection techniques are usually focused at identifying patterns which do not conform to expected behavior. However, according to [24] the challenge lies in the fact that: (i) there is no well-defined boundary between what is normal and what is considered abnormal; (ii) there is a high possibility of a normal behavior evolving to an abnormal representation in the future; (iii) it is difficult to apply anomaly detection techniques developed in one field to another field due to difference in applications and concepts; (iv) presence of noise in the data makes it difficult to distinguish between noise points and the real anomalous points.

3   Problem Statement and Methodology

3.1   Problem Statement

The vehicles of a Cooperative Intelligent Transport Network (C-ITS) exchange a lot of messages. Each message contains an identifier of the transmitting vehicle. In order to protect the privacy of users, each vehicle's identifiers are updated periodically. Given the various identifiers assigned to a vehicle, we wish to investigate whether it is possible to group all identifiers which belong to the same vehicle. We adopt the definition of [9] for Trajectory User-Linkability problem:

Let $T_{vi} = m_{i1}, m_{i2}, \ldots, m_{in}$ denote a trajectory generated by the vehicle v_i during a time interval, where $m_{ij}(j \in [1, n])$ is a message sent from a specific location at time t_j. Given that the identifier is changed after a time period, trajectory $T_x = m_1, m_2, \ldots, m_y$ generated by the same vehicle in the next time interval with a different identifier is considered unlinked. TUL can thus be defined as:

Suppose we have a number of unlinked trajectories $T = t_1, \ldots, t_m$ generated by a set of vehicles $V = v_1, \ldots, v_n(m \gg n)$, TUL learns a function that links unlinked trajectories to the vehicles: $T \to V$.

Information on the presence of obstacles on the road is useful to road operators as it can enhance road safety through planned interventions to treat them. We intend to detect anomalies which are as a result of stopped cars and potholes on the road.

3.2   Methodology

In a C-ITS environment cooperative awareness is achieved through exchange of CAMs which contain position information. This can serve as a privacy risk especially in a scenario where an eavesdropper is able to recreate a comprehensive mobility pattern of the driver. In order to lessen the risk, pseudonyms are used to provide anonymous communication. To ensure unlinkability of actions, multiple pseudonyms are used per vehicle [25]. This involves the periodic change of pseudonyms so as to prevent linkability of one pseudonym to another which can in turn result in the identity of a vehicle and consequently that of the driver being revealed if one is able to identify the home address.

We begin by grouping as much as possible the different identifiers which represent sub-trajectories of one vehicle. A complete grouping with all the identifiers of each vehicle may be difficult to obtain but grouping some identifiers can be achieved. For example, if the last message of an identifier is spatially and temporally close to the first message obtained with another identifier and the change in attributes like speed and heading angle is consistent, then the change of identifier from the last message to the first one is obtained for the same vehicle. Thus the two identifiers are linked and belong to the same vehicle. In this example, the work consists in defining a reliable link between two messages with different identifiers.

Then we detect the contradictions between messages. For instance, if two messages give the same localization at the same time, then their identifiers cannot belong to the same vehicle. These contradictions help to define the group of identifiers for each vehicle by rejecting the identifiers leading to a contradiction. The framework to be followed in the analysis is shown in Fig. 1.

Definition: *Trajectory*: A raw trajectory consists of a sequence of n points $T = [p_1, p_2, \ldots, p_n]$, in which $p_i = x, y, z, t, A$, where x, y ,z represent the position of the moving object in space, t is the timestamp and A represents other attributes associated with the point (i.e. speed, heading angle and drive direction).

In this study a trajectory is considered as the consolidation of messages uniquely identified by a single identifier. The second step is to detect obstacles on the road where we are interested in concept drifts with a sudden appearance (stopped vehicle scenario) and those of a slow appearance (growing pothole scenario). The assumption is that an obstacle will block the whole lane requiring the other vehicles to change lane as they avoid it.

3.3   Dataset Description

In our study we used a real dataset of Cooperative Awareness Messages (CAM) generated by the OMNET simulator together with SUMO, artery plug-in. A vehicle sends CAMs to its neighbourhood using Vehicle-to-Vehicle (V2V) or Vehicle-to-Infrastructure (V2I) communications. The frequency of CAM message generation varies 10 Hz 1 Hz (100 milliseconds to 1000 milliseconds). Each CAM is uniquely defined by a stationid (Pseudonym) and timestamp. In this

Fig. 1. Trajectory mining framework.

dataset each vehicle has a defined stationid which changes periodically in order to guarantee privacy of drivers.

In this study, each message is defined by eight variables: an identifier associated with the transmitting vehicle, a timestamp, the location of the vehicle (latitude, longitude and altitude), speed, heading angle and the drive direction. The speed, heading angle and drive direction variables are used as descriptive variables of the behavior of the transmitting vehicle.

4   Performance Evaluation

In order to link the trajectories we consider the following conditions for triggering CAM generation as specified in ETSI EN 302 637-2 standard [26]:

- If the absolute difference between the current heading value of the vehicle and the heading value included in the last transmitted CAM by the same vehicle exceeds 4 degrees;
- If the distance between the current position of the vehicle and the position included in the last transmitted CAM by the same vehicle exceeds 4 m;
- If the absolute difference between the current speed of the vehicle and the speed included in the last transmitted CAM by the same vehicle exceeds 0.5 m/s.

We performed trajectory mining using PostgreSQL database with the spatial extension PostGIS used for storing and processing spatial data. We also used Quantum GIS (QGIS) an open-source cross-platform desktop geographic information system application that supports viewing, editing, and analysis of geospatial data. QGIS was majorly used for visualization and map matching of the trajectories as a validation step.

Considering the fact that each vehicle was assigned multiple identifiers, we sort out to group identifiers which occurred on the same day by comparing origin and destination pairs. Taking the destination points, we extracted the nearest origin point within 170 m (since the highest speed recorded in the dataset was 163m/s) and also filtered out the results by implementing the CAM generation trigger conditions as additional constraints. The distance computation was done using the *ST_DistanceSpheroid* function in PostgreSQL which gives the linear distance between two longitude/latitude points. We also used the CAM generating frequency of 100–1000 milliseconds as a constraint in order to get exact matches in time and space.

4.1   Obstacle Detection

In our study we have performed anomaly detection mainly focusing on road obstacle detection. We handle the data collected from vehicles as a data stream.

There can be different kinds of change in a data stream. From time to time an outstanding value appears, this is called an outlier. When the data is changing from one behavior to another, this is called a concept drift. A concept drift detector is designed to find when the data is changing from one concept to another, but it should be robust to outliers so as to avoid false positive detection. Different concept drift detection approaches are used for different kinds of data and streams. The parameters of these algorithms are used to tune the algorithm to avoid a trigger on outliers. However, too restrictive parameters can result in the algorithm not triggering at all. Parameters are varied depending on the context.

To handle data streams, the algorithms can store some global value relative to the stream that are updated for each new data or rely on a window model to store part of the stream and calculate the values on the stored data. In a window model, data is stored until the window is full and since the memory is limited older data will be removed from the window [28]. Here are some window models that can be used:

Sliding window model: In this window model the data is treated in a first-in first-out manner. The size of the window can be fixed or variable but when the window is full, oldest data are deleted so new data can be treated.

Damped window model: This window model associates an exponentially decaying weight to the observations and delete the data at the point when the weight is equivalent to zero.

Landmark window model: The landmark model rely on chunks of data separated by landmarks. A landmark can be a time value (hour, day, month, ...) or a number of observed elements. Every data in the landmark is treated until the next landmark is reached. When it is reached, the old data is removed and replaced by the new one.

In this study, we used two algorithms: Page-Hinkley and ADWIN. These are really popular approaches due to their effectiveness on many types of data, and we aim to know if they are adapted to our type of data:

The Page-Hinkley algorithm [27,29] analyzes the data sequentially to detect change and does not use a window model since no data is stored except a mean and a sum. It recalculates the mean value of the data at each input. And it also recalculates the sum of the difference to the mean with the alpha and the delta parameters to adjust the sensitivity. The alpha and the delta parameters help to mitigate outliers both in different ways, the greater they are the more outliers will be needed to detect a drift. If this sum passes over the lambda threshold value then a drift signal is raised. The greater the threshold is, the fewer false positives are but actual errors could be missed or the detection delayed. Also the higher the alpha and delta values are the harder it is to detect small variations. Page-Hinkley consumes very few resources since it is not storing any part of the data stream. But its strongest issues are its sensitivity to outliers when trying to detect concept drift on low varying data and its delay on the detection of concept drift when tuned to resist to outliers.

The ADaptative WINdowing (ADWIN) algorithm [30] is based on a sliding window system. The size of the window, instead of being fixed, is recomputed: if a drift is detected, the window is reduced, if not, it is growing to its maximal size defined by the user. To change the window size, it is made into a bucket list that is split in bucket rows of the same size, and these bucket rows contains buckets. The algorithm takes data as input, stores it in a bucket that is put in the last bucket row. If the bucket list is full, the two oldest bucket rows are reduced and merged. The process to detect the drift is triggered every *clock* number of new data, only if the length of the window is greater than the minimal sub-window length. To detect a drift, the buckets are separated in two sub-windows, one containing the oldest data (this one is bigger than the second one) and the other containing newer data. If the data between these two windows are too different (according to the delta value) then a drift signal is raised, and the window size is reduced. ADWIN has a small memory consumption due to its bucket system and can detect quickly concept drift since part of the stream is stored. But since a small part is stored long and slow drift is hard to detect because the buckets are updated with more and more drifting data without noticing it. And if the algorithm is more sensitive to detect such change the rate of false-positive will be higher. In order to detect avoiding behaviors and the change of frequency of them, we use ADWIN, and Page-Hinkley algorithms.

Figure 2 presents the results for the Page-Hinkley algorithm for the stopped car scenario. And Fig. 3 the result of Page-Hinkley on the pothole scenario. The red dots represent the number of messages with an avoiding behavior (real drift) in the last 600 messages and the blue dots, the number of drifts detected by the algorithm. The x-axis represents the generation time (corresponding to the number of messages). The y-axis represents the number of messages detected that contain an avoiding behavior.The higher on the y-axis the dots are, the stronger the change is on the period.

For the Page-Hinkley algorithm, it is difficult to have an accurate detection of large changes because the detection is highly delayed. That is why we used parameters to detect the smallest changes. This allows us to track the frequency of changes in the overtaking behaviors. We can see that the frequency increases as we enter the period when the overtaking rate is the highest. But by design, the Page-Hinkley algorithm has a certain delay in detecting new concepts, so the points do not directly follow the change. The performance of this algorithm is encouraging for the stopped car scenario since we can see the increase in the number of detections when the change occurs. But the delay in the detection of the events is a strong backlash because we need a filtering step that will delay the detection even more. For the pothole scenario, we can see a slight increase in the detection rate of changes with few spikes but this is not enough to be significant. And with the delay in detection, it is not possible to have a correct view of the detection until the concept stabilizes.

Figure 4 presents the results for the ADWIN algorithm for the stopped car scenario and Fig. 5 the result for ADWIN on the pothole scenario.

For the ADWIN algorithm, in the stopped car scenario, there is little detection in the low avoiding rates, but they do not hide the high number of detections when large changes occur. In this scenario, the results are really convincing and should be tested in real cases. But in the case of the pothole scenario, the detection is not accurate. Initially, the algorithm manages to detect the change, but

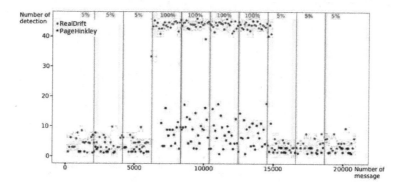

Fig. 2. Detection of Page-Hinkley algorithm for stopped car scenario

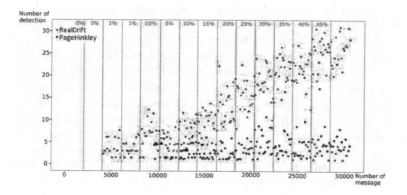

Fig. 3. Detection of Page-Hinkley algorithm for pothole scenario

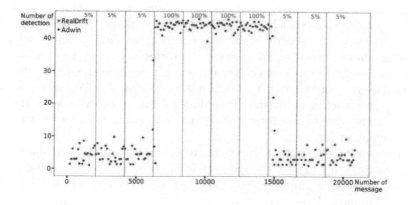

Fig. 4. Detection of ADWIN algorithm for stopped car scenario

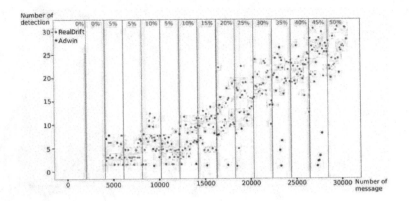

Fig. 5. Detection of ADWIN algorithm for pothole scenario

when the avoidance rate reaches 25%, the algorithm cannot detect the changes correctly. This is because the algorithm is designed to adapt to changes, and then, it fails to detect the next changes accurately because the avoiding behavior has become part of the concept it has learned and the difference in rates is no longer large enough for it to detect them. For this type of behavior, other algorithms may be better suited. Such algorithms should use a window model with a fixed historical window as a basis for learning since we want to detect abnormal behavior compared to typical behavior. But the loss of adaptability to change will require reconfiguration of the history window each time a change is made to the road, its environment, or driver behavior (the latter change could be due to an increasing number of C-ITS, automated vehicles or other technical improvements or recommendations).

5   Conclusion

In this work we considered the trajectory-linking problem and applied it to messages generated by vehicles in C-ITS in order to detect anomalies described by obstacles on roads. Based on our analysis, if other distinguishing attributes and background information on message generation are taken into account, it is possible to link trajectories to the vehicle which generated them. The detection of anomalies is achieved thanks to data stream analysis. We have shown in this study that such analysis should be done off-line in order to learn the main behavior of the system and later it could be run on-line in order to detect any dis-functioning at any time.

As future work, we plan to semantically enrich the trajectories and perform frequent pattern mining on the data. It is foreseeable that autonomous vehicles will need to communicate with C-ITS enabled vehicles which do not have embedded cameras. It is then interesting to detect obstacles using C-ITS data and for future works these obstacles could be confirmed by processing images captured by autonomous vehicle cameras.

References

1. Shekhar, S., Xiong, H., Zhou, X. (eds.): Encyclopedia of GIS. Springer, Cham (2017). https://doi.org/10.1007/978-3-319-17885-1
2. Zheng, Y.: Trajectory data mining: an overview. ACM Trans. Intell. Syst. Technol. **6**(3), 1–41 (2015). https://doi.org/10.1145/2743025
3. Valdés, F., Güting, R.H.: A framework for efficient multi-attribute movement data analysis. VLDB J. **28**(4), 427–449 (2018). https://doi.org/10.1007/s00778-018-0525-6
4. Alesiani, F., Moreira-Matias, L., Faizrahnemoon, M.: On learning from inaccurate and incomplete traffic flow data. IEEE Trans. Intell. Transport. Syst. **19**(11), 3698–3708 (2018). https://doi.org/10.1109/TITS.2018.2857622
5. Wu, T., Qin, J., Wan, Y.: TOST: a topological semantic model for GPS trajectories inside road networks. IJGI **8**(9), 410 (2019). https://doi.org/10.3390/ijgi8090410
6. Cao, Y., et al.: Effective spatio-temporal semantic trajectory generation for similar pattern group identification. Int. J. Mach. Learn. Cybern. **11**(2), 287–300 (2019). https://doi.org/10.1007/s13042-019-00973-y
7. Yan, Z., Chakraborty, D., Parent, C., Spaccapietra, S., Aberer, K.: Semantic trajectories: mobility data computation and annotation. ACM Trans. Intell. Syst. Technol. **4**(3), 1 (2013). https://doi.org/10.1145/2483669.2483682
8. Nishad, A., Abraham, S.: SemTraClus: an algorithm for clustering and prioritizing semantic regions of spatio-temporal trajectories. Int. J. Comput. Appl. 1–10 (2019). https://doi.org/10.1080/1206212X.2019.1655853
9. Gao, Q., Zhou, F., Zhang, K., Trajcevski, G., Luo, X., Zhang, F.: Identifying human mobility via trajectory embeddings. In: Proceedings of the Twenty-Sixth International Joint Conference on Artificial Intelligence, Melbourne, Australia, pp. 1689–1695 (August 2017). https://doi.org/10.24963/ijcai.2017/234
10. Zhou, F., Gao, Q., Trajcevski, G., Zhang, K., Zhong, T., Zhang, F.: Trajectory-user linking via variational autoencoder. In: Proceedings of the Twenty-Seventh International Joint Conference on Artificial Intelligence, Stockholm, Sweden, pp. 3212–3218 (July 2018). https://doi.org/10.24963/ijcai.2018/446
11. Feng, J., et al.: DPLink: user identity linkage via deep neural network from heterogeneous mobility data. In: The World Wide Web Conference on - WWW 2019, San Francisco, CA, USA, pp. 459–469 (2019). https://doi.org/10.1145/3308558.3313424
12. Vicenzi, F., Petry, L.M.: Exploring frequency-based approaches for efficient trajectory classification. In: Proceedings of the 35th Annual ACM Symposium on Applied Computing - SAC 2020, March 30-April 3, pp. 624–631 (2020). https://doi.org/10.1145/3341105.3374045
13. Yu, Q., Luo, Y., Chen, C., Chen, S.: Trajectory similarity clustering based on multi-feature distance measurement. Appl. Intell. **49**(6), 2315–2338 (2019). https://doi.org/10.1007/s10489-018-1385-x
14. Sabarish, B.A., Karthi, R., Gireeshkumar, T.: Clustering of trajectory data using hierarchical approaches. In: Hemanth, D.J., Smys, S. (eds.) Computational Vision and Bio Inspired Computing. LNCVB, vol. 28, pp. 215–226. Springer, Cham (2018). https://doi.org/10.1007/978-3-319-71767-8_18
15. Ferrero, C.A., Alvares, L.O., Zalewski, W., Bogorny, V.: MOVELETS: exploring relevant subtrajectories for robust trajectory classification. In: Proceedings of the 33rd Annual ACM Symposium on Applied Computing-SAC 2018, Pau, France, pp. 849–856 (2018). https://doi.org/10.1145/3167132.3167225

16. Vlachos, M., Kollios, G., Gunopulos, D.: Discovering similar multidimensional trajectories. In: Proceedings 18th International Conference on Data Engineering, San Jose, CA, USA, pp. 673–684 (2002). https://doi.org/10.1109/ICDE.2002.994784

17. Chen, L., Özsu, M.T., Oria, V.: Robust and fast similarity search for moving object trajectories. In: Proceedings of the 2005 ACM SIGMOD International Conference on Management of Data - SIGMOD 2005, Baltimore, Maryland, p. 491 (2005). https://doi.org/10.1145/1066157.1066213

18. Kang, H.-Y., Kim, J.-S., Li, K.-J.: Similarity measures for trajectory of moving objects in cellular space. In: Proceedings of the 2009 ACM symposium on Applied Computing - SAC 2009, Honolulu, Hawaii, p. 1325 (2009). https://doi.org/10.1145/1529282.1529580

19. Ying, J.J.-C., Lu, E.H.-C., Lee, W.-C., Weng, T.-C., Tseng, V.S.: Mining user similarity from semantic trajectories. In: Proceedings of the 2nd ACM SIGSPATIAL International Workshop on Location Based Social Networks - LBSN 2010, San Jose, California, p. 19 (2010). https://doi.org/10.1145/1867699.1867703

20. Furtado, A.S., Kopanaki, D., Alvares, L.O., Bogorny, V.: Multidimensional similarity measuring for semantic trajectories: multidimensional similarity Measuring for Semantic Trajectories. Trans. in GIS **20**(2), 280–298 (2016). https://doi.org/10.1111/tgis.12156

21. Lehmann, A.L., Alvares, L.O., Bogorny, V.: SMSM: a similarity measure for trajectory stops and moves. Int. J. Geogr. Inf. Sci. **33**(9), 1847–1872 (2019). https://doi.org/10.1080/13658816.2019.1605074

22. Chandola, V., Banerjee, A., Kumar, V.: Anomaly detection: a survey. ACM Comput. Surv. (CSUR) **41**(3), 1–58 (2009)

23. Wang, X., Fagette, A., Sartelet, P., Sun, L.: A probabilistic tensor factorization approach to detect anomalies in spatiotemporal traffic activities. In: 2019 IEEE Intelligent Transportation Systems Conference (ITSC), pp. 1658–1663. IEEE (October 2019)

24. Wang, H., Bah, M.J., Hammad, M.: Progress in outlier detection techniques: a survey. IEEE Access **7**, 107964–108000 (2019)

25. Petit, J., Schaub, F., Feiri, M., Kargl, F.: Pseudonym schemes in vehicular networks: a survey. IEEE Commun. Surv. Tutorials **17**(1), 228–255 (2015). https://doi.org/10.1109/COMST.2014.2345420

26. ETSI E. 302 637–2 V1. 3.1-Intelligent Transport Systems (ITS); Vehicular Communications; Basic Set of Applications; Part 2: Specification of Cooperative Awareness Basic Service. ETSI (September 2014)

27. Page, E.S.: Continuous inspection schemes. Biometrika **41**(1/2), 100–115 (1954)

28. Golab, L., Özsu, M.T.: Issues in data stream management. ACM Sigmod Rec. **32**(2), 5–14 (2003)

29. Gama, J., Sebastião, R., Rodrigues, P.P.: On evaluating stream learning algorithms. Mach. Learn. **90**(3), 317–346 (2012). https://doi.org/10.1007/s10994-012-5320-9

30. Bifet, A., Gavalda, R.: Learning from time-changing data with adaptive windowing. In: Proceedings of the 2007 SIAM International Conference on Data Mining, pp. 443–448 (2007)

Leveraging GPS Data for Vehicle Maneuver Detection

Abdallah Aymen[1]([✉])[iD], Jemili Imen[1][iD], Mabrouk Sabra[1][iD],
and Mohamed Mosbah[2][iD]

[1] Faculty of Sciences of Bizerte, University of Carthage, Tunis, Tunisia
{abdullah.aymen,imen.jmili,sabra.mabrouk}@fsb.u-carthage.tn
[2] University of Bordeaux, Bordeaux, France
mohamed.mosbah@u-bordeaux.fr

Abstract. Due to the huge number of accidents, improving driving safety around the world is becoming a priority. Providing efficient and cost effective solutions to detect driving behavior is quite a challenging research topic worldwide. Exploring several technologies including big data, machine learning, data mining and data analysis in general can help researchers to track vehicles and monitor drivers, since several sensors and devices can feed us with a huge amount of data. In this paper, we propose a GPS based method to track vehicles and detect different driving events. The main idea consists on exploiting GPS data to recognize several vehicular motion and proving the feasibility and efficiency of using GPS data in the driving events detection; Obtained results for the proposed method are promising.

Keywords: Driver behaviour monitoring · GPS · DTW · Hausdorff distance · Vehicle maneuvers

1 Introduction

Nowadays, over populated cities and urban areas are facing several transportation issues such as traffic congestion [1,2] which is steadily showing a growing trend and road accidents pushed up by drivers carelessness. In fact, although the rules and regulations imposed for road safety, the road accidents are one of the major causes of death injury and disability in all over the world, both in developed and developing countries. According to the statistics published in February 2020 by the World Health Organization (WHO)[1], approximately 1.35 million people die each year due to road traffic accidents. As far as there is no alarming system to educate drivers about their driving style, the consequences of the vehicle crashes, mainly due to driver distraction, abrupt steering, carelessness, or dangerous driving, are always getting worse. Fortunately, most vehicles today are equipped with several sensors which provide a huge number of

---

[1] https://www.who.int/news-room/fact-sheets/detail/road-traffic-injuries.

© Springer Nature Switzerland AG 2020
F. Krief et al. (Eds.): Nets4Cars/Nets4Trains/Nets4Aircraft 2020, LNCS 12574, pp. 39–54, 2020.
https://doi.org/10.1007/978-3-030-66030-7_4

information about acceleration, speed, positioning and direction or about visual attributes to detect drowsiness and fatigue state [3,4]. This data can be used to analyze driver behaviors, identify risky events and create an alarming system to warn about dangerous drivers and thus help in improving safety. Providing solutions for safety road issues, such as dangerous driving detection system or driving assistance system, helps to reduce the number of road crashes and their tragic consequences and to raise driver's awareness.

In this context, several researches have been done in order to improve driver's safety and monitor driving behaviors using data from several sources such as external sensors, in-vehicle devices [5] or hybrid technologies. Some works are based on driver attributes, mainly visual features to characterize the driver's vigilance. Images from in board camera can be analyzed to extract some facial features such as the movements of the driver mouth in order to identify the yawning fatigue state [4] or to extract the pose face and the eyelid movements [3]. Other works used driving attributes collected directly from the CAN-BUS [6–8] or from external sensors. Some approaches rely on exchanged information between vehicles (V2V communication) or video sequences from road side cameras to monitor and record driving events [9]. Gathering data from these external sensors needs an implementation of some software and requires an expensive infrastructure to ensure the communication between vehicles and the road stations or to record events using a video-surveillance system along roads. Setting up such infrastructure may be impossible in some developing countries. The recourse to data extracted from in vehicle or smartphone sensors constitutes an efficient solution.

Over the last ten years, owning a Smartphone has become a necessity; thanks to its helpful services and with the evolution of its associated industry, several useful applications in various fields involved the Smartphone use. In the driving behavior detection context, the Smartphone was widely employed thanks to its various sensors, reduced cost, ease of use and the possibility to install a smartphone-based system in any vehicle. Some extracted features from Smartphone sensors data, such as speed, acceleration, heading angle, position, are widely used [10,11]. Valuable features can be also extracted from Global Positioning System (GPS) data which does not require expensive devices or complicated infrastructure. In this work, we propose a cost-effective approach accessible by everyone and able to operate even with a typical smartphone or within a vehicle with basic functionalities. The basic idea is to compare the real time vehicle trajectory obtained by the GPS with a reference trajectory in order to detect the lateral maneuvers. Such knowledge is relevant to inform the drivers when driving behaviors are risky. To this end, we need to create the model trajectory for each lane in the road. Parameters in our work have a huge impact on the detection accuracy that's why several experiences have been made to properly choose the parameters values.

This paper is organized as follows: In Sect. 2, we present a review on GPS based approaches designed for detecting driving behaviors. Section 3 describes our approach relying on GPS data for vehicle maneuvers detection. In Sect. 4, we expose our dataset and the experimental study. Conclusions and future work are presented in the last section.

2   Related Works

Several works used data from GPS to monitor vehicle driving behaviors. Some of them installed a GPS device in the vehicle to collect data. In [12], the authors proposed a system that detects abnormal drivers automatically using GPS data sent from in-car transponder to a monitoring station. The detection algorithm compares the driver behavior with normal driving defined with fixed thresholds on speed and lateral position changing. In [13], the authors exploited GPS data and some derivative indicators extracted from the speed and the acceleration measurements to identify the risky events and classify drivers into five categories according to the different levels of risk. They used a Differential Global Positioning System (DGPS) to collect speed and acceleration with high accuracy. Cameras have been used to record driving behaviors which are analyzed by experts in order to extract dangerous events and to construct a set of rules. Another system based on GPS is proposed in [14], the authors developed a real time vehicle tracking system called GIPIX-102B based on GPS technology and GSM/GPRS data transmission to collect GPS positions, speed and time values for later analysis. They extracted a set of parameters such as mean value and standard deviation for speed, acceleration, positive acceleration and barking. Then, they exploited the Principal Component Analysis algorithm to reduce the parameters space dimension and the Hierarchical Clustering algorithm to classify drivers into groups according to the aggressiveness degree from not aggressive to very aggressive. An algorithm for driving style economy estimation is presented in [15]. The main idea is to calculate the energy spent by the driver and compare it with the one obtained from profile references. It is based on the speed and the position collected by a GPS and the longitudinal and lateral accelerations collected by an automotive Inertial Measurement Unit (IMU).

Other works have used the Smartphone GPS for their studies. Wolverine in [16] exploited Smartphone sensors like data from GPS, accelerometer and magnetometer to monitor traffic state. The author applies machine learning techniques such as K-means and SVM[2] to detect bump and braking events and to classify the road into smooth road or bumpy road. In [17], two algorithms were proposed to detect 13 driving events divided into laterals and longitudinal which are right/left turn (normal/aggressive), right/left lane change (normal/aggressive), U-turn, braking (normal/ aggressive) and acceleration (normal/aggressive) using data obtained from Smartphone sensors. The first algorithm is based on GPS data, it sets thresholds on both acceleration and heading angle values to identify driving events. The second algorithm deploys DTW[3] to compare templates created for each event with incoming data from the accelerometer and the magnetometer. Experiences results show that the DTW based algorithm has better

---

[2] SVM: Support Vector Machine.
[3] DTW: Dynamic Time Warping.

performance than the rule-based algorithm in the detection for both lateral and longitudinal events. In [18], the authors propose to divide events into two categories lateral and longitudinal and detect them using a fusion of sensors data from accelerometer, magnetometer, GPS and camera. First, templates have been created for each aggressive event. After that, the authors determined the segment that corresponds to the maneuver using end-point detection algorithm and then use DTW to recognize lateral events while longitudinal events have been easily recognized using thresholds. GPS data in this work allows to determine the speed and the occurred event position, and the camera is used to record driving video for later review. This work distinguishes events with similar movements after examining the accuracy of using pure data from each sensor and proposing a combination of values from accelerometer, gyroscope and Euler rotation angle values to properly detect events. In [19], authors presented DriveSafe, a driver safety application for iphones that uses computer vision and pattern recognition to detect drowsiness and distraction states and gives feedbacks to drivers. The rear camera and the microphone were used for drowsiness state detection, while the accelerometer and the gyroscope were used for the distraction state detection in addition to the GPS which is used to estimate the vehicle speed and the road curvature.

As we can note, previous methods always use GPS jointly with other sensors such as the accelerometer, orientation sensor, gravity sensor etc, which requires more calculations and a technical infrastructure that may be not available in all vehicles or devices. To overcome these difficulties, we propose a cost-effective approach accessible by everyone and able to operate even with a typical smartphone or within a vehicle with basic functionalities.

3   GPS Based Method for Vehicle Maneuver Detection

Nowadays, manufacturers are putting much efforts to provide smart cars able to give a feedback about driving behaviors and to interact with the entourage in order to make decisions or give some directives to the driver. With innovative technological assets, these cars implement and accomplish specific actions to assist drivers like parking and take measures like reducing excessive and inappropriate speed. Exploiting such assets to improve road safety is a very attractive solution; upgrading a typical car with some sensors can be cost-effective while providing similar solutions and functionalities.

In this paper, we propose a GPS based method to detect vehicle maneuvers; GPS data can be obtained from the smartphone sensor or from a GPS integrated in the vehicle. Our aim is to investigate the effectiveness of such solution and later quantify its performances in terms of accuracy. The main idea is to compare the driver trajectory to a model trajectory associated to the taken road. To this end, we create a model trajectory for each road, referring typically to a good driving behavior along this road. For each vehicle, we retrieve its GPS coordinates over time to extract the vehicle trajectory. Then, we compare the test vehicle trajectory with the model one in order to detect events. The steps of our method are presented in Fig. 1.

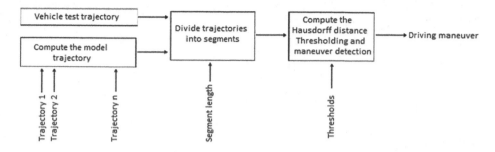

Fig. 1. The GPS based method process.

3.1   Creation of the Model Trajectory

This step consists in extracting a reference trajectory by combining several vehicle trajectories of the same road segment. This reference trajectory will be compared with the vehicle test trajectory in order to detect driving maneuvers. In this context, we used a DTW-based method [20]. Let's consider that we have two trajectories: T1 = [t11, t12, ..., t1n] and T2 = [t21, t22, ..., t2m], where t1i and t2i refers to the ith point respectively in the trajectory t1 and t2. Firstly, we construct an (n, m) matrix where the (ith, jth) element of the matrix corresponds to the distance d(t1i, t2j) between the points t1i and t2j. Then, we find the path which represents the shortest cumulative distance between the two trajectories. The path will be used to generate the combined trajectory. Each point in the path is defined with two indices corresponding to the points from the DTW inputs (trajectories). For each point in the path, we compute the mean between the two trajectories points to produce a new point in the new trajectory. This process is illustrated in Fig. 2.

To explain the DTW functional behavior, let's suppose that we have t1 and t2 two trajectory time series with a number of points n and m respectively. The first step in the DTW algorithm consists on constructing a matrix of n*m cells where the (i^{th}, j^{th}) element of the matrix corresponds to the squared distance, $d(t1_i, t2_j) = (t1_i - t2_j)^2$. The next step is finding the path P which minimizes the cumulative cost. The cumulative cost is calculated as follows:

$$\sigma(i,j) = d(t1_i, t2_j) + min(\sigma(i-1, j-1), \sigma(i-1, j), \sigma(i, j-1)) \quad (1)$$

where d(i, j) is the distance in the current cell, and $\sigma(i,j)$ is the cumulative distance of d(i, j) and the minimum cumulative distances from the three adjacent cells.

An example presented in Fig. 3 [23] describes the several steps for the application of the DTW algorithm on two time series A and B.

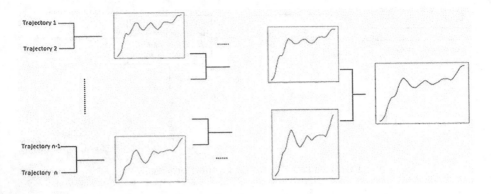

Fig. 2. Model trajectory process.

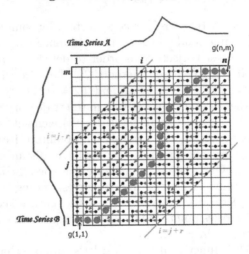

Fig. 3. Illustration of how DTW works. (Color figure online)

We start with the calculation of $g(1, 1) = d(1, 1)$, then we calculate the first row $g(i, 1) = g(i-1, 1) + d(i, 1)$ and the first column $g(1, j) = g(1, j) + d(1, j)$. After that, we move to the second row $g(i, 2) = \min(g(i, 1), g(i-1, 1), g(i-1, 2)) + d(i, 2)$ and we save for each cell the index of this neighboring cell, which gives the minimum score (red arrows). We carry on from left to right and from bottom to top with the rest of the grid. The final step is to find the best path by starting from $g(n, m)$ and moving to $g(1, 1)$ following the red arrows.

3.2   Division of the Vehicle Trajectory Data into Segments

Having a model trajectory for each lane in the road and after collecting data from the GPS, the vehicle trajectory is divided into segments in order to identify where the event occurs. The same fragmentation process is applied to the model trajectory. As a result, we have two sets of sub-trajectories having the same length. As the length of a sub-trajectory will have a deep impact on the detection process accuracy, the appropriate length will be discussed in the experimental study section. The next step is the Hausdorff distance calculation which is presented in the next subsection.

3.3 Hausdorff Distance Calculation

In order to be able to detect vehicles maneuvers, we track vehicle progress and we compare the vehicle trajectory against the reference one. Once the vehicle trajectory moves away from the model path by a defined distance, we can trail the vehicle maneuvers. To this end, we compute the Hausdorff distance for each pair of sub-trajectories from the vehicle test data and the model trajectory data. After comparing results with predefined thresholds, if an event occurs, the corresponding segment is identified.

The Hausdorff distance is given by the Eqs. (1) and (2).

$$H(A, B) = max(h(A, B), h(B, A)) \tag{2}$$

Where

$$h(A, B) = max(min(d(a, b))) \tag{3}$$

where d(a, b) is the Euclidean distance between a and b. Figure 4 [21] presents an example of calculating the Hausdorff distance. A and B consists of five and four points respectively. All distances from a3 to B are calculated. The distance from a3 to b1 is the smallest. In the same way, the other minimum distances from a to b are calculated and the maximum among them is h(A, B) in Eq. (2).

4 Experimental Study

In order to assess the proposed approach for maneuver detection, we first present, in this section, the used dataset in our experiments. Then we study the different parameters values and their impact on the method performance. Once the appropriate parameters are fixed, we evaluate our approach performance.

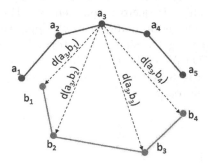

Fig. 4. An example of calculating Hausdorff distance.

4.1 Dataset

In this work, we use a dataset published by the United States Department of Transportation (US Dot) Federal Highway Administration (FHWA) for the Next Generation Simulation (NGSIM) program [22]. Data are collected on the southbound US 101 in Los Angeles, CA, on June 15th, 2005. Eight synchronized digital video cameras mounted from the top of a 36-story building adjacent to the freeway recorded vehicles on a 640 m area (approximately 2100 ft) during 45 min divided into three 15-min periods. The collected data provided X, Y coordinates of each vehicle, every $1/10^{th}$ of a second in relative space. It also specifies the vehicle ID, the lane ID, the vehicle class (motorcycle, truck or auto), the vehicle instantaneous acceleration in feet/second square and more other attributes. In this work, we are mainly interested in the X and Y coordinates used to detect the vehicle trajectory trace and to identify the maneuvers. From the description provided in [22], the Local X attribute presents the lateral (X) coordinate of the vehicle front center in feet with respect to the left-most edge of the section in the travel direction and the Local Y is the longitudinal (Y) coordinate of the vehicle front center in feet with respect to the entry edge of the section in the travel direction.

In our experiments, we consider 2097150 measurements for 3309 vehicles collected between 7:50am and 8:20am in a summer day. We classify vehicles according to the number of lane changes, thus, we can distinguish the following lateral events:

- One lane changing: a vehicle changes from the current lane to the neighbor lane without coming back, as shown in Fig. 5a.
- Lane changing with comeback: the vehicle changes the lane and quickly comes back to the initial lane. It can be an overtaking event, as illustrated in Fig. 5b.
- Lane changing several times, as shown in Fig. 5c.

4.2 Trajectory Model Computation

All the experiences carried out in this work are based on the trajectory data from the database previously presented. The first step is to compute a model trajectory from several vehicle trajectories on each lane. Having n trajectories for vehicles moving on a lane without changing it, we apply the DTW combination iteratively in pairs until we get a single trajectory that represents the model. The application of the DTW method on vehicles on Lane 1 gives the model trajectory presented in Fig. 6. With the same process, we create a trajectory model for each lane in the road.

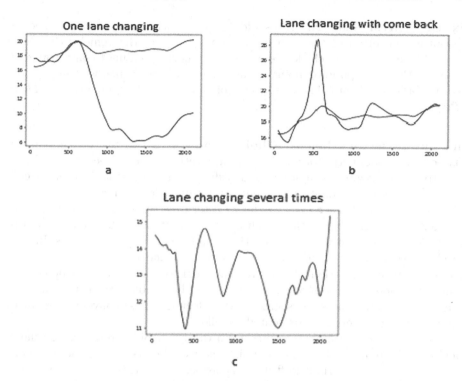

Fig. 5. Vehicle maneuver examples.

4.3   Choice of the Parameters' Values

For our work, thresholds and segment length have a huge impact in detection accuracy, therefore, some experiences are conducted to properly select their values.

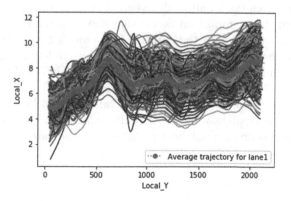

Fig. 6. The model trajectory for Lane 1.

Fix the Thresholds. The threshold for a lane changing event is fixed by computing the mean of the Hausdorff distances for all the vehicles that have changed lanes. For each vehicle, we fix the point corresponding to lane changing, we search the corresponding point in the model trajectory then we compute the distance between points. The fixed threshold for a lane changing event is $Th = 5.92\,ft$.

The Sub-trajectory Length Choice. To apply a two by two comparison between the model trajectory and the vehicle test trajectory, we need to divide trajectories into segments in order to identify in which segment the event occurs and approximately estimate the event start time. The segment length is the object of study in this section in order to determine the most optimal one. We consider three segment lengths which are 50 ft, 75 ft and 100 ft. Our aim is to maintain a trade off between computational and accuracy performances. In fact, too short segments result in longer execution time and too long segments lead to maneuvers misdetection. An appropriate segment size allows to detect the maneuver made by the vehicle and to reduce the probability of two or more events occurring on the same segment. We select the most convenient segment length based on experiences presented as follows.

In order to compute the distance from the threshold, we determine the Y Local coordinate of the lane change point and we label its corresponding frame. Then, we compare the Hausdorff distance associated to this frame with a fixed threshold. The optimal length gives the smallest difference between the Hausdorff distance for the lane change point and the threshold. For example, for vehicle number 529, the segment that corresponds to the lane change for the 3 segment lengths tested is presented in Fig. 7, the Hausdorff distance for this frame is equal to 7.75 for the 50 ft, 6.44 for 100 ft and 6.42 for 75 ft.

Table 1 presents the average Hausdorff distance for vehicles that have changed lane once and the difference between the threshold and the computed average distance. In this experience, the threshold for a changing lane event is 5.92 ft. Results show that dividing trajectories into sub-segments of 75 ft seems the right choice because it gives the smallest difference so the highest precision.

Execution time is an important factor that should be considered. In order to assess this factor, we compute the runtime for vehicles that have changed lane once. All algorithms were implemented with Python under the same conditions using a laptop with Intel Core i5-5200U CPU @ 2.20 GHz RAM 8.00 Go. Results are given in Table 2. As shown, average runtime for 75 ft frame length is very close and almost equal the average for 100 ft frame length. While for 50 ft frame length, the runtime is slightly longer. Results relative to the runtime are very similar, thus the runtime cannot be a length choice indicator.

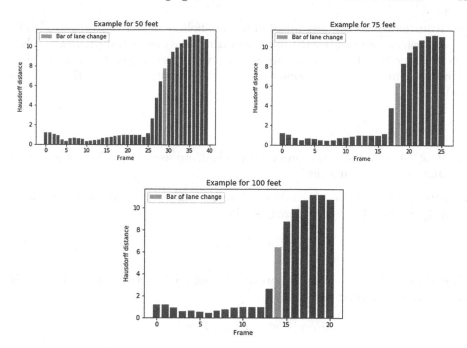

Fig. 7. An example of Hausdorff distance for a set of 50, 75 and 100 ft sub-trajectories.

Table 1. Difference between Hausdorff distances and threshold.

Sub-trajectory length	50 ft	75 ft	100 ft
Average Hausdorff distance	6.95	6.14	6.30
Difference between avg and threshold	1.03	0.22	0.38

Table 2. Runtimes (s).

Sub-trajectory length	50 ft	75 ft	100 ft
Runtime	2.36	2.04	2.05

5   Maneuvers Detection Evaluation

Having the model trajectory for each lane, the threshold and the sub-trajectory
length, we can apply our algorithm to detect vehicle maneuvers. In this work,
we focus on detecting lateral events, the main event to be detected is the lane
changing and from which we can detect other maneuvers. To detect the vehicle
maneuvers, we use a thresholding technique. The first step is to identify in which
lane the vehicle is moving. Then, we divide trajectories into segments using the
fixed length, 75 ft. Having two equal sets of sub trajectories, we compute the
Hausdorff distance for each couple of sub trajectories to compare it with the
threshold. If the condition is satisfied, the event will be detected. We apply the

algorithm iteratively until we investigate the whole vehicle trajectory. As a result for each vehicle, we identify the list of changing lane events and where and when each event occurs. In the next sub-sections, we present several metrics used to evaluate the maneuvers detection and then, we present and discuss the obtained results.

5.1   Evaluation Metrics

To quantitatively assess the proposed method, we used the following standard information retrieval metrics:

Recall: It refers to the proportion of actual positive results that have been correctly identified, it is computed as follows:

$$Recall = TP/(TP + FN). \tag{4}$$

Precision: It measures the proportion of positive detections that are actually correct. It is computed as follows:

$$Precision = TP/(TP + FP). \tag{5}$$

Accuracy: It measures the proportion of positive detections that are actually correct. It is computed as follows:

$$Accuracy = (TP + TN)/(TP + FP + TN + FN). \tag{6}$$

Where TP (True Positive) means the number of events correctly detected, FN (False Negative) which represents the number of missing events (events not detected by the system). FP (False Positive) is the number of no events labeled by the system as events and TN (True Negative) is the number of no events labeled correctly by the system.

F1 score: The use of F1 score is recommended when we had an uneven class distribution. It is the weighted average of Precision and Recall and it is computed as follows:

$$F1score = 2 \times (Recall \times Precision)/(Recall + Precision). \tag{7}$$

5.2   Results and Discussion

Our aim is to evaluate the performance of the proposed method relying on extracted trajectories from GPS data to detect vehicles maneuvers. To this end, we consider a total of 3309 vehicles moving along the same road segment and behaving differently according to Table 3.

Table 4 exposes results relative to all events where we consider 1272 events made by 704 vehicles and 2605 vehicles with no lane changing.

Table 3. Vehicles number for each event.

	Vehicles number
Vehicles with no lane changing	2605
Vehicles with one lane changing	396
Vehicles with two lane changing	168
Vehicles with lane changing several times (3 or more)	140
Total	3309

Table 4. Obtained results when considering all events.

	Recall (%)	Precision (%)	Accuracy (%)
Lane changing event	67	93	88

As we can notice, using GPS data allows us to detect events with a precision rate over 92% and 87.76% for the accuracy rate while the recall rate is less satisfying due to the FN. The system failed to detect all events. The system inability to detect all events could be justified by the fact that the location data retrieved from the GPS may not be sufficiently accurate.

In Table 5, we present results obtained for the considered metrics regarding the defined classes in Table 3. For each vehicle, we verify if all events are correctly detected, except for a vehicle with more than 3 lane changes, we considered it TP if 90% or more of events are correctly detected. Otherwise, it is considered as a FN.

Table 5. Obtained results when considering distinct event classes.

	Recall (%)	Precision (%)	Accuracy (%)	F1 score
Vehicles with no lane changing	99	97	97	98.159
Vehicles with one lane changing	90	75	95	82.161
Vehicles with two lane changing	39	67	96	49.390
Vehicles with lane changing several times	26	52	96	34.427

As expected, measured results for all metrics decrease as the number of lane changes increases. Accuracy is the least impacted factor; it maintains a rate over 95% which means that our system succeeds to correctly predict the majority of classes. Less satisfying results are observable for the recall, precision and F1 score, specially when the lane changes number exceeds 2. This decline is due to successive close events which may mislead the system. In fact, some risky events are not detected as the driver barely enters another lane and his distance from the trajectory model of the taken lane remains over the threshold.

By combining the per-class F1 scores into a single number, we compute the **weighted-F1** in which we weight the F1-score of each class by the number of samples from that class.

$$Weighted \ \ F1 = \sum_{i=1}^{k} w_i \times F1_{score_i}. \tag{8}$$

Where K is the number of classes and w_i is the ith class weight. In our case, the obtained **weighted-F1** is equal to 91.072 which is considered as a good performance indicator.

6   Conclusion

Tracking vehicles to analyze driving behaviors in order to detect abnormal ones has a huge impact on improving road safety. To this end, detecting the events occurrence is the first required step before classifying them. Indeed, several driving monitoring systems have been developed based on various technologies and exploiting multiple data sources, in particular in-vehicle and smartphone sensors are widely used. Among the most available sensors, the GPS is commonly used to detect the event occurrence position but not for the event detection. In this work, we proposed a GPS based method to detect vehicle maneuvers, our aim is to evaluate the feasibility of a such method using only GPS data. Coordinates from GPS were used to draw vehicles trajectories, which are then compared to a model trajectory obtained by DTW combination method. In order to detect an event occurrence, a thresholding is applied on Hausdorff distances computed between test sub-trajectories and model ones. The performance of the lane changing detection was evaluated and experiments showed that 70% of events are correctly detected. For successive lane changes, the accuracy value is less satisfying.

Unquestionably, more experiments are required to better ascertain the effectiveness of this approach. In fact, the accuracy of a GPS based method is closely related to the accuracy of GPS data. Many factors can degrade GPS positioning accuracy such as satellite signal reflection due to buildings and trees, which gives a wrong position of the vehicle and consequently a wrong distance estimation from the model trajectory. Although new technologies can provide better positioning accuracy within a few centimeters, we intend, in future work, to build our own dataset through collected data from a smartphone or from in-vehicle GPS, in order to more assess the performance of the proposed method. Besides, we will investigate the choice for the threshold on the performances. We intend also to enhance the proposed solutions by exploiting relevant information from the combination of several data sources, when required, such as the speed and the orientation in order to properly identify more events and to classify them.

References

1. Chetouane, A., Mabrouk, S., Jemili, I., Mosbah, M.: Vision-based vehicle detection for road traffic congestion classification. Concurr. Comput.: Pract. Exp. e5983 (2020)

2. Chetouane, A., Mabrouk, S., Jemili, I., Mosbah, M.: A comparative study of vehicle detection methods in a video sequence. In: Jemili, I., Mosbah, M. (eds.) DiCES-N 2019. CCIS, vol. 1130, pp. 37–53. Springer, Cham (2020). https://doi.org/10.1007/978-3-030-40131-3_3

3. Bergasa, L.M., Nuevo, J., Sotelo, M.A., Barea, R., Lopez, M.E.: Real-time system for monitoring driver vigilance. IEEE Trans. Intell. Transp. Syst. **7**(1), 63–77 (2006)

4. Rongben, W., Lie, G., Bingliang, T., Lisheng, J.: Proceedings of the 7th International IEEE Conference on Intelligent Transportation Systems (IEEE Cat. No. 04TH8749). IEEE (2004)

5. Ksouri, C., Jemili, I., Mosbah, M., Belghith, A.: Data gathering for Internet of Vehicles safety. In: 2018 14th International Wireless Communications & Mobile Computing Conference (IWCMC), pp. 904–909. IEEE (2018)

6. Choi, S., Kim, J., Kwak, D., Angkititrakul, P., Hansen, J.H.: Analysis and classification of driver behavior using in-vehicle can-bus information. In: Biennial Workshop on DSP for In-Vehicle and Mobile Systems, pp. 17–19 (2007)

7. Van Ly, M., Martin, S., Trivedi, M.M.: Driver classification and driving style recognition using inertial sensors. In: 2013 IEEE Intelligent Vehicles Symposium (IV), pp. 1040–1045. IEEE (2013)

8. Fugiglando, U., et al.: Driving behavior analysis through CAN bus data in an uncontrolled environment. IEEE Trans. Intell. Transp. Syst. **20**(2), 737–748 (2018)

9. Sun, Y., Zhu, H., Liao, Y., Sun, L.: Vehicle anomaly detection based on trajectory data of ANPR system. In: 2015 IEEE Global Communications Conference (GLOBECOM), pp. 1–6. IEEE (2015)

10. Ouyang, Z., Niu, J., Liu, Y., Rodrigues, J.: Multiwave: a novel vehicle steering pattern detection method based on smartphones. In: 2016 IEEE International Conference on Communications (ICC), pp. 1–7. IEEE (2016)

11. Wu, X., Zhou, J., An, J., Yang, Y.: Abnormal driving behavior detection for bus based on the Bayesian classifier. In: 2018 Tenth International Conference on Advanced Computational Intelligence (ICACI), pp. 266–272. IEEE (2018)

12. Mohamad, I., Ali, M.A.M., Ismail, M.: Abnormal driving detection using real time global positioning system data. In: Proceeding of the 2011 IEEE International Conference on Space Science and Communication (IconSpace), pp. 1–6. IEEE (2011)

13. Fu, R., Liu, T., Guo, Y., Zhang, S., Cheng, W.: A case study in China to determine whether GPS data and derivative indicator can be used to identify risky drivers. J. Adv. Transp. **2019**, 1–16 (2019)

14. Constantinescu, Z., Marinoiu, C., Vladoiu, M.: Driving style analysis using data mining techniques. Int. J. Comput. Commun. Control **5**(5), 654–663 (2010)

15. Manzoni, V., Corti, A., De Luca, P., Savaresi, S.M.: Driving style estimation via inertial measurements. In: 13th International IEEE Conference on Intelligent Transportation Systems, pp. 777–782. IEEE (2010)

16. Bhoraskar, R., Vankadhara, N., Raman, B., Kulkarni, P.: Wolverine: traffic and road condition estimation using smartphone sensors. In: 2012 Fourth International Conference on Communication Systems and Networks (COMSNETS 2012), pp. 1–6. IEEE (2012)

17. Saiprasert, C., Pholprasit, T., Pattara-Atikom, W.: Detecting driving events using smartphone. In: Proceedings of the 20th ITS World Congress, p. 11 (2013)

18. Johnson, D.A., Trivedi, M.M.: Driving style recognition using a smartphone as a sensor platform. In: 2011 14th International IEEE Conference on Intelligent Transportation Systems (ITSC), pp. 1609–1615. IEEE (2011)

19. Bergasa, L.M., Almería, D., Almazán, J., Yebes, J.J., Arroyo, R.: DriveSafe: an app for alerting inattentive drivers and scoring driving behaviors. In: 2014 IEEE Intelligent Vehicles Symposium Proceedings, pp. 240–245. IEEE (2014)
20. Vaughan, N., Gabrys, B.: Comparing and combining time series trajectories using dynamic time warping. Proc. Comput. Sci. **96**, 465–474 (2016)
21. Jeong, H., Srinivasan, S.: Fast selection of geologic models honoring CO2 plume monitoring data using Hausdorff distance and scaled connectivity analysis. Int. J. Greenhouse Gas Control **59**, 40–57 (2017)
22. U.S. Department of Transportation Intelligent Transportation Systems Joint Program Office (JPO): Next Generation Simulation (NGSIM) US Route 101 Dataset (2016)
23. https://medium.com/datadriveninvestor/dynamic-time-warping-dtw-d51d1a1e 4afc

Analysis and Comparison of IEEE 802.11p and IEEE 802.11bd

Badreddine Yacine Yacheur[1,2]([⊠]) [iD], Toufik Ahmed[1]([⊠]) [iD], and Mohamed Mosbah[1]([⊠]) [iD]

[1] LaBRI CNRS UMR5800, Univ. Bordeaux, Bordeaux INP, 33400 Talence, France
byyacheur@u-bordeaux.fr, {tad,mosbah}@labri.fr
[2] Ecole nationale Supérieure d'Informatique, BP 68M, 16309 Oued Smar, Algiers, Algeria
fb_yacheur@esi.dz

Abstract. As the interest to improve road safety and traffic management is growing, a new generation standard for Vehicular Ad-hoc Networks (VANETs) need to be defined to enhance the performances of the vehicular networks' communications, in terms of reliability, latency, and throughput. Nowadays, the IEEE 802.11p related systems such as ITS-G5, are the most used C-ITS technologies in Europe. However, these radio access technologies (RATs) fall short of supporting many advanced vehicular applications' communication requirements as high reliability, low latency, and high throughput. In this context, the IEEE 802.11bd is being defined as an amendment to IEEE 802.11p to fulfill these requirements. In this paper, we first analyze the introduced mechanisms in IEEE 802.11bd. Then, to assess its performances compared to the IEEE 802.11p, we propose a simulation-based approach by implementing this new RAT in the OMNeT++ simulator. This implementation will be tested and evaluated. We show that IEEE 802.11bd can enhance the network quality of service performance compared to IEEE 802.11p. This will allow improving road safety.

Keywords: Cooperative intelligent transport systems · IEEE 802.11p · IEEE 802.11bd · OMNeT++

1 Introduction

Vehicular communications have an eminence potential to improve road safety. It allows vehicles to exchange awareness messages with their surroundings. This cooperative aspect will procure a set of applications to build an awareness system for better road safety and traffic management. These messages must be sent reliably, quickly, and with high throughput to promise a better safety service. Nowadays, V2X communication technologies (i.e. ITS-G5 and WAVE) are based globally on the standard IEEE 802.11p™-2010. This latter is derived from the IEEE 802.11a™-2009. However, during the past decade, IEEE 802.11 technology has been improved, from IEEE 802.11a™-2009, to IEEE 802.11n™-2009, IEEE 802.11ac™-2013 and the ongoing IEEE 802.11ax™ amendment, which offers very high throughput, as well as, improved communication range and higher reliability. So, to benefit from these enhancements and to scale the vehicular

F. Krief et al. (Eds.): Nets4Cars/Nets4Trains/Nets4Aircraft 2020, LNCS 12574, pp. 55–65, 2020.
https://doi.org/10.1007/978-3-030-66030-7_5

performances, a new Study Group called the IEEE 802.11 Next Generation V2X was formed in March 2018 [1] to create the IEEE Task Group 802.11bd (TGbd) in Jan. 2019. This task group aims to build a new V2X communication standard, namely the IEEE 802.11bd standard. This latter will be the definition of new PHY and MAC specifications based on new and existing IEEE 802.11 WLAN PHY/MAC (IEEE 802.11ac and IEEE 802.11ax) standards. The IEEE 802.11bd standard is supposed to replace the IEEE 802.11p standard and to provide a vehicular ad-hoc environment with performance enhancement compared to IEEE 802.11p in terms of throughput, latency, reliability, and communication range.

The IEEE 802.11ac standard was implemented (by Inzillo et al.) [2] in the Discrete Event Simulator OMNeT++. This implementation focused on the INET Framework which is an open-source OMNeT++ model suite for wired, wireless, and mobile networks. Implementing the IEEE 802.11ac in OMNeT++ bought improvements in the simulator's features such as the very high throughput (VHT) mode and the multiple-input multiple-output (MIMO) antennas. The IEEE 802.11p standard was implemented in the INET framework too. This implementation was used by the Artery framework [3] as the PHY and MAC layers of the ITS-G5 technology.

The objective of this paper is to provide analysis and performance comparison between IEEE 802.11p and IEEE 802.11bd in meeting the new generation V2X application requirements. We can evoke some theoretical evaluations that treat the same subjects as ours. The finding in [4] presents an evaluation of the performance of V2X technologies by modeling their complete PHY features in MATLAB. Adding to that most studies that dealt with C-V2X performance derived their results from simulation platforms [10]. Our comparison is performed through the OMNeT++ simulation platform. We used the Artery framework to simulate ITS-G5 technology (i.e. IEEE 802.11p. Furthermore, since OMNeT++ doesn't provide an IEEE 802.11bd implementation like many other discrete event based-simulation tools. We will follow the OMNeT++ improvement move and enhance the features of both INET and Artery by implementing the IEEE 802.11bd standard in the INET framework. Thus, make it available in the Artery. We built a basic implementation of the IEEE 802.11bd standard in to be able to simulate IEEE 802.11bd based V2X communications. The remainder of this paper is structured as follows. In Sect. 2, we will present an overview of each technology with an emphasis on how each of them will enhance message delivery reliability. Next, in Sect. 3, we will present, in detail, the implementation and validation of the IEEE 802.11bd standard. Finally, we will conclude with a road safety perspective on how these improvements will enhance road safety.

2   Overview of C-ITS Technologies

In this section, we detail the most relevant specifications of each technology that have an impact on the reliability of message delivery.

2.1   Overview of the IEEE 802.11p Standard

The IEEE 802.11p is based on the IEEE 802.11a standard, to which it brings some changes to adapt it for the vehicular environment. This standard supports relative velocity up to 200 km/h, a response times of around 100 ms, and a communication range of up to 1000 m. However, due to interferences and noise effects, this standard doesn't assure good reliability of message delivery. As presented in [5], the estimated average delivery reliability of IEEE 802.11p is 78%. This is due to the abovementioned Physical and MAC layers specifications.

The physical layer of IEEE 802.11p is based on the Orthogonal Frequency Division Multiplexing (OFDM) similar to most 802.11 standards. The main difference as compared to IEEE 802.11a is in the carrier spacing and bandwidth, which are reduced by a factor of two (10 MHz of bandwidth and 156.25 kHz sub-carrier spacing). IEEE 802.11p uses binary convolutional coding (BCC) that is a weak coding mechanism compared to the low-density parity-check coding (LDPC) or the turbo coding. BCC loses its capability to recover erroneous messages once we augment the modulation and coding schemas (MCS) in a high communication range (i.e. >50 m). The MAC layer of the IEEE 802.11p uses the Enhanced Distributed Channel Access (EDCA) method which uses carrier sense multiple access with collision avoidance (CSMA/CA) with no exponential back-off and no message acknowledgment [6]. To provide low latency, the IEEE 802.11p standard is operating in the out-of-context of a basic service set (OCB). This means that there is no association nor authentication before sensing the channel. Besides, the standard does not allow message retransmission. Consequently, a loss in message delivery reliability is observed.

2.2 Overview of the IEEE 802.11bd Standard

IEEE 802.11bd standard is based on the IEEE 802.11ac (a.k.a. Wi-Fi 5) which makes it more powerful than its predecessor IEEE 802.11p. According to the project authorization report (PAR) [7], the IEEE 802.11bd standard should assure twice the performance of the IEEE 802.11p with a tolerance for twice the MAC throughput of 802.11p, relative velocities up to 500 km/h, and twice the communication range of 802.11p. In the IEEE 802.11bd PHY layer, a 20 MHz bandwidth channel is used for communication instead of 10 MHz in IEEE 802.11p. The modulation and coding scheme (MCS) profile can reach 256-QAM, and multiple-input multiple-output antenna can help in providing very high throughput. To maintain reliability in an environment of 500 km/h velocity and using 256QAM MCS, IEEE 802.11bd uses the LDPC coding mechanism and Midambles which are similar in form to a preamble but are used in-between the OFDM data symbols to estimate the channel variation. Thus, this reduces the interference effects on message integrity. *IEEE* 802.11*bd*^{DC} is a variant of the IEEE 802.11bd and is based on the IEEE 802.11ax standard. The *bd*^{DC} implements the dual-carrier modulation (DCM) which augments its communication range. IEEE 802.11bd MAC layer is also based on the EDCA method to access the channel. However, with a 20 MHz bandwidth and a 256-QAM MCS, we can allow message retransmissions by sending each OFDM symbol over two different sub-carriers. This latter, combined with each of LDPC and midambles, will help to achieve better reliability of message delivery as compared to the IEEE 802.11p standard performances.

3 Implementation and Model Validation

In this section, we propose to implement the IEEE 802.11bd important building blocks in the OMNeT++ simulator. Then, we validate our implementation by comparing the simulator's output with the theoretical specification of the standard.

3.1 IEEE 802.11bd Implementation

The first step of this implementation was to study and test what was implemented as VHT specifications in the physical layer models of the INET framework. Next, we adopt these specifications to build a new "bd" operating mode, that reflects the IEEE 802.11bd standard implementation. Furthermore, we use this implementation in the Artery framework to benefit from an enhanced throughput in our VANET simulation scenarios.

In the INET Framework

The two micro-layers that are concerned with these modifications are the IEEE 802.11 "mode" modules and the "packet-level" modules. The "mode" modules are both the "IEEE 802.11 mode" module and the "IEEE 802.11 band" module. The "mode" module defines the Modulation and coding schemas (MCS), the number of streams, and the preamble format used to achieve the wanted data rate values. As the "bd" mode requires a Very High Throughput (VHT). We use the "VHT Mode", thus, supporting modulation schemes up to 256-QAM. The "IEEE 802.11 band" module defines the frequency band and its respective channel bandwidth. And as the IEEE 802.11bd operates on a channel bandwidth of 20 MHz in the 5.9 GHz band, we had to add the definition of these channel parameters to the "band" module. In Fig. 1, we illustrate the concerned modules in the process of adding the "bd" operation mode. This operation mode had to be added in each of these modules to have a complete PHY layer that can support the "bd" mode.

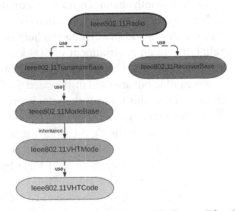

Fig. 1. The concerned modules with the modifications.

To be able to send and receive messages in a 20 MHz channel bandwidth we had to define a 5.9 GHz band with two 20 MHz bandwidth channels. The 5.9 GHz can hold up to two 20 MHz channels. The central frequencies of these two 20 MHz channels are 5.875 GHz and 5.905 GHz. We defined this band as an "Ieee80211EnumeratedBand" structure that takes as parameters the name of the band and the central frequency of each channel as shown below from the "Ieee80211Band.cc" code source:

```
Const Ieee80211EnumeratedBand
  Ieee80211CompliantBands::band5_9GHz20MHz("5.9 GHz&20 MHz",
  {                                          .
    GHz(5.875),
    GHz(5.905),
  });
```

With these modifications done we could modify the OMNeT++ Network Description Files (NEDs) to add the operation mode "bd" and the band name 5 GHz&20 MHz as depicted in the following extract of the "Ieee80211TransmitterBase.ned" source file.

```
module Ieee80211TransmitterBase extends NarrowbandTransmitterBase
{
    parameters:
        string opMode @enum("a", "b", "g(erp)", "g(mixed)",
"n(mixed-2.4Ghz)", "p", "ac", "bd");
        string bandName @enum("2.4 GHz", "5.9 GHz", "5.9 GHz&20
MHz", "5 GHz","5 GHz&20 MHz","5 GHz&40 MHz","5 GHz&80 MHz","5
GHz&160 MHz");
        int channelNumber;
        modulation = default("BPSK");
}
```

In the Artery Framework

Artery modules are responsible for the Application and the Facilities layers in the ITS station architecture (see Fig. 2). The component that manages the message forwarding between these layers and the lower ones is the Artery middleware, which acts also as an abstraction and data provisioning layer for VANET applications (services in Artery's terminology). Artery provides a flexible framework for the implementation of services (applications). It offers the possibility of creating many services in a VANET node and each service can operate with a multi-channel policy [3]. These services are created according to an external definition as an XML configuration file (services.xml file). This XML file lists the services for a group of vehicles, with their respective port and operating channel numbers. By default, the channel number is set to the Control Channel (i.e. CCH: central frequency = 5.9 GHz) as defined in the ITS-G5 standard.

To introduce the IEEE 802.11bd standard operating mode that we added in the INET framework, we modified the "application", "inet" and "utility" packages of the Artery Framework. The "application" package represents the application layer related modules. The "inet" package represents the modules that are related to the INET framework. The "utility" package represents the definition of some basic elements that are essential for

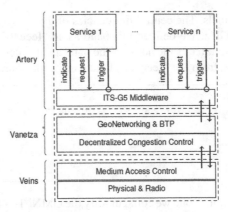

Fig. 2. Artery's ITS architecture [3].

the operation of other Artery modules. To send messages, the Artery middleware needs to find a network interface that operates on the appropriate service's channel. And to receive a message, it needs to find which service should this message be delivered to. If not specified in both the "omnet.ini" and the "services.xml" files of the simulation scenario, the middleware sends and receives messages according to the default parameters (i.e. the IEEE 802.11p network interface). So, to be able to send and receive messages in the newly defined "5.9 GHz&20 MHz" channel, we added its definition in the "utility/channel" module under the name of SCH0_BD and SCH1_BD as listed in the following extract of the "channel.h" source file.

```
constexpr ChannelNumber SCH0_BD = 0;
constexpr ChannelNumber SCH1_BD = 1;
```

To differentiate between a service that will use the IEEE 802.11p PHY layer and a service that will use the IEEE 802.11bd PHY layer in Artery. We added the "channel-bd" parameter to the service in the "services.xml" configurations file as listed in the following extract of the source file.

```
<?xml version="1.0" encoding="UTF-8"?>
<services>
  <service type="artery.application.CaService">
    <listener port="2001" channel="180" channel-bd="0" />
  </service>
  <service type="artery.application.ExampleService">
    <listener port="4711" channel="180" channe-bd="0"/>
    <listener port="4712" channel="176" channel-bd="1"/>
    <filters>
      <penetration rate="0.5" />
    </filters>
  </service>
</services>
```

To resume this implementation process, we modified both the INET and Artery frameworks to implement the basic specifications of the IEEE 802.11bd standard. In the INET framework, we used the VHT modules from the IEEE 802.11ac implementation to build an IEEE 802.11bd mode-set. We also defined a new 5.9 GHz band, namely the "5.9 GHz&20 MHz". In the Artery framework, we adapted the service's definition in the "services.xml" file and the Artery middleware to send and receive messages via a network interface that uses the IEEE 802.11bd standard. The network interface configuration under the "bd" mode is listed in the following extract of the "VanetNic.ned" source file. The "opMode" parameter indicates the IEEE 802.11 standard. Both "bandName" and "bandwidth" parameters define the band used to transmit and receive messages.

```
module VanetNic extends Ieee80211Nic
{
    parameters:
        macType = "Ieee80211Mac";
        mgmtType = "Ieee80211MgmtAdhoc";
        opMode = "bd";
        bitrate = default(52 Mbps);
        **.opMode = opMode;
        mac.modeSet = opMode;
        mac.qosStation = true;
        mac.rx.typename = default("ChannelLoadRx");
        radioType = default("VanetRadio");
        radio.bandName = "5.9 GHz&20 MHz";
        radio.bandwidth = 20 MHz;
        radio.channelNumber = default(0);
        radio.antenna.numAntennas = 8;
        radio.receiverType = default("VanetReceiver");
    ...}
```

3.2 Model Validation

Our implementation is intended to make a simulation-based comparison between IEEE 802.11-based C-ITS technologies (IEEE 802.11p and IEEE 802.11bd). This comparison has to be aligned with what was studied in the theoretical and analytical comparisons such as [4]. In this context, we first compare the IEEE 802.11bd theoretical performances with the obtained simulated results in terms of data bitrate (i.e. net bitrate). Next, we compare the performance of this new generation standard with its predecessor IEEE 802.11p in terms of bitrate, latency, and packet reception ratio (PRR) while varying the modulation and coding schemes and the distance between vehicles. Furthermore, to avoid interoperability and fairness issues, we consider evaluating these technologies in an isolated simulation environment. In all the simulation scenarios, we consider an urban road type and we assume that the IEEE 802.11bd standard will be published by the end of 2021 [11]. Simulation parameters are Summarized in Table 1. Our evaluation scenario is based on the Manhattan urban grid road type, where V2V communication is considered according to these characteristics:

Table 1. Main simulation parameter set.

	IEEE 802.11p	IEEE 802.11bd	LTE-V2X
Simulation time		120s	
Message length		From 200 Bytes to 1400 Bytes.	
Channel bandwidth	10 MHz	20 MHz	20 MHz
MCS	Up to 64-QAM with ¾ coding	Up to 256-QAM with ¾ coding	Up to 64-QAM
Num. NSS		1	
Receiver sensitivity	-85 dBm	-85 dBm	-85 dBm
Noise	-110 dBm	-110 dBm	-110 dBm
Receiver energy detection	-85 dBm	-85 dBm	-85 dBm
Transmit power	23 dBm	23 dBm	15 dBm

- Max vehicle speed: 40 km/h
- Between vehicles Gap: 0.5 m (meter)
- Vehicle acceleration: 0.8 m/s^2
- CAM message (Cooperative Awareness Message) and alert/warning messages: 10 messages per second (10 Hz).

The throughput depends on the number of data subcarriers, and this latter is tightly related to the bandwidth [4]. So, with a 20 MHz channel bandwidth, we will have 52 data subcarriers out of 64 OFDM subcarriers. With these resources, the IEEE 802.11bd will be able to realize the presented theoretical net bitrate in Table 2.

Table 2. Obtained simulation results compared to theoretical ones.

Modulation	Coding	Net bit rate (Mbps)	Simulation Net bit rate (Mbps)
BPSK	1/2	7.2	6.5
QPSK	1/2	14.4	13
QPSK	3/4	21.66	19.5
16-QAM	1/2	28.88	26
16-QAM	3/4	43.33	39
64-QAM	2/3	57.78	52
64-QAM	3/4	65	58.5
64-QAM	5/6	72.22	65
256-QAM	3/4	86.66	78

To calculate the net bitrate (*Rdata*), we used the same equation used in the IEEE 802.11ac standard as presented in [8].

$$Rdata = \frac{N_{DPBS}}{T_{Symbol}}$$ (1)

The N_{DPBS} is the number of data bits per OFDM symbol and T_{Symbol} is the symbol duration. The N_{DPBS} is determined by the number of data subcarriers and the MCS, while T_{Symbol} is determined by the employed bandwidth and the guard interval (GI) [8]. When we implemented the IEEE 802.11bd standard, we defined a set of modes. Each mode represents a combination of a modulation and coding scheme (MCS), a guard interval duration, and spatial streams. Each mode is associated with a specific data rate. After retrieving these simulation data rates and comparing them with the calculated theoretical ones, we found that the simulated bitrate confidently approaches the theoretical bit rate (see Table 2).

After comparing the calculated net-bitrate and the simulated one, we analyze this metric against the IEEE 802.11p. To do so, we launched two separate simulation runs, one using the IEEE 802.11bd standard (256-QAM), and the other using IEEE 802.11p (64-QAM). In this simulation runs, we vary the packet length from 50 bytes to 1300 bytes, and we fix the distance between two vehicles to 50 m.

From Fig. 3(a), we can see that the IEEE 802.11bd outperforms IEEE 802.11p in all cases. These results are aligned with the MATLAB ones presented in [4]. In Fig. 3(b), we recorded a transmission latency of 0.4 ms for IEEE 802.11p and 0.2 ms for IEEE 802.11bd (for a 1200 packet length). Thus, we notice a remarkable transmission latency drop of 50% between the two technologies.

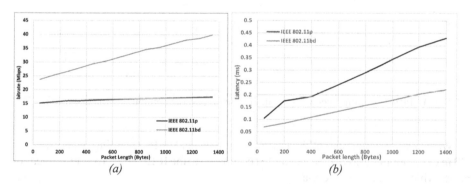

Fig. 3. Throughput (a) and Latency (b) comparison of IEEE 802.11bd and IEEE 802.11p.

Now that our implementation is validated, we compare the PRR between the IEEE 802.11-based C-ITS technologies (i.e. IEEE 802.11p and IEEE 802.11bd) to make some baselines for the road safety comparison that will follow this work.

3.3 Packet Reception Ratio Comparison

The packet reception ratio (PRR) is defined as the ratio of packets received successfully to the total number of transmitted packets. The PRR is commonly used by the vehicular community to evaluate the maximum range of technology over the distance and to find out how reliable is a technology in terms of packet delivery. To better reflect the performances of the IEEE 80211bd, we compare its simulation PRR results with the IEEE 802.11p ones. At this stage, it is worth noting that our implementation of the

802.11bd standard in OMNeT++ doesn't include LDPC coding. Thus, to obtain an accurate PRR comparison, we have integrated into our simulation results the finding in [9] which affirms that LDCP offers a gain of 1–4 dB over the Binary Convolutional Codes (BCC). This can be translated to a 20% PRR gain over BCC. In Fig. 4 the PRR obtained from different simulation runs is plotted according to the bitrate and to the communication distance. In Fig. 4(a), we fixed the communication distance to 50 m to compare the two technologies at the best of their performances. In Fig. 4(b), we fixed the MCS (2/3 64-QAM) due to Signal to Noise Ratio (SNR) variations. We can observe from Fig. 4(a) that a higher value of PRR is obtained using IEEE 802.11bd. It is interesting to see that the same values of PRR that can be reached with IEEE 802.11p are reachable by the IEEE 802.11bd with high throughput. In Fig. 4(b), we can notice that with a value of 64-QAM MCS the PRR of the "bd" is always higher than the "p" one, especially in lower distances.

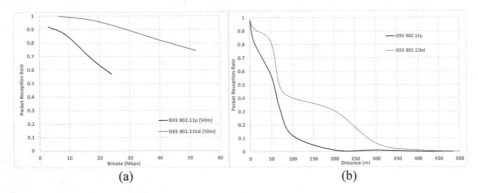

(a)   (b)

Fig. 4. PRR variations according to the bitrate (a) and the communication distance (b).

We can see the outcome of the LDPC coding instead of BCC coding, where an extra 100 m of communication range, are added compared to the IEEE 802.11p communication range, which is reaching the x-axis at 150 m.

4   Conclusions

In this paper, we assessed and compared the performances of IEEE 802.11p and IEEE 802.11bd in terms of bitrate, latency, and PRR. First, we implemented the basics of the 802.11bd PHY layer in OMNeT++ simulator, to assess its performance with the 802.11p. Then, to validate our implementation, we compared the theoretical network bitrate, with the simulation-based one. Finally, performance comparison showed that IEEE 802.11bd provides enhanced performance in the OMNeT++ simulator and thus it is more suitable for supporting more V2X applications efficiently. We noticed that a better throughput and low transmission latency are obtained using an IEEE 802.11bd-based PHY layer in Artery. On the other hand, our PRR study demonstrates an average message delivery reliability of 75% for the IEEE 802.11p and 88% for the IEEE 802.11bd. To achieve road safety, several factors should be considered among which the driver's behavior but also the message delivery reliability of the used in-vehicle awareness systems. In this context, and towards a road safety study, we envision using the obtained PRR results to assess the ability of the IEEE 802.11bd to help to avoid more road accidents compared to the IEEE 802.11p. We will also use the road safety 5G Automotive Alliance (5GAA) assessment model [5] to compare the relative performance of the IEEE 802.11p, IEEE 802.11bd, and in regards to improving road safety in the EU roads. Our implementation in Artery was based on INET 3.x version. However, a new version of INET (4.x) is now available but not compatible with Artery. The IEEE 802.11bd implementation source code may be requested by sending an email to one of the authors of this paper.

References

1. IEEE P802.11-TASK GROUP BD (NGV) Group. http://www.ieee802.org/11/Reports/tgbd_update.htm. Accessed 30 May 2019
2. Inzillo, V., De Rango, F., Ariza Quintana, A.: Supporting 5G wireless networks through IEEE802.11ac standard with new massive MIMO antenna system module design in OMNeT++. In: Proceedings of 8th International Conference on Simulation and Modeling Methodologies, Technologies and Applications, vol. 1. SIMULTECH, Porto (2018)
3. Riebl, R., Günther, H.J., Facchi, C., Wolf, L.: Artery extending veins for VANET applications. In: 2015 Models and Technologies for Intelligent Transportation Systems (MT-ITS), Budapest, Hungary, June 2015 (2015)
4. Anwar, W., Franchi, N., Fettweis, G.: Physical layer evaluation of V2X communications technologies, 5G NR-V2X, LTE-V2X, IEEE 802.11bd, and IEEE 802.11p. In: Vodafone Chair Mobile Communications Systems (2019)
5. 5G Automotive Association: An assessment of LTE-V2X (PC5) and 802.11p direct communications technologies for improved road safety in the EU, 5 December 2017 (2017)
6. Hassan, M.I., Vu, H.L., Sakurai, T.: Performance analysis of the IEEE 802.11 MAC protocol for DSRC safety applications. IEEE Trans. Veh. Technol. **60**, 3882–3896 (2011)
7. Sun, H.B., Zhang, H.: 802.11 NGV proposed PAR. IEEE 802.11-18/086lr8 (2018)
8. Liao, R., Bellalta, B., Barcelo, J., Valls, V., Oliver, M.: Performance analysis of IEEE 802.11ac wireless backhaul networks in saturated conditions. EURASIP J. Wirel. Commun. Network. **2013**, 226 (2013)
9. Sharama, P., Cao, R., Zhang, H.: LDPC investigation for 11bd. Marvell, 14 March 2019 (2019)
10. Naik, G., Choudhury, B., Park, J.-M.: IEEE 802.11bd & 5G NR V2X: evolution of radio access technologies for V2X communications. The Bradley Department of Electrical and Computer Engineering, Virginia Tech, Blacksburg, VA 24060, USA, vol. 7, pp. 70169–70184, 10 June 2019 (2019)
11. Moerman, K.: Next generation vehicular networks IEEE 80211bd. NXP, 6 March 2019 (2019)

An Investigation of the Bits Corruption in the IEEE 802.11p

Sébastien Bindel$^{(\boxtimes)}$ iD, Dorine Tabary iD, Soumia Bourebia,
Frédéric Drouhin iD, and Benoît Hilt iD

Université de Haute-Alsace, IRIMAS UR 7499, Mulhouse, France
`sebastien.bindel@uha.fr`

Abstract. Data rate management algorithms aim to perform a proper selection of the signal modulation and the coding rate to avoid the corruption of data bits. This paper describes a preliminary investigation on the bit corruption pattern related to the IEEE 802.11p standard. Measurements have been acquired with an experimental test-bed made up with a couple of software radios to perform white-box tests. Software radios are stationary and operate on the same channel without disturbances coming from concurrent communication. The aim of this experimental test-bed is to represent a static scenario where vehicles are stationary such as a crossroad situation. The data analysis shows that a data length reduction as an impact as much as a decrease of the data rate. A deeper analysis of the data bit corruption distribution highlights that some bits are more corrupted than others, rejecting the independent and identically distributed assumption for some situations. This opens a perspective to design algorithms dealing with multiple constraints, even if they are **NP**-complete.

Keywords: IEEE 802.11p · Bit corruption · Combinatorial problem

1 Introduction

Vehicular communications are a building block for automotive applications. Each vehicle can stay connected and broadcast information to the neighbourhood or send unicast messages to a target destination. Vehicle can communicate with each other but include also the infrastructures, the pedestrians, leading to introduce the concept of Vehicle-to-Everything (V2X). The IEEE 802.11p is an amendment of the IEEE 802.11 standard related to Dedicated Short Range Communication (DSRC) and define communication between Vehicle-to-Vehicle (V2V) and Vehicle-to-Infrastructure (V2I) [1]. It uses a physical layer close to the one defined from the IEEE 802.11a, with a change on communication operating in the 5.9 GHz band and a bandwidth of 10 MHz. However, the IEEE 802.11a has been developed for indoor environments with relatively stationary entities, as the result the performance of the 802.11p might suffer since vehicles are moving in the outdoor.

© Springer Nature Switzerland AG 2020
F. Krief et al. (Eds.): Nets4Cars/Nets4Trains/Nets4Aircraft 2020, LNCS 12574, pp. 66–77, 2020.
https://doi.org/10.1007/978-3-030-66030-7_6

The main causes of these impairments can be related either to the settings of the materials or to the implemented physical layer. The first one includes the gains of antennas, the transmission/reception power, but the transmission power represents the major challenge, since it determines the amount of energy to send the signal. However, only the receiver is able to determine if the transmission power was sufficient to receive and decode the signal, leading to develop a costly feedback mechanism due to the time varying nature of the channel. The second one covers all process related to the physical layer from the signal coding to its parsing to decode data. Before the transmission, the 802.11p standard let to the transmitter the proper selection of the modulation and the coding rate which have an impact on the data rate and the probability on the data bit corruption. This selection is performed without taking into account the data length since, the physical layer performs a channel estimation for decoding data and can be quickly outdated due to the time-varying nature of the channel. Therefore, the primary challenge is to determine the impact of the following couple, data rate and data length to the packet error rate. This study goes deeper by pointing out the bit error patterns and determines the computational complexity of the related combinatorial problem to deal both with the data rate and the data length.

The investigation details in this article is based on some articles described in Sect. 2. The Sect. 3 details the experimental test-bed which aims to perform measurements on the IEEE 802.11p, made up with software radios (USRP B210) to perform white-box tests and avoid side effects generated by proprietary radio chipsets. A discussion is opened on the impact of the data rate and data length and is extended to the bit error pattern in the Sect. 4. From this discussion, an investigation of the related combinatorial problems is developed in the Sect. 5 and shows the **NP**-completeness when some constraints arise. The Sect. 6 ending this article, opens a perspective on online algorithms related to the related combinatorial problem.

2 Overview of the 802.11p Performance

The physical layer of the 802.11p uses as transmission technique the Orthogonal Frequency-Division Multiplexing (OFDM). The OFDM frame structure is composed of three parts, the preamble, the signal and data, as illustrated in the Fig. 1. The preamble is split in two parts, the short training symbols for the signal detection and the long training symbols for the channel estimation. The signal part gives information for decoding the payload including the signal modulation and the coding rate. At the end, the payload[1] is divided and coded into OFDM symbols according to the coding scheme detailed in the Table 1.

The reception process being sequential, each part must be decoded without error to trigger the next one. Major impairments of the reception process are

---

[1] In the IEEE 802.11p the payload is the whole MAC frame including the header, data and the tail.

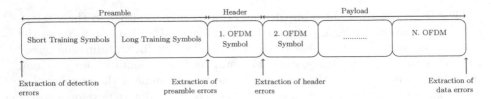

Fig. 1. OFDM packet structure

related to the long training symbols used by the channel estimation process. Fernandez et al. [6] point out the performance of the channel estimation algorithm used for the demodulation. They argue that in a dynamic environment, the channel estimation is outdated before the complete reception of data especially with the Least-Square (LS) method, as the result they have designed a new one called Spectral Temporal Averaging (STA). Such a method require to perform modifications in the physical layer meaning, the development of a specific hardware prototype. Authors have hinted, that the data length has a significant impact, since a shorter length means a shorter reception time and so an higher chance for the channel estimation to not be outdated.

A second strategy is a proper selection of the modulation and the coding rate, because they have an impact on the Bit Error Rate (BER) and the data rate. Several approaches attempt to design data rate management algorithms based on a piece of information related to the incoming signal or the frame loss ratio [2], to maximise the data rates and avoid the bit corruption. The first kind of algorithms use a signal quality indicator either the Received Signal Strength Indicator (RSSI) or the Signal to Noise Ratio (SNR), however a calibration setup is required. The second kind of algorithms attempt to adapt the data rate according to the frame loss threshold. Some of them try to interpret the causes of lost to get an accurate management of the data rate. More complex approaches attempt to deal with additional constraints such as the power transmission [5]. Some further investigations have been performed on the bit corruption to understand the distribution, find some patterns and open strategies, including the important study performed by Han et al. [7]. In this article is described some preliminary results on the impact of the data rate and the packet size on the loss ratio with an investigation on the bit corruption. The results illustrated in this article confirm partially those obtained by Han et al. [7].

The proposed approach is a preliminary study and continue the investigations performed by Han et al. [7]. In contrast with their study, the 802.11p is taking into account and only software radios are used to avoid side effects generating by proprietary radio chipsets. The approach is also motivated by the observations of Fernandez et al. [6] pointing out the impact of the couple data rate and data length on the packet error rate. This one is confirmed by the study of Bourebia et al. [4] which have investigated the rate of OFDM errors triggered during the reception process and show that the errors related to the decoding payload are the most important. These ones are confirmed by our results detailed in

Information :

scale: 1/200

Legend :

△ Receiver USRP

▽ Transmitter USRP

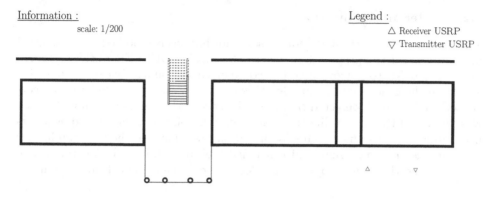

Fig. 2. Map of the test-bed

Sect. 4. This kind of errors is related to the data bit corruption detected at the MAC layer with the Frame Check Sequence (FCS) algorithm using the Cyclic Redundancy Check (CRC) in the tail. The proposed study focuses on the current version of the 802.11p standard with an experimental test-bed embedding only an open source physical layer within a static environment representing some static vehicular scenarios.

3   Experimental Test-Bed

The experimental outdoor test-bed aims to represent a scenario wherein entities are static and the communication channel is stable. In order to perform white-box testings, software radios are used and embed an open source IEEE 802.11p transmitter. They have been customised and configured to log all incoming MAC frames, including the corrupted ones.

3.1   Materials

All experiments have been performed with a couple of USRP (Universal Software Radio Peripheral) B210 managed by laptops under ArchLinux, one being the transmitter, the other being the receiver. Each radio is equipped with an omnidirectional antenna supporting two frequency slots, 2.4−2.5 GHz and 4.9−5.9 GHz with a gain of 3 dBi. Software radios have been programmed with the GNURadio 3.8 and embed the IEEE 802.11 a/g/p transmitter module developed by Bloessel et al. [3]. This one, called gr-ieee802-11, details all physical components of the OFDM transmitter from the signal detection to the MAC frame retrieval. Once MAC frame data are retrieved, these ones are logged into a pcap file thanks to a companion module, called gr-foo, plugged after the gr-ieee802-11 module.

3.2 Material Modifications

The source code of the GNURadio software has been modified and compiled manually to set the preprocessor macro GR_FIXED_BUFFER_SIZE[2] to 128Kb instead of 64Kb to not overflow the communication buffers between successive blocks in the gr-ieee802-11 module. This one has been also modified to log corrupted MAC frames detected by the FCS algorithm[3]. The last but not the least was the log of the SNR value through a floating point number instead as a natural number in pcap files[4]. This modification takes place in the radiotap header wherein the antenna signal field (unsigned 8 bits) contains the integral part of the SNR and the floating part is encoded in the antenna noise field (unsigned 8 bits).

3.3 Experiment Settings

The test-bed is made up of a couple of nodes situated along the administrative building as illustrated in the Fig. 2. Each experiment has been scheduled during the daytime on weekdays and radio have operated on the same channel, 5860 MHz, without any interference generated by a wireless device. The transmitter sends periodically MAC frames containing either 42 bytes or 1500 bytes of data, corresponding to the minimum length without bit stuffing and the maximum length regardless the Jumbo frames. Data bytes enclosed in MAC frames are set to 0x00 and each field in the MAC header have a fixed value, except the sequence number, increased by one after each sending. The periodical sending has been defined at 100 ms which is lower than the coherence time which represents the time duration over the channel is not varying. The FCS algorithm identifies the presence of errors thanks to a CRC field. This one is a 32 bits CRC value positioned at the tail of the MAC frame. Its computation is based on the XOR operation which is the simplest scheme for error handling, without a correction possibility. The transmitter and the receiver being software radios, they embed only the physical layer of the IEEE 802.11p, as a result any additional services are provided including the MAC re-transmission scheme when a frame is lost. The channel equalisation in the IEEE 802.11p hardware is responsible to perform a channel estimation for improving the signal demodulation. The time varying nature of the channel tends to disturb the channel equalisation process since the estimation can become outdated. The couple of software radios implement the Least Squares (LS) estimator and uses the long training symbols (depicted in the Fig. 1) to estimate the channel [6]. The LS estimator has the benefit to have a low computational complexity but the estimation can be outdated before the complete packet reception. However, the couple of radios being static, the channel should be enough stable to not impair the channel estimation.

---

[2] Defined in the gnuradio-runtime/lib/flat_flowgraph.cc file.
[3] The source code is available at https://github.com/sbindel/gr-ieee802-11.
[4] The source code is available at https://github.com/sbindel/gr-foo.

4   Data Analysis

Each experiment has been achieved with all modulations and coding rates, summarised in the Table 1. The transmitter broadcasting periodically a fixed bits sequence, the receiver is able to determine if data are lost or received. In the last case, the receiver compares the received bits sequence with the reference to find out the position of corrupted bits. This analysis aims to point out the impact of the data rate and the length of data on the received rate of MAC frames by investigating the first kind of data. It also shows that some data sets related to selected data rate are more interesting to investigate the corruption of data bits. A surprising observation is the bit corruption distribution is not uniform and open a perspective on the minimisation of MAC frame lost without reduce the data rate.

Table 1. IEEE 802.11p coding scheme

Coded bit rate (Mb/s)	Data rate (Mb/s)	Modulation	Coding rate	Coded bits per sub-carrier	Data bits per OFDM symbol
6	3	BPSK	1/2	1	24
9	4.5	BPSK	3/4	1	36
12	6	QPSK	1/2	2	48
18	9	QPSK	3/4	2	72
24	12	16-QAM	1/2	4	96
36	18	16-QAM	3/4	4	144
48	24	64-QAM	2/3	6	192
54	27	64-QAM	3/4	6	216

4.1   Data Set Selection

Regardless the bit corruption, the receiver computes for each incoming frame the SNR, the ratio between the power of the incoming signal and the power of the background noise. By definition, it depends on the environment but not on the modulation, the coding rate and the length of data, as a result, it is used to determine if a couple of data sets have been getting within a same environment. The Fig. 3 depicts the distribution of the SNR for a couple of scenarios within the data length is different and confirms the previous assumption. This couple of scenarios have been selected, since their data set contain the most relevant data for this analysis. The SNR distribution appears barely different with a few outliers since the median (central line of the box plot) and the mean (diamond symbol) are approximately equal.

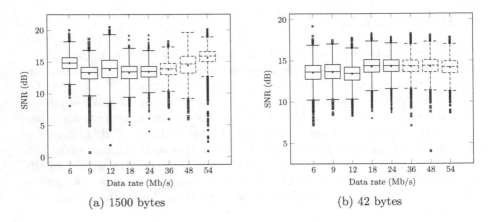

Fig. 3. Distribution of the SNR

4.2   Impact of Data Length and the Data Rate

The Fig. 4 depicts the statics and the ratios of the reception states of the incoming packets. The state *Received* covers the MAC frames which have been well received, beside if data are corrupted the frame is considered as *Corrupted*, the rest is declared as *Lost*. In both scenarios, few data are considered as lost since the receiver stays in the transmission range of the transmitter. As expected, when the data rate increases the number of corrupted packets increases too, since there is a positive relationship between the SNR and the Bit Error Rate (BER). However, it differs according the data length. The most significant difference is at 24 Mb/s where the ratio of received frames is ~ 0.48 with a data length of 42 bytes, meanwhile almost all frames with a length of 1500 bytes are corrupted. MAC frame embedding less data than a bigger one are more robust to corruption for a same modulation. It is more surprising to note that the ratio of received frames for a smaller frame is often higher than the bigger sent with the previous lower data rate. This highlight the importance of data length on the reception rate even more to decrease to a lower data rate.

4.3   The Bits Corruption

The investigation of the bit corruption is performed by plotting the normalised bit corruption frequency. Depicted in the Fig. 5, it is computed for each bit as the ratio between the number of corruption occurrence and the total number of corrupted frames. The bit corruption frequency for the frames with a length of 1500 bytes is clearly not uniform a reveal the presence of peaks, regardless the data rate. These peaks indicate that some bits are more sensible to the corruption, but their positions and their strengths differ between the couple of scenarios. However, the bits position can be incorporated to a pool of bits according to these peaks. For the 18Mb/s scenario, a first removal from the max corrupted bit situated on the last peak (bit position at 10821) to the last bit, the number

Data rate	Receveid	Corrupted	Lost	Total
6	4617	6	0	4623
9	3280	18	4	3302
12	4564	599	27	5190
18	3177	997	2	4176
24	0	4073	0	4073
36	0	4217	0	4217
48	0	2994	0	2994
54	0	3735	21	3756

(a) Statistics of reception states (1500 bytes)

Data rate	Received	Corrupted	Lost	Total
6	4385	0	0	4385
9	1890	0	0	1890
12	2734	2	2	2738
18	4170	26	0	4196
24	2543	2680	1	5224
36	55	4722	1	4778
48	0	4092	0	4092
54	0	3962	2	3964

(b) Statistics of reception states (42 bytes)

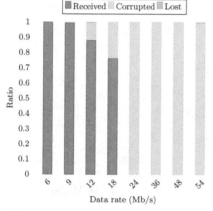

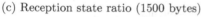

(c) Reception state ratio (1500 bytes)

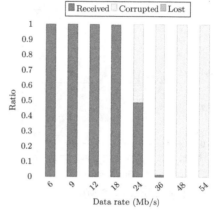

(d) Reception state ratio (42 bytes)

Fig. 4. The impact of packet size and the data rate on the reception state

of corrupted MAC frames decreases by 3.5%. Another removal from the second peak (bit position at 3445) to the last bit, the number of received MAC frames without corruptions increased by 52%. This confirms that a proper reduction of the data length can improve significantly the rate of received MAC frames without corrupted bits. However, such a strategy has a limit, since plots related to the corruption of MAC frames with a length of 42 bytes do not highlight the presence of peaks.

5 Theoretical Framework for Data Rate Selection Problems

In the previous section, experimental results have shown that a proper selection of the data rate and the data length have a significant impact. However, a theoretical framework is required to determine the hardness of the computation related to the data rate and the data length selection problem under some constraints. In this article, the problem is modelled with a complete k-partite

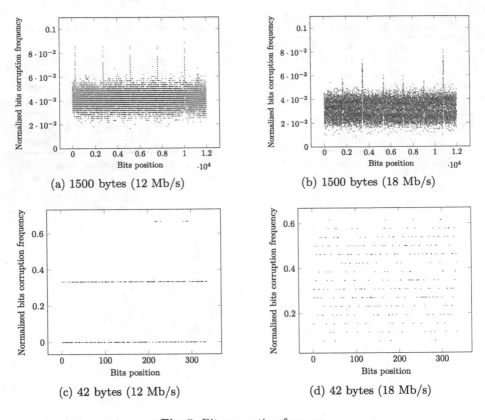

Fig. 5. Bit corruption frequency

graph, each partite being an occurrence of transmission. Each one shares the same size and represents the number of available data rates. An illustration of the modelled problem is depicted in the Fig. 6. Two variants of the problem can be considered, one without constraint and another with constraints.

5.1 Combinatorial Optimisation Without Restriction

Let G a complete k-partite graph, where each partite V_i have the same size n such as $V_1 \cup \ldots V_k = V(G)$. A couple of vertices (u, v) are connected by an arc, $A_{u,v} \in A(G)$ if $\forall u \in V_i,\ \forall v \in V_j,\ j = i + 1$. Each vertice in the same partite have a weight, $w : v \to \mathbb{R}^+$, such as $w(v_1) < \ldots < w(v_n)$, $\{v_1, \ldots, v_n\} \in V_i$. In addition, $\forall u \in V_i,\ \exists y \in V_j,\ j = i + 1$ such as $w(v) = w(y)$. The presence (e.g. absence) of an arc is the result of the following function $\Gamma : A \times x \to [0, 1]$ with $x \in [0, 1]$. Each arc, A, has also a weight such as $w(A_{u,v}) = w(v)$. A path, p, in a the k-partite graph has a weight denoted $w(p)$. This weight is a function of its individual arc is given by a function, such as $f : (w(A_{i,j}),\ , w(A_{j,k}), \ldots,\ w(A_{y,z})) \to \mathbb{R}^+$. The aim of an algorithm is to find a path p, crossing all partites, which maximises

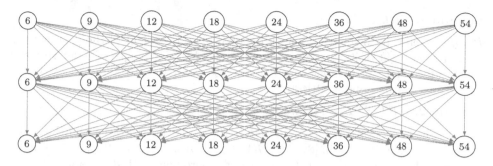

Fig. 6. An instance of the data rate selection problem

its weight and takes into account the presence (e.g. absence) of its arc denoted A_i, such as :

$$max\ w(p) = \sum_{i=1}^{k} (w(A_i) \times \Gamma(A_i)).$$

Consider now a complete k-partite graph and a Bernoulli random variable, X, used by the Γ function such $\Gamma : A \times X$. Now the time-complexity of an algorithm which aims to find an optimal path[5] can be expressed.

Theorem 1. *The time complexity of the maximisation path computation where the presence of arcs is determined by a Bernoulli random variable is $\mathcal{O}(nk)$.*

Proof. The proof is trivial. The algorithm has to find sequentially the best weight of an available arc, however in the worst case, the latest checked has the best weight and is available.

5.2   Combinatorial Optimisation with Transmission Restrictions

The previous analysis determines the time complexity of an algorithm that computes the path which has the maximal weight. In practise, an algorithms has to deal with a sequence of bits and has to choose a packet size for each transmission in order to minimise the number of transmissions. Most of the time, the data rate must satisfy a minimal rate to satisfy an application. As a result, the number of transmissions through a path, p is denoted $t(p) \le Th_t$ with Th_t a given threshold. Beside, the weight of the path w(p) must satisfy $\frac{1}{w(p)} \le Th_w$ with Th_p a given threshold. We now define the Selection of data Rate and data Length problem, denoted SRL, which aim to satisfy the couple of constraints on the minimal data rate, Th_w and data length Th_t given by a path p.

---

[5] An optimal path is a path with a maximal weight.

Lemma 1. *SRL* ∈ **NP**.

Proof. Given a path p with a length denoted $|p|$. The weight of the path is the sum of the weight of its arcs and compared to Th_w. The length of p determines the number of transmissions and can be also compared to Th_t. All of these operations can be done in $\Theta(|p|)$.

Lemma 2. *OPT SRL is* **NP**-*hard.*

Proof. This proof is based on a reduction to the n additive metrics with LEQ constraints problem detailed in [8]. Let $(G(V, E), d_1(p), d_2(p), Th_1, Th_2)$ an instance of the n additive metrics with LEQ constraint problem with $d_1(p)$ and $d_2(p)$ a couple of additives metrics ans their related constraints given by Th_1 and Th_2. The instance of the *SRL* problem can be performed as following. Each adjacent vertices of V are placed in a different partite. Two nodes are in a same partite if they are adjacent with a same node. Since all partites must have the same given size, dummy vertices are added to satisfy this condition, this part can be done in polynomial time. All edges $e_{(i,j)} \in E$ between two node are split into a couple of arc such as the first metric is the weight of arc $d_1(e_{i,j}) = w(A_{i,j}) = w(A_{j,i})$. The same process is used for the second metric, this part can be done in polynomial time. At the end, all edges with dummy nodes are notified absent with the Γ function, the rest is notified present, this part can be done in polynomial time. To find the path with a minimum number of transmission and maximise the data rate implies to find a path p with the costs $d_1(p)$ and $d_2(p)$ and satisfying the minimum of the couple of thresholds Th_1 and Th_2. This completes this proof.

Theorem 2. *The SRL problem is* **NP**-*complete.*

Proof. According to the couple of Lemmas 1 and 2, the *SRL* problem is **NP**-complete.

6   Conclusion

In this paper some preliminary results about the impact of the data rate and the length of data have been discussed. They also show that the decrease of the data rate is not the only way to increase the packet reception rate, but the data length reduction can be also considered. Fortunately, the distribution related to the bit corruption is not uniform and some clusters arises. As a result, the design of an algorithm performing on the data length do not have to inspect each bit but clusters to split data. Even if all algorithms which attempts to maximize the packet reception rate dealing the data rate and additional constraints are **NP**-complete, the split of data can be performed according to a pool of bits and not on the bit itself.

This study must be extended to additional experiments both on the length of data and in different scenario to confirm the observations detailed in this article. However, obtained results are sufficiently close to the observations made by Han et al. [7] to confirm that our data set is not a outlier. Concerning the algorithm part, the study of the optimal strategy opens the perspective to study if c-competitive online algorithms can be designed.

References

1. IEEE standard for information technology–telecommunications and information exchange between systems local and metropolitan area networks–specific requirements - part 11: Wireless LAN medium access control (MAC) and physical layer (PHY) specifications. IEEE Std 802.11-2016 (Revision of IEEE Std 802.11-2012), pp. 1–3534 (2016)
2. Biaz, S., Wu, S.: Rate adaptation algorithms for IEEE 802.11 networks: a survey and comparison. In: 2008 IEEE Symposium on Computers and Communications, pp. 130–136 (2008)
3. Bloessl, B., Segata, M., Sommer, C., Dressler, F.: An IEEE 802.11a/g/p OFDM Receiver for GNU Radio. In: ACM SIGCOMM 2013, 2nd ACM SIGCOMM Workshop of Software Radio Implementation Forum (SRIF 2013), pp. 9–16. Hong Kong, China (August 2013)
4. Bourebia, S., et al.: A belief function-based forecasting link breakage indicator for VANETs. Wirel. Netw. **26**(4), 2433–2448 (2020)
5. Chevillat, P.R., Jelitto, J., Truong, H.L.: Dynamic data rate and transmit power adjustment in IEEE 802.11 wireless LANs. Int. J. Wirel. Inf. Netw. **12**(3), 123–145 (2005)
6. Fernandez, J.A., Borries, K., Cheng, L., Vijaya Kumar, B.V.K., Stancil, D.D., Bai, F.: Performance of the 802.11p physical layer in vehicle-to-vehicle environments. IEEE Trans. Veh. Technol. **61**(1), 3–14 (2012)
7. Han, B., Ji, L., Lee, S., Bhattacharjee, B., Miller, R.R.: Are all bits equal?-experimental study of IEEE 802.11 communication bit errors. IEEE/ACM Trans. Netw. **20**(6), 1695–1706 (2012)
8. Wang, Z.: On the complexity of quality of service routing. Inform. Process. Lett. **69**(3), 111–114 (1999)

Measurements of Communication Channel in Different Scenarios with the Channel Characterization Tool System

Nerea Fernández-Berrueta[1,2]([⊠]), Iker Moya[1,2], Javier Añorga[1,2], Mario Monterde[1,2], Jaione Arrizabalaga[1,2], and Jon Goya[1,2]

[1] CEIT-Basque Research and Technology Alliance (BRTA), Manuel Lardizabal 15, 20018 Donostia /San Sebastián, Spain
{nfernandez,imoya,jabenito,mmonterde,jarrizabalaga,
jgoya}@ceit.es
[2] Universidad de Navarra, Tecnun, Manuel Lardizabal 13, 20018 Donostia/San Sebastián, Spain

Abstract. Nowadays, the wireless networks have an important role in the deployment of several means of transports, platforms and applications. In the particular case of roads and vehicle area, some ideas are starting gaining importance such as the autonomous vehicle. In order to reach this ambitious goal, the wireless networks are a strategic issue for the communication between vehicles (V2V) and between infrastructure and vehicles (V2I), generally known as vehicle-to-everything (V2X). In this current moment, the most deployed cellular network is LTE (Long Term Evolution), progressing to 5G technology. Because of this, this paper shows the measurement of the LTE technology and the phenomena that affects this technology at IP level. To reach this last goal, the on-site testing of a measurement system is needed allowing to quantify network impairments of a communication channel in a given road environment. In this paper, the system capable of measuring a communication channel is explained and it is shown how an on-site testing of the communication channel of a specific road has been measured in terms of the RTT network impairment. As well, the results of the measurement has been analysed and explained. Finally, some conclusions are presented.

Keywords: Communication channel · Network impairments · Roads · Cellular wireless network · Wireless · On-site testing

1 Introduction

In the last years, the world is more and more connected due to the implementation and the deployment of different communication technologies, applications and the need to exchange information. Moreover, European cities are more and more overcrowded with vehicles, facing unpleasant everyday phenomena such as traffic congestions, as well as unpredicted emergencies and accidents. This situations cause enormous losses of time, decrease in the level of safety for both vehicles and pedestrians, high pollution, degradation of quality of life, and huge waste of nonrenewable fossil energy. These

© Springer Nature Switzerland AG 2020
F. Krief et al. (Eds.): Nets4Cars/Nets4Trains/Nets4Aircraft 2020, LNCS 12574, pp. 78–88, 2020.
https://doi.org/10.1007/978-3-030-66030-7_7

inefficiencies bring up the need to develop systems to reach a more efficient and safer mobility [1].

In this respect, ITS (Intelligent Transportation System) is an emerging area that aims to solve of these issues. It refers to a new set of information and communication technologies that allow vehicles to exchange information with each other (V2V, vehicle-to-vehicle) and with the infrastructure (V2I, vehicle-to-infrastructure) to improve road safety, traffic efficiency, and travel comfort [2]. This environment can be called the connected vehicle environment or vehicle-to-everything (V2X) which have a significant role to play in optimizing road traffic and improving road safety [3, 2]. In this context, two standards have emerged, ITS-G5 (IEEE 802.11p) [4] and C-V2X (3GPP Long Term Evolution Release 14) [5]. This last technology allows its users to communicate leveraging the existing LTE infrastructure and in future, the use of 5G mobile network [6].

In this paper, the target technology chosen is LTE because is the current technology used for the cellular wireless technology for the V2X. The purpose of this paper is to show the CCT tool, by means of a field test example. CCT is capable of measuring different network impairments on-site with an on-board system geo-localizing them in order to check the performance of this technology on the several road environments. As the LTE is a mature technology and, as well, totally deployed, the measurements are possible by just choosing an operator of cellular networks. Moreover, some of the different phenomena, which affect to the communication channel, are exposed in order to understand how and why the communication channel varies along the road.

This paper is structured as follows.

- Section 2 shows the main objectives of the developed measurement system
- Section 3 exposes the road environment and the phenomena that affect to the communication channel.
- Section 4 describes the measurement campaign.
- Section 5 shows the results obtained.
- Finally, Sect. 6 presents conclusions.

2 Measurement Equipment: CCT

The measurement equipment used to carry out the different measurements along the roads is explained in this section.

The equipment applied for the measurements is the one called Channel Characterization Tool (CCT). The main objective of the CCT system is to measure different IP network impairments (such as RTT or bandwidth) of a communication channel, along the roads. The benefit that it brings is allowing to understand how the road environment can affect the communication channel. Moreover, there is additional functionality of the system: in order to allow a user-friendly system, other services have been implemented such as the configuration of different type of tests by the user including the start and end hour, which allows the different test automation. In addition, the system permits to monitor the diverse network impairments that the user choses in the test configuration and to visualize the different results of the on-site testing.

This system consists of three different parts: agent, server and CI (Control Interface) as Fig. 1 shows. The agent is the on-board part of the system; it contains the LTE modem, which allows sending/receiving the data to/from the server that is placed in a fix network. The server is the responsible of forwarding the corresponding tests that the user configured in the CI to the agent. Moreover, it is as well responsible of measuring the communication channel with the agent and processing the data of the obtained results from tests, which will be visualized in the CI. The CI is the web interface for specifically the user in order to firstly, configure the different tests and send them to the CCT server, which will be reproduced on-site and secondly, monitor and visualize the results of the on-site testing obtained by the CCT server.

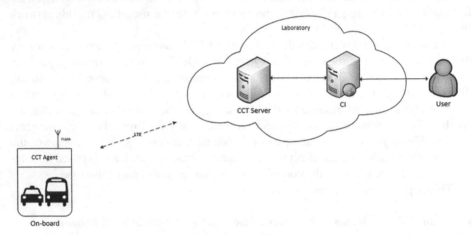

Fig. 1. CCT system architecture

3   Main Environments and Phenomena in Road Communications

Before carrying out the different measurements with the CCT system along several roads, it has to be exposed that there are a number of possible effects that could affect the communication channel in a negative way. This allows understanding why the communication channel varies along the road.

Road environment can be considered demanding according to the communications. The wireless communication channel can be affected by different external influences. Some of these impairments are the following ones:

1. Weather conditions
2. Environment scenarios
3. Speed of the vehicle
4. Interferences
5. Coverage

This section shows the state of art of the different phenomena affecting the communication channel. This state of art is shown from the LTE technology point of view since it is the target technology chosen.

3.1 Road Environment: General Scenarios

The ground vehicles, such as cars and buses, pass through different type of environment depending on the geographical area of the region, affecting differently to the communications.

The general environments in which every scenario could be classified are the following ones shown in the Fig. 2:

Fig. 2. Different environments or scenarios in the road domain

- Urban [7]: high presence of numerous obstacles (building, trees, etc.) can strongly influence the received signal levels.
- Semi-urban: not as many obstacles as the urban area and as well not the same number of antennas therefore different coverage.
- Open sky [8]: open road with unlimited line of sight (LOS).
- Canopy [9]: discrete scatterers in the forest such as the randomly distributed leaves, twigs, branches and tree trunks can cause attenuation, scattering, diffraction, and absorption of the radiated propagating waves.
- Rural area [10]: areas where low population density and noncontinuous delivery of wideband services are experienced.
- Tunnel: these areas are characterized normally due to lack of coverage (no antennas inside the tunnel).

These scenarios carry different propagation effects to the radio signal such as multipath effect, which causes delay between the first ray and the others, and, as well, attenuations that could cause no coverage in the worst case.

3.2 Weather Conditions

Depending on the frequency of the communication channel technology, weather conditions could affect to it in terms of attenuation and multipath effect. Some of the weather conditions could be rain, snow or fog.

One of these weather conditions, according to the recommendation ITU-R P.838-3 [11], is the rain attenuation which affects to frequencies greater than 10 GHz since the rainfall impact on the electromagnetic wave attenuation is reduced at lower frequencies.

Therefore, the effect in this particular cellular LTE network will be lower, than in other technologies places in high frequency bands. However, even if the effect is lower that in other frequency bands, it has to be taken into account as [12] exposes.

On the other hand, regarding the fog effect and according to the Rec. ITU-R P.840-8 [13], attenuation due to this effect may be significant just at frequencies of the order of 100 GHz and above.

As already stated before, these specific influences are not affecting to the target communication channel of this paper, as it is LTE with frequency bands lower than those affected. However, as the CCT is an adaptable system regarding the technologies to be measured, it is important to take into account these different phenomena. As the successor of LTE is 5G NR (mmwave), the next target communication channel could be this one which will be affected by these influences.

3.3 Speed of the Vehicle

The main issue due to the speed of the vehicle regarding to the road communications is the consequence of handover. The handover is a crucial factor to maintain high reliability and availability of mobile communication. The handover addressed in this paper, refers to the horizontal handover due to the fact of the exclusive use of LTE. This type of handover maintains the use of the same technology and consists in changing the connection from one base station to another. As well, different types of handovers exist depending on when the detach and attach process from/to the base stations is done. In the particular case of LTE, hard handover is the one implemented for the tests.

The hard handover is a break-before-make method; it means that a new wireless link connection with the target base station should be set up after the release of the connection with the source base station. Therefore, there is a time (Detach Time) when the user equipment is not connected to the systems which carries a no connection and packet loss in the communication channel [14]. Thus considering then that handover creates an interruption time in the user plane, the handover performance in terms of success rate and delay of execution is of high importance [15].

As well, Doppler effect could affect the communication channel depending the frequency of the technology selected and the speed of the vehicle. If variation of received frequency occurs, it is possible as variation factor of carrier frequency recognize as a loss of received signal without compensation for Doppler effect. Therefore, a loss of received signal supposes a loss of information from the information of the vehicle [16].

3.4 Coverage

The coverage of the LTE technology depends fundamentally on the network operator directly on the deployment of the cellular network such as the strength of the signal or the number of antennas, and, as well, on the road environment mentioned before.

Because the network operator coverage can differ, two different have been selected for the later example of measurements with CCT.

3.5 Interferences

In general, interferences lead to malfunction of the network in terms of call drops, signaling errors, traffic throughput loss and decrease of data rates among others [17,15,18,19]. In cellular networks, these interferences could be classified in intra-cell interferences, inter-cell ones or interferences generated by another source.

Regarding the LTE specific system, there are no intra-cell interferences thanks to orthogonal character of used OFDM-based schemes; this method supports intra-cell orthogonality, therefore the most important interference which affects system performance is inter-cell interference. Inter-cell interference scenarios typically involve User Equipments (UE) in neighboring cells being scheduled on the same Resource Block. The transmission rate of UE which the location is at the cell edge will be degraded mostly due to inter-cell interference [20].

As well, other interferences out of the own technology, in this case LTE, could disturb the target communication channel. For example, LTE technology in the European Union is allocated for mobile operators to deploy in the 800 MHz frequency band. However, for Northern European countries frequency interoperability issue arises due to neighboring Russia and Belarus using the same frequency band for aeronautical radio navigation services [19].

3.6 Summary

After analyzing all the different external conditions, it is clear that they could affect the communication channel and the effects that produce in the communication, as Fig. 3 summarizes. This is reflected into the network impairments and parameters that are used to characterize the communication channel.

The network-measured parameters that are affected by the different external influences are defined below:

- RTT (Round Trip Time): is the duration that it takes for a network to send a request from a starting point to a destination and back again to the starting point.
- Jitter: the variation between the maximum delay and minimum delay within a specific time window [21].
- Bandwidth (BW): is used as a synonym for data transfer rate, the amount of data that can be carried from one point to another in a given time period.
- Throughput: the amount of data transferred from an interface of a source node to an interface of a destination node over some time interval, expressed as the number of bits per second.
- Packet loss: the failure of a packet to traverse the network to its destination [21].

Therefore, the effects in the communication channel carry, at physical level, such as attenuation or multipath and, at IP level, they affect to the network impairments stated before.

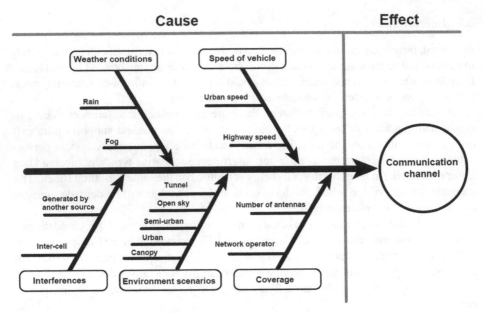

Fig. 3. Fishbone diagram of the different phenomena affecting the communication channel

4 Measurement Campaign

The measurements made with the CCT on-board unit in order to check the network impairments of the communication channel have been carried out in San Sebastian (Spain). The objective of measurement campaign performed by CEIT is to characterise a communication channel by means of the RTT parameter (Round Trip Time) along the specific roads already mentioned. This testing route, shown in Fig. 4, involve the general environments explained before in Sect. 3 such as a short tunnel, semi-urban, urban and canopy area.

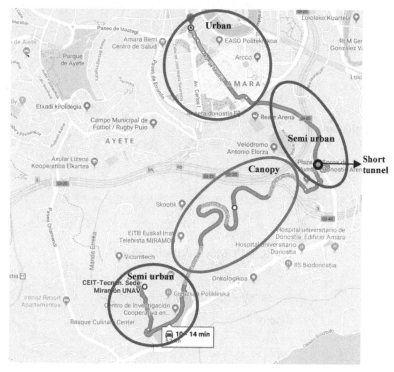

Fig. 4. Testing route

Regarding the speed of car, the maximum speed that the vehicle reaches, as there is no highway in the testing route is 50 km/h. As well, the factor of the coverage is another important point that can vary depending on the network operator. For that, two public cellular wireless networks offered by two Spanish operators have been chosen offering LTE technology, as the target technology, in a maximum date rate depending on the coverage available in each point of the road. In Sect. 5, the results of the RTT measurements obtained from these tests are shown.

5 Results

The next figures shows the results of measuring with CCT: how the RTT network impairment vary along the time due to the different conditions, such as the road environment or network operator, in the same testing road. The mapping of the environments to the RTT network impairment is possible to the geo-localization special feature of the CCT (Fig. 5 and 6).

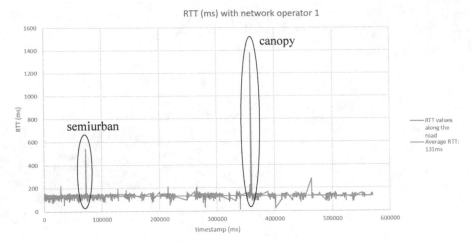

Fig. 5. RTT with network operator 1

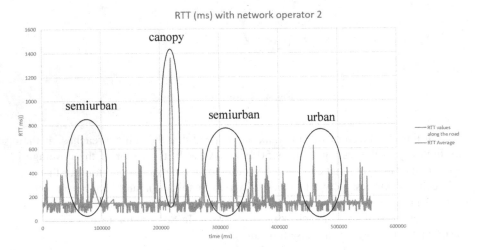

Fig. 6. RTT with network operator 2

The peaks in the graphics represents a high value of RTT, which normally means that an external influence has affected to the desired signal. According to the obtained results, these peaks correspond with certain conflictive areas, such as canopy areas, that the multipath effect could have affected the signal and, because of that, the RTT impairment or even the lack of base stations in this area causing a handover. Other conflictive area that coincide with an elevate value of RTT is the entrance in an urban area including many different obstacles in this area which produces multipath effects and, as well, having a big population connected. This last issue is related with the management of the network operator; the user capacity of the closer base station could be overpassed (high system occupancy) sending the user to a further base station. As well, different interferences working in the same LTE frequency band can affect the signal.

Moreover, the different measurement in each area done with different network operators vary; the different network operators do not have the same coverage, for example, not the same amount of antennas installed. In this specific case and as the figures show, network operator 2 has a higher variance in terms of RTT than network operator 1.

6 Conclusions

Road V2X communications can be affected by different external influences e.g. signal interferences, without forgetting, the environment where the vehicle passes through (tunnels, open space, etc.). The different disturbances, affecting the channel, could come from different sources such as the vehicle itself due to the speed of the vehicle and the different roads, therefore, different environments. These different influences cause the modification of the parameters in the communication channel such as RTT, bandwidth or throughput. The result of these disturbances in the channel are reflected in a worse communication channel than the ideal one (only free space losses) which, in the worst case (a large tunnel, for instance), leads in a channel that could be impossible to transmit through.

The CCT is a system capable of measuring network impairments such as RTT and geo-localizing them into, in this case, a road. This tool allows configuring different test, measure the communication channel and monitoring it. In the measurement, that it is shown as an example of how it would work, the technology selected is LTE but could be any available due to the adaptability of the tool to others technologies. For example, as nowadays 5G technology is being deployed, the CCT could test it in order to analyse how the environment would affect to the technology.

In this paper, as an example of how the CCT works, field measurement with CCT has shown that each measurement can be different due to different conditions. The results show that the area where the vehicle is passing through is an important point to take into account due to the different effects that they can cause such as attenuation or multipath. That is, its mapping of geo-localization and measured parameters helps to understand the behaviour of the communication channel (e.g. lack of coverage because a tunnel). However, the testing road chosen for the measurements does not contain every type of area. Others type of area, such as a larger tunnel or a rural area could be other conflictive areas for the desired signal that could be interesting to be analysed; the particular characteristics of these areas would affect to the signal in a different way than the already analysed ones. It can be concluded that the RTT of a specific technology depends on different factors, some of them more controllable and known such as the map coverage of the network operator, and others not controllable such as the interferences in the same frequency band or the environment that can be different due to changes such as a forest or network system capacity.

References

1. Dimitrakopoulos, G., Demestichas, P.: Intelligent transportation systems: Systems based on cognitive networking principles and management functionality. IEEE Veh. Technol. Mag. **5**(1), 77–84 (2010)
2. Calabuig, J., Monserrat, J.F., Gozálvez, D., Klemp, O.: Safety on the roads: LTE alternatives for sending ITS messages. IEEE Veh. Technol. Mag. **9**(4), 61–70 (2014)
3. Mannoni, V., Berg, V., Sesia, S., Perraud, E.: A comparison of the V2X communication systems: ITS-G5 and C-V2X. In: IEEE Vehicle Technological Conference, April 2019, pp. 1–5 (2019)
4. ETSI (European Telecommunications Standards Institute): Draft ETSI EN 302 663 v.1.2.0 - Intelligent Transport Systems (ITS). Access layer specification for Intelligent Transport Systems operating in the 5 GHz frequency band, pp. 1–24 (2012)
5. 3GPP TS 22.185 V14.4.0 (2018-06): 3rd Generation Partnership Project. Technical Specification Group Services and System Aspects, Service requirements for V2X services
6. Costandoiu, A., Leba, M.: Convergence of V2X communication systems and next generation networks. IOP Conf. Ser. Mater. Sci. Eng. **477**(1), 1–18 (2019)
7. Gozalvez, J., Sepulcre, M., Bauza, R.: IEEE 802.11p vehicle to infrastructure communications in urban environments. IEEE Commun. Mag. **50**(5), 176–183 (2012)
8. Böhm, A., Lidström, K., Jonsson, M., Larsson, T.: Evaluating CALM M5-based vehicle-to-vehicle communication in various road settings through field trials, pp. 613–620. Proc. Conf. Local Comput. Netw., LCN (2010)
9. Meng, Y.S., Lee, Y.H., Chong Ng, B.: Study of propagation loss prediction. Prog. Electromagn. Res. B **17**, 117–133 (2009)
10. Giuliano, R., Monti, C., Loreti, P.: WiMAX fractional frequency reuse for rural environments. IEEE Wirel. Commun. **15**(3), 60–65 (2008)
11. ITU-R Recomendation: P.838-3. Specific attenuation model for rain. Rec. ITU-R P.838-3, pp. 1–8 (2005)
12. Thiagarajah, S.P., Pillay, S., Darmaraju, S., Subramanian, R., May Fung, M.F.: The effect of rain attenuation on S-band terrestrial links. In: IEEE Symposium on Wireless Technology Application ISWTA, pp. 192–197 (2013)
13. ITU: Attenuation due to clouds and fog P Series Radiowave propagation, vol. 6 (2013)
14. Han, J., Wu, B.: Handover in the 3GPP long term evolution (LTE) systems. In: 2010 Global Mobile Congress, GMC 2010, pp. 1–6 (2010)
15. Dimou, K., et al.: Handover within 3GPP LTE: Design principles and performance. In: IEEE Vehicle Technological Conference (2009)
16. Fernandez, N., et al.: Survey of Environmental Effects in Railway Communications", Nets4Cars/Nets4Trains/Nets4Aircraft. Communication Technologies for Vehicles, pp. 56–67 (2018)
17. Černý, J., Masopust, J.: Interference optimization and mitigation for LTE networks. In: International Conference on Applied Electronics (2017)
18. Chamorro, L., Reyes, A.F., Paredes-Paredes, M.C.: Interference evaluation in LTE heterogeneous networks. In: 2018 IEEE 3rd Ecuador Technical Chapters Meeting ETCM 2018, pp. 1–6 (2018)
19. Juskauskas, M., et al.: Experimental investigation of radar interference into LTE system at 1800 MHz frequency band. In: Proceedings Paper of 2013 21st Telecommunication Forum Telfor, TELFOR 2013, pp. 28–30 (2013)
20. Chang, P., Chang, Y., Han, Y., Zhang, C., Yang, D.: Interference analysis and performance evaluation for LTE TDD system. In: Proceedings of 2nd IEEE International Conference on Advanced Computing Control. ICACC 2010, Vol. 5, pp. 410–414 (2010)
21. ITU-T: Rec. ITU-T Y.2617, June 2016

Survey on Decision-Making Algorithms for Network Selection in Heterogeneous Architectures

Ali Mamadou Mamadou[✉], Mouna Karoui, Gerard Chalhoub,
and Antonio Freitas

LIMOS-CNRS, University Clermont Auvergne, Aubière, France
{ali.mamadou_mamadou,mouna.karoui,gerard.chalhoub,antonio.freitas}@uca.fr

Abstract. Access technologies are one of the fundamental assets of networking. Indeed, they are usually designed to optimize network performance in a given context and are therefore only well suited for targeted applications. Meanwhile, the paradigm of recent generation networks such as 5G is expected to revolutionize communication techniques by supporting a wide range of new applications that compel low latency and high data rates for both indoor and outdoor use cases. In this context, answering how should a user select an access technology at a given time while guaranteeing application needs, and leading to efficient utilization of network resources is an open research area. We survey in this paper decision-making algorithms for network selection in heterogeneous communication architectures. We also propose a taxonomy of these algorithms and carry out a discussion about common design challenges related to their applicability.

Keywords: Decision-making · Network optimization · Heterogeneous architectures

1 Introduction

The high demand for mobile traffic and the diversity of future applications motivates the evolution and revolutions of current communication techniques toward ubiquitous radio access. Thus, improved spectrum efficiency and innovative heterogeneous network deployments with astute resource sharing are essential to meet traffic demands expected in the near future [1].

Cooperative Intelligent Transport Systems (C-ITS) use cases such as autonomous driving and critical safety are one of the most promising services that will revolutionize mobility and transport field. These services require ultra-reliable communications and are expected to rely on technologies standards such as IEEE 802.11p, IEEE 802.11bd, LTE-V2V and NR-V2X [2]. Massive deployment of base stations and access points of different Radio Access Technologies (RATs) are therefore required to achieve robust and reliable connectivity solutions as well as the capability of seamlessly connecting all devices.

© Springer Nature Switzerland AG 2020
F. Krief et al. (Eds.): Nets4Cars/Nets4Trains/Nets4Aircraft 2020, LNCS 12574, pp. 89–98, 2020.
https://doi.org/10.1007/978-3-030-66030-7_8

In these heterogeneous networks, when a new session or handover session arrives, a decision must astutely be made as to which technology it should be associated with. This is called RAT selection. Overall, there are two approaches to tackle this problem, centralized and decentralized. In centralized approaches, the issue of RAT selection is formulated as a centralized optimization task (e.g. using linear and nonlinear programming models) which objective is to maximize throughput or equivalently minimize delay. These centralized approaches are the most straightforward to apprehend the issue of RAT selection, but the requirements and practical intractability of optimal solutions make them difficult to implement in real life. Whereas in distributed approaches, mobile users try to improve their performance by themselves, without a central coordinator, generally using heuristic rules. This does not always guarantee optimal solutions for mobile users but has the advantage of not requiring extra signaling for coordination, unlike centralized approaches.

The issue of RAT selection can be formulated also as a multiple attribute decision making (MADM) problem concerning considered criteria [3]. The typical MADM algorithms are Hierarchical Analysis Process (AHP), Fuzzy Analytic Hierarchy Process (FAHP), Technique for Order Preference by Similarity to an Ideal Solution (TOPSIS) and Entropy. In addition to these schemes based on MADM, many Artificial Intelligence-based algorithms have also been applied for this issue, such as Artificial Neural Network (ANN) and Q-Learning. However, these so-called intelligent algorithms must be iterated many times by probabilistic and heuristic rules to gradually obtain optimal results. Without enough iterations, any intelligence of algorithms will not be reflected, undesirable, or even bad, results may yield. Compared to AI-based algorithms, MADM algorithms are relatively simple and straightforward without any random factors in the whole runtime. They can obtain the definite result almost directly, relying only on their corresponding formulas rather than multiple loops. Although the results may be less intelligent, they can quickly complete the vertical transfer decision process and select the best target network.

In this paper, we propose a classification of RAT selection mechanisms into two main categories namely deterministic methods based on MADM schemes, and Artificial Intelligence (AI) based decision-making methods based on probabilistic and heuristic rules. We also review recent proposals on RAT selection mechanisms according to this categorization and identify open issues related to this topic.

This paper summarizes recent studies in Multiple Attribute Decision Making and Artificial Intelligence-based network selection methods. It also fills a research gap by summarizing common design challenges regarding the applicability of these methods.

The remainder of this paper is organized as follows. In Sect. 2 we describe network models and mechanisms of some representative and recent proposals on RAT selection. In Sect. 3, we carry out a discussion regarding challenges and issues in designing mechanisms of RAT selection. Finally, we conclude the paper in Sect. 4.

2   A Taxonomy of Decision-Making Algorithms

Modern wireless devices tend to contain multiple RAT interfaces that are cooperatively used to provide seamless connectivity. In this context, we propose a taxonomy of different decision-making algorithms for selecting the best RAT which we grouped into two categories: deterministic and AI-based. Tables 1 and 2 summarize the studied papers.

2.1   Deterministic Decision-Making Methods

In this section, we describe some representative decision-making algorithms without any random factors in the whole runtime which we classify as deterministic methods. We end the section with a summary table of these proposals.

A RAT selection mechanism considering the user and the network context is derived in [4]. It adopts the Analytical Hierarchical Process (AHP) for weighing the importance of selection criteria and the Technique for Order Preference by Similarity to an Ideal Solution (TOPSIS) for ranking available RATs. The framework consists of a *context provider* collecting network information from a *context manager* and user preferences and status form a *context consumer* to apply mechanisms toward decision making for the target RAT.

A centralized algorithm that applies the TOPSIS method on network attributes and user preferences to rank network association alternatives WiMAX, LTE, or WLAN is proposed in [5]. Simulation results indicate that the proposed algorithm reduces handover failure probabilities when compared to a network decision algorithm based on Received Signal Strength (RSS) only.

Authors in [6] propose a network selection algorithm combining three typical MADM methods as follows. FAHP is first used to calculate subjective weights of network attributes (e.g. bandwidth) and subjective utility values of all alternatives of four traffic classes (conversational, interactive, streaming, and background). Then Entropy and TOPSIS are used to respectively get the objective weights of network attributes and the objective utility values of all alternatives.

Authors in [7] propose a utility function based RAT selection mechanism taking into account user preferences, channel state information as well as network loads and service cost into account. The mechanism consists of central modules that periodically collect and broadcast network loads as part of the input of a normalized user utility function taking into account the quality of service requirements per service. Then the network having the largest utility function is selected for access.

The approach in [8] is motivated by guaranteeing QoS for different service flows with diverse QoS requirements. The authors propose a handover framework with QoS architecture with scheduling and admission control mechanisms in the MAC layer. The work proposed to extend the Media Independent Handover framework in the IEEE 802.21 standard by a cross-layer architecture with new modules in different layers and new service primitives to facilitate the communication. Whereas in [9], an optimization approach to RAT selection problem using a linear programming model considering the downlink of a heterogeneous network with two broadband RATs (Wi-Fi and LTE) is first proposed. Then heuristic approaches that are based on simple decisions made by the users that necessitate no signaling information are proposed.

Table 1 summarizes the proposals and their main approaches, features and findings. We note that most of the work proposes decision algorithms based on MADM algorithms and are evaluated with LTE and Wi-Fi simulation models.

Table 1. Summary table of deterministic methods in related work

Reference	Decision methods	Networks	Traffic classes	Criteria	Signaling message	Findings
[4]	AHP, TOPSIS	LTE-A, Wi-Fi	Baseline class	RSS, Network load, User velocity	Yes	Improvement of throughput and delay compared to another link quality based handover mechanism
[5]	TOPSIS	WiMAX, LTE, Wi-Fi	Baseline class	Number of nodes associated, User velocity, Service price, RSS	Yes	Handover success probability is increased by considering multiple criteria compared to RSS only based method
[6]	TOPSIS, FAHP, Entropy	GSM, UMTS, LTE-A, Wi-Fi	Conversation, streaming, interaction, background	Bandwidth, latency, delay jitter, packet loss rate, service price	No	Combination of the MADMs reduces vertical handovers and provides better QoS compared with existing hybrid algorithms
[7]	Based on cost function	LTE, Wi-Fi	Voice, Streaming	Throughtput, Network load, Service cost	Yes	Load balancing and user throughput improvement compared with a baseline scheme
[9]	An optimization approach	LTE, Wi-Fi	Baseline class	Throughput, Network load, RSS	No	Proposed distributed algorithms give efficient results compared to the centralized optimal approach
[8]	Cross-Layer architecture	LTE, Wi-Fi	Real time, background	Bandwidth, Delay, SNIR, user velocity	Yes	Conducted simulations demonstrate the effectiveness of the proposed cross-layer handover architecture

2.2 Artificial Intelligence-Based Decision-Making Methods

In this section, we survey some Artificial Intelligence (AI) based network selection algorithms. We begin with a brief description of the operating principles of these algorithms. We then review the proposals and classify them into two main groups: Machine Learning (ML) and Swarm Intelligence (SI). We end this section by giving a classification and findings summary of these proposals in Table 2.

ML-based solutions are divided in three main subcategories: (i) Supervised Learning (SL), (ii) Unsupervised Learning (UL), and (iii) Reinforcement Learning (RL). SL and UL are offline ML algorithms where the prediction model has to be built prior to use. Indeed, SL techniques learn on a labeled data set, providing key elements that the algorithm can use to evaluate its accuracy on training data. In contrast to UL techniques that provide unlabeled data in which the algorithm attempts to make sense by extracting useful features. Whereas, RL approaches are generally classified as online ML algorithms which differ from SL and UL in not needing learning data beforehand. It is mainly based on how software agents ought to take actions in an environment to maximize the notion of reward (i.e. feedback).

SI-based techniques were also used to formulate network selection problem in heterogeneous architectures. SI algorithms are biologically inspired by the behavior of social insects like ants and bees. It is mainly based on collective intelligence behavior of agents which are able to communicate with each other through the shared environment to cooperatively learn its properties.

To begin with, we review Artificial Neural Network (ANN) based techniques included in SL subcategory. Many papers used ANN to predict the optimal network based on multiple input criteria. ANN algorithms are inspired by the biological neural networks that constitute human brains. Targeting the goal of achieving uninterrupted connectivity taking into account multiple criteria, authors in papers [10,11], proposed ANN-based solutions. In paper [10], authors' findings showed an improvement of QoS performance compared to traditional RSS-based scheme. Authors of [11] also showed the benefits of their ANN-based scheme in reducing the number of handovers.

Clustering is a UL technique frequently used to resolve network selection problem. In the context of wireless sensor networks (WSNs), papers [12,13] used clustering techniques for decision-making in centralized architectures. Authors in [13] compared Grouped Vertical Handover (GVHO) scheme with traditional vertical handover for single user where each mobile station just selects the best network without considering the influence from other concurrent handover decision making users. GVHO scheme has been introduced to avoid simultaneous decision-making for mass handover users. Other papers adopt the game theory to analyze the network selection problem where the focus is to design an efficient Multi-Agent Reinforcement Learning (MARL) algorithm to solve it. In this context, authors of paper [14] proposed a network selection problem formulation based on Tag-of-war (TOW) algorithm which is inspired by the behavior of the amoeboid organism. The algorithm is based on observing the performance of selected network and deciding whether the rewards or the punishments is to be given.

In an attempt to resolve the radio access technologies selection game in 5G HetNets, authors in paper [15] proposed an ML-based framework where the throughput is the main objective function. Indeed, authors tackled the problem of determining which RAT standard and spectrum to utilize and which Base stations or users to associate within the context of 5G HetNets. The proposed framework combined different machine learning algorithms.

Authors in papers [16,17] proposed SI-based solution for network selection based on Artificial Bee Colony (ABC), Particle Swarm Optimization (PSO), and Ant Colony (ACO) algorithms.

Most cited papers highlight benefits of using machine learning techniques for network selection. However, the efficiency of these AI-based algorithms need to be proven using realistic implementations and experimental demonstrations in different environments.

Table 2. Summary of AI-based decision-making techniques in literature

Reference	Learning technique	Networks	Traffic class	Criteria	Findings
Supervised learning					
[10]	Neural Network Based Handover Management Scheme (NNBHMS)	LTE WiMAX Wi-Fi	Real-time, and Data services	Data rate, coverage, Mobility, BER, Cost, and packet process	QoS enhancement
[11]	Learning Vector Quantization Neural Networks (LVQNNs)	LTE WLAN	Multimedia	RSSI, Bandwidth, mobile speed, monetary cost	Handover reduction and network usage increase
Unsupervised learning					
[12]	Fuzzy c-means clustering	WSNs	Web usage	QoS	Low energy and low cost constraints are targeted
[13]	Fuzzy clustering	General context of HetNets	Real-time, Non real-time	Data rate, delay, affordable cost	Handover blocking probability reduction
Reinforcement learning					
[14]	Multi-armed bandit	IEEE 802.11 ac/n LTE	Base line	Throughput, delay	Throughput increase with experimental demonstrations
[15]	Q-learning based framework with clustering and classification process	5G multi-rat architecture	Base line	Throughput, number of users	Low overhead
Swarm intelligence					
[16]	ABC-PSO	LTE, WiMAX, Wi-Fi	Streaming, Conversational	QoS	Lower cost and delay, Higher available bandwidth and less number of handovers
[17]	Update version of ACO	4G, Wi-Fi	Base line	Available bandwidth, monetary cost, security level, power consumption, and RSS	Better bandwidth Less cost and power consumption

3   Challenges and Key Issues

Apart from this representative MADM and Artificial Intelligence-based methods in the literature presented in Sect. 2, we identify in this section open issues concerning design challenges and applicability of decision-making algorithms for network selection. Key issues for both proposed decision-making method categories are then summarized in Fig. 1.

3.1   Deterministic Methods Related Issues

Typical MADM algorithms currently available are Simple Additive Weighting (SAW) method; Analytic Hierarchy Process (AHP); Technique for Order Preference by Similarity to the Ideal Solution (TOPSIS) Multiplicative Exponent Weighting (MEW). Each of these algorithms has its advantages and disadvantages and none can solve all MADM problems perfectly so far [3]. Hence, the question related to choosing one MADM instead of another is among the number of first challenges to consider in using MADM in the context of RAT selection. This should depend on targeted needs.

In the context of RAT selection and MADMs, different types of applications such as conversation, streaming, interaction, or background traffic may simultaneously be considered together with different attributes such as bandwidth, packet jitter, packet loss, or service cost. Thus, how to astutely define dominant attributes while considering user preferences remains also challenging.

3.2   Artificial Intelligence-Based Methods Related Issues

Limitations of offline machine learning techniques (i.e. SL and UL) are manifested in two aspects: lack of data, and lack of good data. In fact, if the training model is poorly fed, it will give inaccurate results. Hence, these techniques require large amounts of data before they begin to give useful results. The quality of data is a key factor affecting the efficiency and the accuracy of these learning techniques. Indeed errors in training data might confuse the algorithm and lower its accuracy. Collecting and labeling data is also a time-consuming task. In addition, the training set needs to cover different network performance situations to avoid modeling a decision based on specific use cases.

RL generally makes use of Markov Decision Process (MDP) and game-theory which are complexity prohibitive, and their convergence to an optimal solution is not always guaranteed. Searching for and finding the optimal solutions is cumbersome, especially in the case of large network topology. In fact, formulating the network selection as an optimization problem with low or moderate computational complexity is not a trivial task and can be in some cases NP-hard problem [18]. So-called intelligent algorithms require an iteration phase before the desired results are obtained since fast convergence is not always ensured. In this case, powerful engines and High Performance Computing (HPC) are essential to minimize the runtime of these algorithms and fit the constraints of vertical handover in terms of latency and quality of user experience (QoE).

Another issue is manifested in different research studies dealing with the misapplication of ML techniques in their problem formulation that leads to blindly use these algorithms for analyzing cases that are either deterministic or stochastic in nature. Applying ML techniques for resolving deterministic problems will succeed, but the algorithm which will not learning the relationship between the two variables, and will not know when it is violating "physical laws".

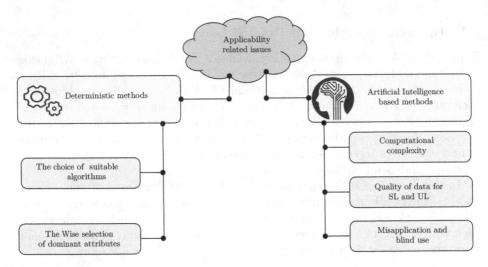

Fig. 1. Summary of decision-making techniques applicability related issues for network selection problem.

4   Conclusion

The increasing demand for mobile traffic and the diversity of future applications are among the main motivations of evolution of current communication techniques toward ubiquitous radio access relying on a heterogeneous architecture. In these heterogeneous networks, when a new session or handover session arrives, a decision has to be made as to which technology it should be associated with. This constitutes the fundamentals of RAT selection problem.

In this paper, we survey RAT selection algorithm proposals in the literature by identifying two main categories namely deterministic methods based on MADM schemes, and methods based on probabilistic and heuristic rules that we called Artificial Intelligence based methods. The advantages of MADM-based methods for the RAT selection problem are simplicity, rationality, comprehensibility, relatively good computational efficiency, and the ability to measure performance for each alternative in a relatively simple mathematical form. However, the main challenge of using MADM-based methods for the RAT selection problem relates to astutely defining network criteria and comprehensive utility values that meet user preferences.

AI-based solutions can easily review large volumes of data and discover specific trends and patterns. As AI algorithms gain experience, they keep improving in accuracy and efficiency gradually with iterations. This enables them to make better decisions. On the other hand, without enough iteration, any intelligence of algorithms will not be reflected, undesirable, or even bad results may yield.

When it comes to performance evaluation, the majority of AI-based proposals for network selection in heterogeneous architecture do not use a realistic simulation model implementing communication protocol stacks. For RL-based decision-making techniques, authors generally build an abstract model of HetNets. For data-driven learning techniques, some of the papers used imported data from network simulators like NS3 and OPNET for a particular context to analyze the network and use these data for their training model to learn an optimal matching between network performance and user demand.

In future work, the taxonomy of RAT selection algorithms we propose may be extended to consider optimization approaches using linear or nonlinear programming models.

Acknowledgement. This work is supported by C-ROADS France European project.

References

1. Mamadou, A.M., Toussaint, J., Chalhoub, G.: Survey on wireless networks coexistence: resource sharing in the 5G era. Mob. Netw. Appl. **25** (2020)
2. Naik, G., Choudhury, B., Park, J.M.: IEEE 802.11bd & 5G NR V2X: evolution of radio access technologies for V2X communications. IEEE Access **7**, 70169–70184 (2019)
3. Trestian, R., Ormond, O., Muntean, G.M.: Performance evaluation of MADM-based methods for network selection in a multimedia wireless environment. Wirel. Netw. **21**(5), 1745–1763 (2015)
4. Habbal, A., Goudar, S.I., Hassan, S.: A context-aware radio access technology selection mechanism in 5G mobile network for smart city applications. J. Netw. Comput. Appl **135**, 97–107 (2019)
5. Abdullah, R.M., Abualkishik, A.Z., Alwan, A.A.: Improved handover decision algorithm using multiple criteria. Procedia Comput. Sci. **141**, 32–39 (2018). The 9th International Conference on Emerging Ubiquitous Systems and Pervasive Networks (EUSPN-2018)/The 8th International Conference on Current and Future Trends of Information and Communication Technologies in Healthcare (ICTH-2018)/Affiliated Workshops
6. Yu, H.W., Zhang, B.: A heterogeneous network selection algorithm based on network attribute and user preference. Ad Hoc Netw. **72**, 68–80 (2018)
7. Wu, X., Du, Q.: Utility-function-based radio-access-technology selection for heterogeneous wireless networks. Comput. Electr. Eng. **52**, 171–182 (2016)
8. Mansouri, W., Zarai, F., Mnif, K., Kamoun, L.: Cross layer architecture with integrated MIH in heterogeneous wireless networks. Comput. Netw. **127**, 126–137 (2017)
9. Khawam, K., et al.: Radio access technology selection in heterogeneous networks. Phys. Commun. **18**, 125–139 (2016). Special Issue on Radio Access Network Architectures and Resource Management for 5G

10. Alotaibi, N.M., Alwakeel, S.S.: A neural network based handover management strategy for heterogeneous networks. In: 2015 IEEE 14th International Conference on Machine Learning and Applications (ICMLA), pp. 1210–1214. IEEE (2015)
11. Kunarak, S., Sulessathira, R.: Vertical handover decision management on the basis of several criteria for LVQNN with ubiquitous wireless networks. Int. J. GEOMATE **12**(34), 123 (2017)
12. Thakur, G.K., Priya, B., Sharma, P.K.: Optimal selection of network in heterogeneous environment based on fuzzy approach. J. Math. Comput. Sci. **10**(3), 554–571 (2020)
13. Ning, L., Wang, Z., Guo, Q., Jiang, K.: Fuzzy clustering based group vertical handover decision for heterogeneous wireless networks. In: 2013 IEEE Wireless Communications and Networking Conference (WCNC), pp. 1231–1236. IEEE (2013)
14. Oshima, K., Onishi, T., Kim, S.J., Ma, J., Hasegawa, M.: Efficient wireless network selection by using multi-armed bandit algorithm for mobile terminals. Nonlinear Theor. Appl. IEICE **11**(1), 68–77 (2020)
15. Naghavi, P., Rastegar, S.H., Shah-Mansouri, V., Kebriaei, H.: Learning rat selection game in 5G heterogeneous networks. IEEE Wirel. Commun. Lett. **5**(1), 52–55 (2015)
16. Goudarzi, S., et al.: ABC-PSO for vertical handover in heterogeneous wireless networks. Neurocomputing **256**, 63–81 (2017)
17. El Fachtali, I., Saadane, R., ElKoutbi, M.: Vertical handover decision algorithm using ants' colonies for 4G heterogeneous wireless networks. J. Comput. Netw. Commun. **2016** (2016)
18. Rouskas, A., Kosmides, P., Kikilis, A., Anagnostou, M.: RAT selection optimization in heterogeneous wireless networks. In: Tomkos, I., Bouras, C.J., Ellinas, G., Demestichas, P., Sinha, P. (eds.) BROADNETS 2010. LNICST, vol. 66, pp. 460–472. Springer, Heidelberg (2012). https://doi.org/10.1007/978-3-642-30376-0_33

Radio Access Technologies Selection in Vehicular Networks: State-of-the-Art and Perspectives for Autonomous Connected Vehicles

Sidoine Juicielle Kambiré[1,2]([✉]), Hasnaâ Aniss[2], Francine Krief[3],
Sassi Maaloul[2], and Marion Berbineau[4][ID]

[1] LaBRI Lab, University of Bordeaux, Bordeaux, France
`sidoine.kambire@labri.fr`
[2] COSYS-ERENA, Univ Gustave Eiffel, IFSTTAR, Marne-la-Vallée, France
[3] LaBRI Lab, Bordeaux INP, Bordeaux, France
[4] COSYS-LEOST, Univ Gustave Eiffel, IFSTTAR, Villeneuve d'Ascq, France

Abstract. Inter-vehicle (V2V) and vehicle to infrastructure (V2I) communication is an active research field in Vehicular Network domain. Each application in these networks presents specific needs in terms of Quality of Service (QoS), reliability and security. Thus, it is important to select in a smart way the various radio access technologies (RAT) to be used to transfer information. In this paper, we present a state of the art related to this subject. Then we propose ideas for a smarter, multi-application, adaptable and secure selection solution of RAT. This approach is essential in the context of autonomous connected vehicle, where vehicles and users always send and receive data from diverse applications.

Keywords: Vehicular networks · Smart RAT selection · V2V · V2I · V2X · Autonomous vehicles · C-V2X · 5G NR

1 Introduction

Vehicles are now able to communicate via network infrastructure with other vehicles and other devices. This results in more connected integrated services with increased data exchanges with other vehicles and with network infrastructure. The more networks grow, the more performances requirements increase. Indeed, connected services integrated into vehicles require mainly high reliability, broadband connectivity, high throughput for some services, security and integrity of exchanged data. These needs become more critical, as we are now entering the autonomous vehicles era with higher Quality of Service (QoS) requirements.

Vehicle applications require different types of data exchanges in the network. For example, a multimedia content broadcasting application will not have the same performance expectations as a traffic safety application. In this context, it is important for each application to communicate via a given Radio Access

© Springer Nature Switzerland AG 2020
F. Krief et al. (Eds.): Nets4Cars/Nets4Trains/Nets4Aircraft 2020, LNCS 12574, pp. 99–112, 2020.
https://doi.org/10.1007/978-3-030-66030-7_9

Technology (RAT) offering the expected performances to answer the needs. In order to deal with the multitude of existing RATs (e.g. Cellular networks, ITS-G5...), vehicles should also know how to choose the best one.

In this paper, we present a state of the art about RAT selection solutions in vehicular networks. We analyze these works to identify their strengths and limits. After that, in order to bring the best QoS satisfaction to autonomous vehicles, as they require better network performances, we propose some new enhanced ideas and concepts to integrate to vehicular networks. This paper is organized as follows: Section 2 summarises applications needs in vehicular networks, and the available radio resources for these networks. Section 3 presents a state of the art of access technologies selection techniques in vehicular networks. Before concluding, Sect. 4 provides directions for future works.

2 Background

2.1 Vehicular Use Cases Needs

Depending on the importance of the exchanged data, the requirements in terms of network performances are different. In [29], authors give an overview of different existing applications in vehicular networks, and the main requirements of each one, according to the use cases type (Road safety, Traffic information, Infotainment and Autonomous vehicles). The classification is as follows:

- **Road safety use cases** have the highest priorities in the network. They are related to users and vehicle safety critical applications. The on-time delivery probability to the destination should be maximized, thus, their requirements are mainly: low latency (100 ms maximum), high reliability of the network, high messages broadcasting frequency (10 Hz minimum).
- **Traffic information use cases** need lower network performances, but still remain an important type of information. They inform users about the road traffic status. For this, they need: good periodicity of messages broadcasting (1 Hz), good reliability, especially for traffic management messages (traffic jams warnings, roadworks, lane changes, *etc.*), less performances in terms of delay (between 100 ms and 500 ms).
- **Infotainment use cases** usually have the lowest priority, because their main goal is to bring more comfort to users. They don't require high network performances for the reliability or the delay, but they generally require more bandwidth than other applications.
- **Autonomous connected vehicles use cases** need the highest network performances, especially in terms of delay. For instance in platooning (when a collection of vehicles travel together [3], actively coordinated in formation), it is essential for vehicles to use networks that are able to provide them with latency lower than 10 ms [5], in order to increase the probability for the information to arrive on-time. We notice the same requirements for remote driving [5].

2.2   Access Technologies in Vehicular Networks

In this section, we will first describe the actual main used RATs in selection solutions, and their future evolutions. Then, we will present some other existing RATs not used yet in RAT selection modules, but offering more choices during the selection process.

Deployed Radio Access Technologies

- **ITS-G5** (Intelligent Transportation Systems) [9] is a communication technology based on the IEEE 802.11p standard allowing vehicles to communicate with their environment, operating in the 5.9 GHz frequency band, able to form a distributed network. It is specifically designed for V2V (Vehicle-to-Vehicle) and V2I (Vehicle-to-Infrastructure) communications. It is characterized by the integration of the DCC (Distributed Congestion Control) functionality for channel control and the definition of four channel access priorities (Voice, Video, Best Effort and Background) thanks to EDCA (Enhanced Distributed mode Channel Access). The new standard, IEEE 802.11bd (NGV: Next Generation V2X) [21], is an evolution of ITS-G5 to meet new requirements in vehicular environments in terms of better throughput, improved reliability and efficiency and extended range.
- **LTE-V2X or C-V2X** LTE-V2X (Vehicle to Everything) [18] or Cellular V2X (C-V2X) is a communication technology standardized by 3GPP [24], which provides V2V, V2I and V2P (Vehicle-to-Pedestrian) communications in the 5.9 GHz band. C-V2X defines two complementary transmission modes: mode 3 and mode 4. The mode 3 uses the Uu (User unit) cellular interface to leverage the LTE infrastructure for communications. In this mode, the cellular network manages the radio resources used by vehicles for their communications. The mode 4 uses the PC5 (Proximity Communication 5) interface for direct V2V communications. In this mode, vehicles autonomously select their radio resources through a Semi-Persistent Scheduling (SPS) mechanism. When the vehicles are not under cellular coverage, mode 4 is used to ensure direct V2V communications.

Upcoming 5G Standard. 5G deployment will be based on 4G networks and will be interoperable with LTE. It should guarantee greater QoS of communications, increased throughput and lower latency. In addition, 5G standard will introduce the possibility to provide specific resources slices (Network Slicing) that can logically isolate network functions and resources, specifically tailored for various applications on a single common network infrastructure [6].

Other RATs that Could Be Integrated. So far, for most of the research works, only a few types of RATs have been considered in RAT selection. Nevertheless, there are other existing RATs, that could be used for some autonomous connected vehicles use cases in different situations. We will briefly present them next.

- **Visible Light Communication (VLC)** [26] is a technology using light from vehicle headlights to communicate over short distances. In their paper [27], authors present a comparative study of VLC with 802.11p showing that this technique can be applied to V2V and V2I communications. The limit of the VLC lies in its great sensitivity to obstacles and weather conditions such as fog. Nevertheless, in optimal conditions, authors conclude that VLC can be more efficient than 802.11p.
- **Ultra-Wide Band (UWB)** [2,19] radio relies on the use of very short pulses in time (typically a few hundreds of picoseconds) that cause a spreading of the radio energy over a very wide frequency band, with a very low power spectral density. This limits potential interference with conventional radio systems, and the high bandwidth can allow very high data throughput for communications devices, or high precision for location. This technique could be very interesting for ITS applications [8].

3   State-of-the-Art Related to Radio Access Technology Selection

This section is an overview of RAT selections techniques in vehicular networks by analysing standards, European projects and research works.

3.1   Standards for Radio Access Technology Selection

Standards about RAT selection in vehicular networks tend to normalize the selection process, by describing some choices and their selection process. ETSI Standard TS 103 301 [11] describes different types of communication profiles that can be available for selection. These profiles stand for the types of RATs and their different settings that can be selected by vehicles. It enumerates five profiles, named CPS (Communication Parameter Settings):

- CPS-001: for transmission over ITS-G5
- CPS-002: for transmission over WLAN 2.4 GHz in infrastructure mode
- CPS-003: for transmission over WLAN 5.8 GHz in infrastructure mode
- CPS-004: for transmission over LTE-V2X sidelink
- CPS-005: for transmission over IP based data services

All profiles are set to use geonetworking [10]. This allows profiles working together in the same network. The standard also describes the particularities of each profile, as the protocols to set up before using them.

The ISO standard [14] related to the selection of communication profiles describes how to make choice efficiently according to application needs. To do so, a variable called *CostObjective* represents the relevance of the profile for a given communication. The values vary from 0 to 255, where 0 means that the communication link will not be relevant at all. The best profile is the one for which the value is the closest to 255.

3.2   European Projects

SCOOP@F[1], InterCor[2], C-ROADS[3] are European projects dealing with C-ITS (Cooperative Intelligent Transportation Systems) deployment considering multiple RATs selection (Fig. 1). Their goals are the drivers and road operators workers safety improvement, better traffic management, optimization of infrastructure costs, and preparation of the infrastructure for future vehicle services including autonomous connected vehicle applications. They all participate to the European harmonisation of services, architectures and evaluations.

Functional and technical architectures described in Fig. 1 are based on several communication RATs: ITS-G5 with geobroadcasting, ITS-G5 over IP (with geobroadcasting header for security matters) and LTE (C-ITS messages are signed at geonetworking layer). Figure 1 shows architecture evolution from a full ITS-G5 architecture (SCOOPwave 1) to an hybrid one (C-Roads). Three communication modes are available for V2V and V2I: only ITS-G5, only LTE, or hybrid communication. In these projects, hybrid communication means that C-ITS messages are sent on all available RATs. The end-user considers only the first received message whatever the used RAT is. Message redundancy is used here to make sure that the end user will receive messages, no matter the network deployment.

3.3   Dynamic Radio Access Technology Selection in the Literature

In [25], authors propose a dynamic RAT selection model, based on genetic algorithms. The selection system called "Attractor Selection Model" matches the applications needs with the RAT characteristics in order to precisely choose the best RAT for each one. The selection results vary depending on possible changes of considered QoS parameters, namely delay, bandwidth and packet loss rate. The concerned RATs broadcast this information periodically to vehicles. The authors assume that each vehicle can access a single RAT interface at the same time, and the selection process is carried out each time an application wants to communicate. The available RATs are classified according to the values of the parameters they return. Authors consider 802.11g, DSRC (Dynamic Short Range Communication), the American version of ITS-G5, and 3G/4G cellular networks. Selection is made by vehicles. The RAT with the best QoS is chosen for the communication. The solution is compared with [13] and [22], showing an improvement of network QoS in terms of requirements satisfaction, for about 10 to 15%.

[7] describes an approach based on Stackelberg's game theory. It aims to select the best RAT, between 3G, WiMAX and DSRC, using SDN (Software Defined Networking) feature. Applications are classified regarding their priority (safety, entertainment...). The selection is made for the application with the

---

[1]   SCOOP project official website: http://www.scoop.developpement-durable.gouv.fr/ [Accessed 27/03/2020].

[2]   Intercor official website: https://intercor-project.eu/ [Accessed 27/03/2020].

[3]   C-ROADS: https://www.c-roads.eu/pilots/core-members/france/Partner/project/show/c-roads-france.html [Accessed 27/03/2020].

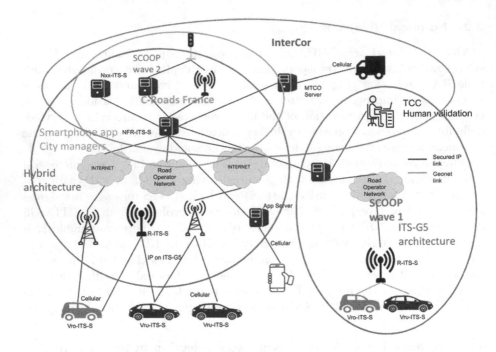

Fig. 1. Projects architecture evolution

highest priority. Parameters used to choose the RAT are bandwidth, latency, bit rate, priority and cost. The solution includes a decision process, a RAT detection manager, a priority manager, a module for the pre-selection of available RATs, and a best RAT Selection module located in the SDN controller. Results show that the solution increases the network performances: end-to-end delay have been improved by 39.32%, average throughput by 34.87%, packet delivery ratio by 30.38%, and routing overhead by 27%.

In paper [15], authors propose a RAT selection approach, for V2I communications with 3G, 802.11p and WiMAX, that considers QoS, energy efficiency and user preferences, using the multi-criteria utility theory. Measured parameters for each RAT are signal strength, bandwidth and latency. RATs are first pre-selected according to the measured parameters and traffic type, then the final RAT is chosen according to energy efficiency, cost and user preferences in terms of QoS parameters. Selection is made by vehicles. The solution is compared with the Simple Addition Weight Algorithm, and the Random Access Selection Algorithm. Results show better performances in terms of needs satisfaction, for up to 10% compared to other works, bandwidth management and latency lowering, with execution times close to 500 ms for 30 traffic requests.

[23] presents a decision algorithm capable of computing at any time the state of more than one RAT, between cellular networks 3G/4G, DSRC and ITS-G5, and the Wi-Fi. They use the Ant Colony Optimization Model. They consider received signal strength, latency, bit rate, and packet loss rate. The algorithm

calculates the satisfaction rate of application needs according to each RAT, and generates a graph based on these rates. The best RAT is the one with the highest satisfaction rate. The solution avoids ping-pong effect, by reducing for among 65% RAT switching, thanks to its stability that is evaluated with the satisfaction rate. Results show that according to the test scenarios, the solution brings more stability in terms of QoS. The solution gives a 62.22% satisfaction, and 15% less ping-pong effect than the one it has been compared with.

[28] offers a smart selection mode between cellular networks 3G/4G, ITS-G5, WiMAX and WiFi which operates with a cloud. Authors takes advantage of the cloud distributed architecture to store information about network entities (vehicles, RSUs (Roadside Units), available access technologies, and some information regarding the location of these entities). The selection based on Coalition Formation Games method, is made by the OBU (OnBoard Unit), which must be able to access the cloud database at any time. The network information available in the cloud is the location of the stations, the free channels, the available bandwidth, the cost, the number of connected vehicles and the network's load. This information is used by vehicles to choose the RAT they will use. They must therefore have permanent access to the cloud. But if they are unable to access the cloud, the OBU will operate the change by traditional handover, based on received signal's strength. Experiments results show that compared to other systems of the same type, the solution gives better throughputs (up to 2 Mbps) and lower delays, less than 5 ms for 1000 nodes.

[4] presents a handover model between cellular and 802.11p in order to improve access to the network. The handover is carried out in two situations: either the power received by the base station or the RSU becomes too low, or one of the neighboring stations offers more power than the serving one. The handover decision is made based on two criteria, the strength of the received signal and the estimated bit rate that the candidate station can provide. A controller is used for RAT selection and management of resource allocation. For simplicity reasons, authors considered only the case of V2I communications. They compared their solution to [22] and [16], and results show that their solution provides a better handover method, by improving choice accuracy and throughput and reducing costs.

A mobility management solution using SDN (Software Define Network) technology is detailed in [20]. The RAT selection, based on 802.11p and LTE-V2X, problem is viewed from the user and from the network. From the user point of view, the controller considers an utility function that takes into account the QoS metrics (throughput and delay) of each V2X application. From the network point of view, the controller solves a cooperative game between the players (candidate RATs) in order to avoid congestion.

Some studies deal with RAT selection module that will integrate the upcoming 5G to raise QoS performances in the network. In [6], authors propose a solution based on network slicing, for Vehicle-to-Everything Services. 5G will offer slicing functionality, described as a set of logical resources and network services, customized to fit with a specific service or application. Authors propose services integrated to this slice, including RAT selection. They do not specifically propose a RAT selection method, but they enumerate requirements that a RAT Selection solution should have such as adaptation to networks changing conditions, or the simultaneous use of multiple RAT. They also propose a network architecture with on-demand deployment of Radio Access Networks (RAN) functions, including the cloud-RAN technology and virtualization. They also propose slicing solution for other entities of the network, such as the core network and the user device in order to improve V2X communications.

Authors in [12] describe a context-aware RAT selection in ultra dense 5G-enabled networks. This work is not specified for vehicular networks, but for every end user that could be able to communicate. A multi-attribute solution is proposed, using the Multi-Attribute Decision Making (MADM) theory. The solution first analyses the network in a hierarchic process mechanism, then selection chooses the best RAT regarding the order preference. During analysis phase, the solution first collects information about signal quality (Signal strength, data rate and user preferences), then combining this information, it defines a priority assignment according to context. After that a context-aware algorithm is processed, and puts weights to each criteria. This leads to the generation of an input decision matrix, which maps criteria and RAT. Then, another context-aware selection algorithm is processed, and the best available RAT is chosen. Experiments considered LTE and DSRC, as 5G is not yet available. Results show that compared to classic multi-attribute decision making integrated solutions, such as Technique for Order Preference by Similarity to an Ideal Solution (TOPSIS), Simple Additive Weight (SAW) and Grey Relational Analysis (GRA). This one reduces useless handover from 11.11% to 22.22%.

Summary of the Works Analysed. Table 1 presents a summary the analysed papers considering: ·

- QoS: ability of the proposed solution to take into account QoS parameters such as delay and throughput.
- Application priority: ability of the solution to choose the RAT regarding the needs of the highest priority applications.
- Multi-application: ability of the solution to satisfy simultaneously the needs of more than one application.
- Guaranteed Access: ability of the solution to make sure that the application will reach at least one RAT, even if with lowest performances.
- Energy efficiency: ability of the solution to ensure energy-efficient use of the resources.
- User preferences: ability of the solution to consider user preferences in the selection process such as cost.
- Final decision: is the final decision made only by the vehicle (local) or in collaboration with other entities in an externalized infrastructure (deported).
- V2V/V2I: ability of the solution to provide V2I and/or V2V communications.
- Used RATs: Radio access technologies that are considered in the selection process.

Table 1. Summary table of studied works

Solution	QoS considered	Selection by priority	Multi-apps	Access guaranteed	Energy efficiency	Users' preferences	Final decision	V2V/V2I	Used RATs
[25]	Yes	No	No	Yes	No	Yes	Local	V2I	DSRC, 802.11g, 3G/4G
[7]	Yes	Yes	No	Yes	No	No	Deported	V2I	DSRC, Wimax, 3G
[15]	Yes	No	No	Yes	Yes	Yes	Local	V2I	Wimax, 802.11p, 3G
[23]	Yes	No	No	Yes	No	No	Local	V2I	DSRC, ITS-G5, 3G/4G
[28]	Yes	Yes	No	Yes	No	No	Deported	V2I	ITS-G5, Wimax, WiFi, 3G/4G
[4]	Yes	No	No	Yes	No	No	Local	V2I	802.11p, 3G/4G
[20]	Yes	No	No	Yes	No	Yes	Deported	V2X	802.11p, LTE-V2X
[6]	Yes	No	Yes	Yes	No	No	Deported	V2X	802.11p, 5G
[12]	Yes	Yes	No	Yes	No	Yes	Local	–	DSRC, LTE, 5G

While studying these works, we noticed a lot of important points, that we present here.

First, all the proposed solutions consider, in the selection process, QoS criterion as delay, throughput or bandwidth. This guarantees a minimal level of QoS while making RAT choice. In some works, QoS Criterion are combined with other types of criterion, as energy efficiency [15], or user preferences [20,25]. This allows more accurate and adapted RAT choice processes, as they consider end-users requirements. QoS is only considered during RAT choice, but authors do not precise if during the communication this QoS is maintained.

In addition, none of the solutions offers the multi-RAT functionality. If more than one application requires to communicate at the same time, with actual solutions considering only one RAT at a time, they will be queued, and a communication order will be established, regarding priority in better cases. This increases latency in the network, and then reduces QoS. Our solution will provide possible redundancy and will improve QoS by reducing latency. Today, this solution is chosen for example in the railway domain in order to ensure redundancy and reliability [1].

We also noticed that depending on the selection module entities, final decision could be done either locally, or in a collaborative way including vehicles, network entities and external entities as controllers or Cloud databases from a common agreement. Decision is made by vehicles when the OBU has the data collection role in the process. The choice is then made regarding network parameters. Deported decisions tend to be more accurate, as they consider not only RATs parameters, but also other vehicles information. Otherwise, deported selection could have some limits, especially when the deported infrastructure becomes unreachable, due to some radio coverage degradation. In this situation, in main of the cloud-based solutions, vehicles will launch an handover process, in order to continue the communication. The QoS performances of the solution will surely be decreased. In the same way, local selection is made exclusively by vehicles, without any external help. This could also be considered as non optimal, because each vehicle will not have an idea of what is going on in its neighboring. As the vehicles are in a common geographic zone, it is very important to take the decisions regarding their neighbors behavior, in order to improve the network's collaborative aspect.

All these works use different mathematical methods such as Stackelberg theory, game theory, genetic algorithms, fuzzy logic, to propose efficient solutions. We can also notice that none of the solutions considers prediction or networks behavior anticipation, which could improve the reliability. In the next section, based on these remarks, we propose some ideas to improve the efficiency of the future solutions.

4   Research Directions for Future Works

Applications dedicated to autonomous vehicles (AV) require higher network performances, especially in terms of throughput, latency and resources availability. To improve the selection of the best RAT adapted to AV requirements, our future works will focus on designing a context/content-aware RAT selection module for C-ITS that will improve the drawbacks highlighted previously. The solution will be *smart, adaptable, programmable, secure and reliable* and will include a good resources management technique. It will also be able to anticipate some networks behaviors to propose a more accurate selection process. In addition, we will develop a *multi-** solution, able to make more than one application communicate (multi-applications) at the same time, to satisfy more than one user (multi-users), and to communicate with different types of devices (multi-device).

4.1   Adaptability and Programmability

The dynamic RAT selection process will be adjusted regarding network behavior and collected information from infrastructure and other vehicles. Network virtualization, Edge computing and software-defined radio (SDR) will allow our solution to be scalable and evolutive.

- **Network virtualization** stands for the principle of designing some network functionalities and features, in a software infrastructure. In vehicular networks, this permits to reduce the number of network physical equipment, and to decouple functions execution from hardware. Thanks to Network Function Virtualization, our solution will have an easy deployment process, as it will only consist in downloading software on existing equipment, avoiding infrastructure installation costs. Upgrade and addition of supplementary services in vehicles and infrastructure will be facilitated. Furthermore, instead of installing all services on every vehicle, it could be possible that if a vehicle needs to use a service that is not installed on its own OBU, this vehicle could ask his neighbors to provide him with this service, for a given time. This will avoid installation latencies, and OBUs CPUs and storage saturation. So, thanks to virtualization, our solution will be suitable for all vehicular networks.
- **Edge computing (EC)** is a distributed computing model, in which IT systems are deployed near the physical location where data is collected and analyzed, rather than on a centralized server or in the cloud. EC brings the

cloud computing capabilities closer, by running services in the Radio Access Network, and also in vehicles, which reduces a lot latency. In the EC infrastructure, we will store networks and vehicles information, so they will be accessible all over the network, allowing vehicles to access to other vehicles and network information without influence on latency. EC will also make data scheduling and dissemination easier, and then the selection process will be more efficient, as the selection module will be able to access all network information for the RAT choice.

- **Software-defined radio (SDR)** is a concept where, all the functions that are generally located and executed by radio interfaces, are now defined in a software way. From the frequency carrier to the bandwidth definition, all radio functionalities and parameters become software defined, making them programmable. Thanks to SDR, our solution will be able to adjust the physical interfaces (frequencies, modulations, *etc.*, making them adaptable for every applications needs, avoiding new interfaces installation costs and optimizing radio resources management.

4.2   Smart Aspect

Smart techniques will be considered to enhance autonomy and self-management of the solution thanks to the Cognitive Radio (CR) concept based on the use of prediction, learning and decision methods. This concept describes a system able to adapt itself to its environment thanks to automatic and dynamic detection of available radio resources and reconfigurability of its physical parameters [17]. CR will allow the use of different RAT in order to guaranty availability.

- **Learning and decision.** In Sect. 3.3, we saw that existing analysed solutions are using some Artificial Intelligence (AI) algorithms, such as Stackelberg theory, game theory, genetic algorithms and fuzzy logic to help dynamic RAT selection process. In our solution, the AI module will be in charge of the RAT selection decision process in order than several application will be able to communicate simultaneously on different interfaces. The learning and decision module will also manage interface access priority to attribute RAT interface to applications regarding their priorities. Energy efficiency will be also taken into account in our solution to suit with electrical vehicles constraints.

- **Prediction** describes the capacity of a system to anticipate network behaviors to avoid operating outages, and then guarantee continuity of service. In our solution, we plan to anticipate vehicles position to know in advance the available radio access network and anticipate new RAT selection but also the use of multiple RAT in parallel. The CR capabilities will be also able to anticipate spectrum occupancy and to select the RAT with the highest QoS.

4.3   Multi-*

As indicated previously, we will allow more than one application/device/user to communicate. So, our solution will be:

- **Multi-Applications:** thanks to virtualization and SDR, we will be able to create virtual programmable interfaces, and to use them simultaneously for communication. Our solution will be able to manage this multi-access, thanks to a priority management module.
- **Multi-Users:** in a vehicle, there could be more than one user profile with different priorities. Our solution will be able to stop a low priority profile, to give access to a higher priority one, for safety and security reasons.
- **Multi-devices/IoV:** as in vehicular networks there are not only V2V communications, it is important to take in consideration the type of device with which vehicle will communicate. Our solution will be able to communicate with connected devices. For this, the type of device will be considered in the RAT selection. This will allow vehicles and our solution to have more information about their environment.

4.4   Reliability and Security

Reliability and Security are important features in vehicular networks. Reliability can be increased thanks to the use of multiple RAT at the same time to send the same information in parallel (solution already mentioned for railways), ensuring redundancy, particularly when safety is concerned. Thanks to the CR module, as already explained, it will be possible to anticipate the selection of two RAT at the same time while the vehicle is moving.

To guarantee integrity and communication security, a context/content-aware security parameter will be integrated to our solution. As we will use decentralized infrastructures such as EC and NFV, we will ensure that the communication between these software and vehicles will be secured by considering security as a parameter in our final decision process. We will also ensure that data stored in the EC will be secured, same in the vehicles.

5   Conclusion

In this paper, we highlighted the importance of dynamic RAT selection in vehicular networks to allow vehicles to always be able to communicate with each other or with other devices. We have presented a state of the art related to dynamic RAT selection. We pointed out the limits of the selected solutions and we proposed ideas and approaches to enhance dynamic RAT selection well adapted to autonomous vehicles requirements. This future solution should be able to satisfy multi applications, multi users and multi devices. Taking into account fast evolution of vehicular networks, it should be smart, adaptable, programmable, secure and reliable, thanks to new features such as: Network Virtualisation, Edge computing, Software Defined Radio and Cognitive radio concept that will facilitate learning, prediction and decision functions.

Acknowledgements. This study has been carried out with financial support from the French State, managed by the French National Research Agency (ANR) in the frame of the "Investments for the future" Programme IdEx Bordeaux - SysNum (ANR-10-IDEX-03-02).

References

1. Allen, B., Eschbach, B., Mikulandra, M.: Defining an adaptable communications system for all railways. In: Proceedings of the 7th Transport Research Arena TRA 2018, TRA 2018, Vienna, 16–19 April 2018 (2018)
2. Benedetto, M.D., Vojcic, B.R.: Ultra wide band wireless communications: a tutorial. J. Commun. Netw. **5**(4), 290–302 (2003)
3. Bergenhem, C., Shladover, S., Coelingh, E., Englund, C., Tsugawa, S.: Overview of platooning systems. In: Proceedings of the 19th ITS World Congress, Vienna, Austria, 22–26 October 2012 (2012)
4. Bi, S., Chen, C., Du, R., Guan, X.: Proper handover between VANET and cellular network improves internet access. In: Proceedings of the 80th IEEE Vehicular Technology Conference, VTC2014-Fall, pp. 1–5. IEEE (2014)
5. Boban, M., Kousaridas, A., Manolakis, K., Eichinger, J., Xu, W.: Use cases, requirements, and design considerations for 5G V2X. arXiv preprint arXiv:1712.01754 (2017)
6. Campolo, C., Molinaro, A., Iera, A., Menichella, F.: 5G network slicing for vehicle-to-everything services. IEEE Wirel. Commun. **24**(6), 38–45 (2017)
7. Chahal, M., Harit, S.: Network selection and data dissemination in heterogeneous software-defined vehicular network. Comput. Netw. **161**, 32–44 (2019)
8. Elassali, R., et al.: Performance evaluation of high data rate M-OAM UWB physical layer for intelligent transportation systems. Wirel. Pers. Commun. **94**(4), 3265 3283 (2016). https://doi.org/10.1007/s11277-016-3776-9
9. ETSI: Intelligent Transport Systems (ITS); Vehicular Communications; GeoNetworking; Part 4: Geographical addressing and forwarding for point-to-point and point-to-multipoint communications; Sub-part 1: Media-Independent Functionality. European Telecommunications Standards Institute (2013)
10. ETSI: Intelligent Transport Systems (ITS); Vehicular Communications; GeoNetworking; Part 4: Geographical addressing and forwarding for point-to-point and point-to-multipoint communications; Sub-part 1: Media-Independent Functionality. European Telecommunications Standards Institute (2014)
11. ETSI: Intelligent Transport Systems (ITS); Vehicular Communications; Basic Set of Applications; Facilities layer protocols and communication requirements for infrastructure services. European Telecommunications Standards Institute (2016)
12. Habbal, A., Goudar, S.I., Hassan, S.: Context-aware radio access technology selection in 5G ultra dense networks. IEEE Access **5**, 6636–6648 (2017)
13. Hasswa, A., Nasser, N., Hassanein, H.: Tramcar: a context-aware cross-layer architecture for next generation heterogeneous wireless networks. In: 2006 IEEE International Conference on Communications, vol. 1, pp. 240–245. IEEE (2006)
14. ISO: Advanced technical ceramics. Monolithic ceramics. Gerneral and textural properties. Standard, International Organization for Standardization (2014)
15. Jiang, D., Huo, L., Lv, Z., Song, H., Qin, W.: A joint multi-criteria utility-based network selection approach for vehicle-to-infrastructure networking. IEEE Trans. Intell. Transp. Syst. **19**(10), 3305–3319 (2018)

16. Lee, S., Sriram, K., Kim, K., Kim, Y.H., Golmie, N.: Vertical handoff decision algorithms for providing optimized performance in heterogeneous wireless networks. IEEE Trans. Veh. Technol. **58**(2), 865–881 (2008)
17. Mitola, J., Maguire, G.: Cognitive radio: making software radios more personal. IEEE Pers. Commun. **6**(4), 13–18 (1999)
18. Molina-Masegosa, R., Gozalvez, J.: LTE-V for sidelink 5G V2X vehicular communications: a new 5G technology for short-range vehicle-to-everything communications. IEEE Veh. Technol. Mag. **12**(4), 30–39 (2017)
19. Molisch, A.F.: Ultra-wideband communications: an overview. URSI Radio Sci. Bull. **2009**(329), 31–42 (2009)
20. Mouawad, N., Naja, R., Tohmé, S.: SDN-based network selection platform for V2X use cases. In: 2019 International Conference on Wireless and Mobile Computing, Networking and Communications, WiMob 2019, Barcelona, Spain, 21–23 October 2019, pp. 1–6. IEEE (2019). https://doi.org/10.1109/WiMOB.2019.8923214
21. Naik, G., Choudhury, B., Park, J.M.: IEEE 802.11bd & 5G NR V2X: evolution of radio access technologies for V2X communications. IEEE Access **7**, 70169–70184 (2019). https://doi.org/10.1109/ACCESS.2019.2919489
22. Nasser, N., Hasswa, A., Hassanein, H.: Handoffs in fourth generation heterogeneous networks. IEEE Commun. Mag. **44**(10), 96–103 (2006)
23. Silva, R., Couturier, C., Bonnin, J.M., Ernst, T.: A heuristic decision maker algorithm for opportunistic networking in C-ITS. In: 2019 5th International Conference on Vehicle Technology and Intelligent Transport Systems (2019)
24. Qualcomm Tech.: Building a unified, more capable 5G air interface for the next decade and beyond. Qualcomm 3GPP Standard (2020)
25. Tian, D., Zhou, J., Wang, Y., Lu, Y., Xia, H., Yi, Z.: A dynamic and self-adaptive network selection method for multimode communications in heterogeneous vehicular telematics. IEEE Trans. Intell. Transp. Syst. **16**(6), 3033–3049 (2015)
26. Uçar, S., Ergen, S.Ç., Özkasap, Ö.: Visible light communication in vehicular ad-hoc networks. In: 2016 24th Signal Processing and Communication Application Conference (SIU), pp. 881–884. IEEE (2016)
27. Uysal, M., Ghassemlooy, Z., Bekkali, A., Kadri, A., Menouar, H.: Visible light communication for vehicular networking: performance study of a V2V system using a measured headlamp beam pattern model. IEEE Veh. Technol. Mag. **10**(4), 45–53 (2015)
28. Xu, K., Wang, K.C., Amin, R., Martin, J., Izard, R.: A fast cloud-based network selection scheme using coalition formation games in vehicular networks. IEEE Trans. Veh. Technol. **64**(11), 5327–5339 (2014)
29. Zheng, K., Zheng, Q., Chatzimisios, P., Xiang, W., Zhou, Y.: Heterogeneous vehicular networking: a survey on architecture, challenges, and solutions. IEEE Commun. Surv. Tutor. **17**(4), 2377–2396 (2015)

Toward the Integration of V2V Based Clusters in a Global Infrastructure Network for Vehicles

Sabrine Belmekki[1]([✉])[iD], Martine Wahl[1][iD], Patrick Sondi[2][iD],
Dominique Gruyer[3][iD], and Charles Tatkeu[1]

[1] COSYS-LEOST, Univ Gustave Eiffel, IFSTTAR, Univ Lille,
59650 Villeneuve d'Ascq, France
`sabrine.belmekki@univ-eiffel.fr`
[2] Univ. Littoral Côte d'Opale, LISIC - EA 4491, 62228 Calais, France
[3] COSYS-PICSL, Univ Gustave Eiffel, IFSTTAR, 77454 Marne-la-Vallée, France

Abstract. Vehicle Ad-hoc Networks (VANETs) is an emerging research area that has received much attention over the recent years. One of the main challenges of VANET is the routing protocol and the development of reliable ad-hoc communications between vehicles. We proposed a cooperative scheme between V2I and V2V communications in the highway scenarios to extend V2I connection in the uncovered areas. The main focus of this primarily work is to evaluate the communication and structure stability of the ad hoc vehicle-to-vehicle (V2V) Chain branch leaf clustering scheme (CBL) in an infrastructure network. The insertion of infrastructure components is materialized by the roadside units (RSU). The results show the adaptation of the vehicle ad hoc network clustering in the presence of roadside units (RSUs).

Keywords: VANET · Clustering · V2X · CBL · Infrastructure · RSU

1 Introduction

Routing information is a major issue considering that VANET networks have a dynamic topology, high mobility and variation in density of nodes. Clustering schemes represent an interesting solution according to the work of [10], it can cope with routing, reducing control trac in the network and simplifying the data referral process. A vehicle to vehicle (V2V) self-organization clustering algorithm has been proposed and developed in the work of [6], the Chain branch leaf scheme has shown impressive results regarding the construction of the structure and the connection time of the moving points. However V2V has its limitations, it may become unreliable in low density trac, or when the number of hops in the communication becomes large and incur long communication delay [12]. Moreover, V2I communications have limited availability due to the limited number of infrastructure points because of the high cost of deployment, particularly in rural areas and in the initial phase of vehicle network deployment [4].

© Springer Nature Switzerland AG 2020
F. Krief et al. (Eds.): Nets4Cars/Nets4Trains/Nets4Aircraft 2020, LNCS 12574, pp. 113–122, 2020.
https://doi.org/10.1007/978-3-030-66030-7_10

The work of [3] explain that V2I communication links are expected to be short-lived and intermittent due to mobility of vehicles and the high cost to deploy a ubiquitous roadside infrastructure. It studies the drive-thru scenario where moving vehicles spend at most a couple of minutes in the coverage area of a RSU. Therefore, V2I and V2V communications have to coexists and complement each other to meet the diverse communication requirements of vehicular networks. By doing qualitative comparison of routing protocols, [1] showed that hybrid communication would be a better choice since it can resolve the major problem of disconnected network by considering V2I communication. In this paper we integrate the infrastructure to the structure of the CBL algorithm in a highway environment in different cases and situations. We start by introducing the CBL scheme in the Sect. 2. Then we define the operation including the infrastructure in the Sect. 4. After that we define the simulation's context in the Sect. 5, we go through several road situations for both first and second case in Sect. 5.1. Finally, we explain the results in the Sect. 6.

2   Related Work

The paper [6] proposes **the chain branch leaf clustering scheme** which is a vehicle-to-vehicle (V2V) fully distributed self-organization algorithm. It takes into consideration the following parameters: position, speed, steering angle. CBL creates a hierarchy between nodes in order to form clusters, so that each node in the cluster can communicate directly with the Cluster Head. CBL specifies two types of nodes: branch nodes and leaf nodes. The branch node is the head cluster which is elected by the other nodes (branch or leaf) in its 1-hop neighborhood. A leaf is an ordinary node that must connect itself to the nearest branch node. Both types of nodes send periodic HELLO messages to dynamically build a structure called "chain", which connects the "branch" nodes, by extension the clusters, in each direction on the longitudinal road, as shown in Fig. 1.

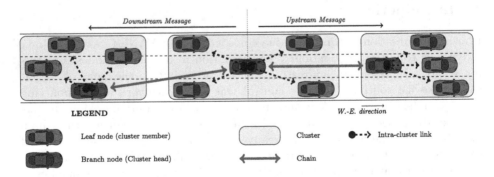

Fig. 1. The chain branch leaf (CBL) structure on a three-lane one-way highway

3   Background

VANETs are used to improve traffic efficiency and safety by collecting and transferring V2V and V2I communication data. Vehicle to infrastructure (V2I) communications may be inappropriate in some contexts and ineffective in specific degraded conditions. It requires an infrastructure equipped with radio access points at regular intervals. Clearly, this could not be guaranteed, for obvious reasons as return on investment, especially on sections of roads that are generally poorly travelled. Moreover, information passing through the infrastructure may present a greater risk of obsolescence compared to direct vehicle-to-vehicle (V2V) communication when the vehicles involved are close by. Ad hoc networks would contribute to the overall reduction of the infrastructure's charge, thus allowing an increase of the global traffic supported by the vehicular network, and bring flexibility to the applications. However, the distributed algorithms for medium access control and the routing protocols in ad hoc networks are more complex, and their addition of energy load. It requires a routing protocol that is able to adapt itself. However, in the presence of an operational infrastructure, driving assistant systems will gain to rely on both V2I and V2V communications [8]. Particularly, all or an important part of distant communications will be supported by the infrastructure. In the paper of [7] the authors study the unicast and probabilistic protocols used for routing in VANET and classify them by: trajectory based forwarding (TBF), geographic based, link stability based, distance Based...ctc. The authors of [11] summarize them by metric-based routing (minimum number of hops, distance, route cost (RCM), packet receive rate (PRR), density, speed, link/route lifetime), and multi-metric routing proposals that use more than one of the previously explained metrics. The work of [7] focus on the requirement for forwarding protocols unicast (Geographic based, Trajectory based and Link Stability based) and probabilistic (Distance based) routing protocols in VANETs. A cooperative communication strategy is proposed in the work of [2], which utilizes V2I and V2V communications, the mobility of vehicles, and cooperation among vehicles and infrastructure only analyzed the relationship between the achieved throughput and the distance between two adjacent infrastructure points without considering helpers readiness. Unlikely, the model of [5] that indicates the interaction of three parameters, such as the inter-RSU distance, vehicles assistance willingness, and the target vehicle's buffer size, with the packet dissemination. The recent works of [6] defined a new routing approach in ad hoc networks (V2V) for VANETs. In terms of application traffic, close communications are needed by vehicles for the sharing of both short real-time messages with information such as position and speed and longer messages with their local perception map, also longer messages are needed between vehicles and infrastructure for road network operators as an example. In the absence of an infrastructure, it offers the services of a virtual backbone dynamically stable to the application layer similar to the one that would be obtained with an infrastructure. Thus, the CBL clustering algorithm can be adapted to have infrastructure components to obtain a coordinated distribution of V2V and

V2I communication tasks in the routing of applications, for the automated road according to the expected traffic loads and the traffic priority.

4   Definition of the Operation Including the Infrastructure

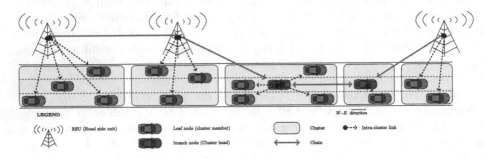

Fig. 2. Proposition of CBL structure with an infrastructure

The research in [9], has shown that a VANET that enables wireless communication between vehicles and between road side units (RSUs) offers the advantage of low transmission delay, rich handling sets of mobile nodes, i.e. vehicles on the move in the coverage area. Based on the CBL routing scheme in ad hoc vehicle networks that has been introduced in Sect. 2 and detailed in paper [6], we introduce the infrastructure components on the side of the highway by inserting RSUs nodes to the simulation environment as shown in the Fig. 2. We study 2 cases: first the "free RSU" then the second case "branch RSU".

5   Simulation context

The road network is modeled in Matlab (R2013a) simulator. It is a three-lane, one-way motorway 5 km long. Three different traffic density are considered (S1, S2, S3) shown in the Table 1. In each one, a ratio of 1/6 trucks and 5/6 cars is considered. For each scenario the RSUs are in 2 different states: **Case 1-Free RSU (C1)** The RSUs are positioned on the side of the road with no particular condition to be a leaf or a branch, that's the reason why it's called Free RSUs, and **case 2-Branch RSU (C2)** RSUs are automatically cluster heads i.e. RSUs nodes are imposed on the branch state. We disable the branch-to-leaf transformation in the CBL algorithm. Several deployment scenarios of RSUs along the road are implemented in each case with each RSU that operate in ad-hoc mode. The first RSU is always at the beginning of the road section then RSU is located every 350 m.

Vehicles travel from West to East. Each vehicle drives to its desired speed, the speed limit is set at 130 km/h, which corresponds to the legal speed limit on motorways in France. Simulation time for each scenario is 500 s. Nodes send a HELLO message every 1 s. The chain formation illustrations in this paper

Table 1. Simulation parameters and values of road traffic

Car traffic (veh/h/direction)	Truck traffic (veh/h/direction)	Density	RSU
500	100	S1 - Low	C1
			C2
2000	400	S2 - Medium	C1
			C2
4000	800	S3 - High	C1
			C2

represent the leaves by green points, the branches by red ones and the chain is the red line formed by the branches. The 3 lanes of the road are represented on the vertical axis, the points aligned on the side of the upper lane are the RSUs at the roadside. The horizontal axis represents the length of the road which is 5 km for a simulation time in seconds.

5.1 Scheme Behavior Description in Case 1 and Case 2

Down below we review the vehicles behavior in several situations for both cases:

(a) **Deployment of RSU along the road every 350 m:** At the initialization of the network the RSUs are already on the road unlike vehicles that enter the road at different times. The first RSU is located at the beginning of the road section (1 m), then a RSU is located every 350 m. In C1 when RSUs are close to each other some of them automatically transform into branches. We consider them to be close to each others if they are at 350 m or less. In C2 The RSU chain is formed at 1 and all vehicles are automatically attached to it, as shown in Fig. 3. While observing the chain formation of the C1, i noticed that the first branch node of the chain tend to turn into a leaf for a few seconds, and this is due to the algorithm programming of the chain formation which is done upstream.

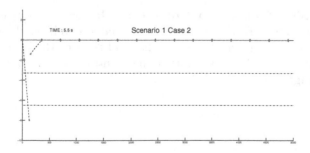

Fig. 3. S1C2 - Chain formation when Branch RSUs present along the way (Color figure online)

(b) **RSU deployed at the beginning of the road:** In C1 vehicles are leaving a RSU area, the chain is built at the beginning of the road by RSUs once the vehicles leaves the RSU coverage area, the last RSU elects the nearest node that fulfills the conditions as downstream branch, this way the chain is maintained. The same happens for C2 A neighboring leaf node is selected to extend the chain at the exit of a RSU zone. The Fig. 4 shows that this mechanism ensures the presence of a chain at different times (inside and outside of the RSU coverage area). Another aspect is that using the infrastructure and V2V communication, does not prevent from having in some situations an isolated node.

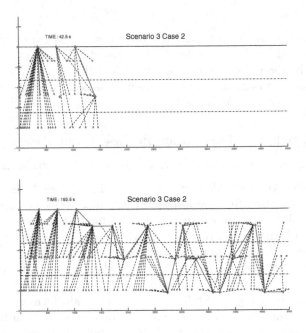

Fig. 4. S3C2 - Chain formation when leaving a RSU area at different times

(c) **RSU deployed at the end of the road:** For both C1 and C2 when vehicles entering a RSUs area we notice that the vehicle chain is built at the road's beginning. On the end of the road the free RSUs already present also form a chain. The two chains connect and form one when entering the RSU coverage area.

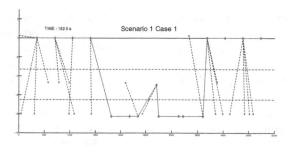

Fig. 5. S1C1 - Chain formation when physical/technical issues on some RSUs

(d) **Physical/technical issues on some RSUs:** RSUs are not present all along the way or if so some of them are out of service. As shown in the Fig. 5 for the (C1) the vehicles connect to the RSU branches. Ones they leave the RSU zone and before entering the second one, we observe for both C1 and C2 that CBL-V2V takes over and the "vehicle" nodes transform to branches to maintain the chain.

(e) **Vehicles pass through a RSU area:** Due to lack of infrastructure deployment on the road or abnormal behaviour on some RSUs. We observe in C1 that when vehicles are out of RSUs area, they transform into branches to form a chain, most of the RSU on the other side also forms a chain. When the vehicles enter the RSU area, the 2 chains collide and become one. We obtain a continuous chain for C2 also.

6 The Results Explanation

RSUs have been successfully introduced to the CBL architecture and are considered vehicles on the side road with zero speed. Every vehicle is equipped by OBU which is used to differentiate between the RSUs and the stationary/broke vehicles at the road side. First of all, when the free RSUs are close to each other, we notice that from the first seconds they turn into branches and form a stable chain, vehicles arriving at different times hang on to them. This shows that when the RSUs are in a free state the distance between RSUs has an impact on there state (leaf or branch), this information must be taken into consideration when deploying RSUs on the road. The following performance metrics are extracted from Matlab (R2013a) simulation. The values reported are picked up when the network is stable (between 150 s and 500 s): S1C2 is more efficient regarding the number of chains in the network, we notice that the chain is built by the branches RSUs at 1 s and that it becomes stable (only 1 main chain) faster after 3 s. In the first case (C1), when the RSUs are free, it takes more time to form the chain. In Fig. 7, more then one chain is formed for (C1) at first, then a single chain becomes stable at 12 s until the end of the simulation. Because there are several stages of election in caparison with C2. As explained in the paper [6] and in the Sect. 2 the leaf node has to find a branch node to connect itself to, if it does not find one, it will elect a leaf node as a branch, thus node must transform itself into a branch, then it will look for an upstream branch node to form a chain with. This requires an adaptation delay compared to C2 where there are already branches, each one of them will look for a branch upstream to form a chain. The number of branch nodes per chain and the number of 1-hop neighbors shows same results for both S1C1 and S1C2 (average of 7 one-hop neighbors) since it's related to the density of the highway, i.e. in a medium density we obtain 16 branches per chain for the S1C1, and 18 branches per chain for the S1C2. The Fig. 8 shows the duration of a node in the branch state in the scenario 1 case 2 (S1C2), where the leaves nodes attachment to their branch start at 1 s so immediately because the chain of branches RSUs is already present on the road from the beginning until the end of the simulation so vehicles connect to them, unlike S1C1 which start later at 10 s because some vehicles nodes need to transform into branches to form the chain. We studied the connection/link stability by measuring the link duration between the leaf and the branch, we notice a difference between the first and the second case since the S1C1 shows a longer link duration about 25 s that we can see in the Fig. 6, thus more transmissions. While in the S1C2, that the duration of the link is about 10 s. Because when RSUs are free, a leaf can be attached to a vehicle branch which gives a longer time connection. Unlike where the branches are only RSUs (C2) there will be disconnection each time the vehicle leaves the RSUs coverage. In the S3C1 it's about 28 s while in the original CBL-V2V, each leaf node remains attached to the same branch for about 30 s.

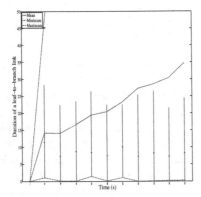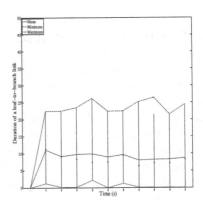

Fig. 6. Scenario (S1) - The leaf to branch link duration for case 1 and case 2

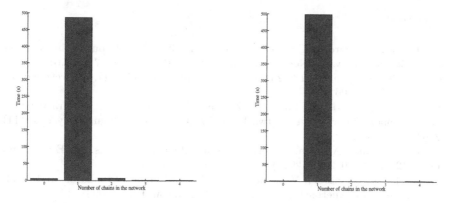

Fig. 7. Scenario (S1) - Number of chain in the network for case 1 and case 2

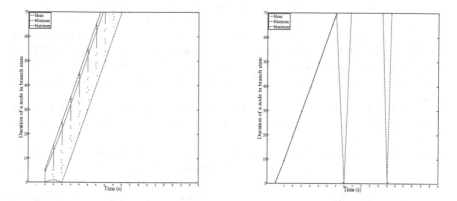

Fig. 8. Scenario (S1) - Node duration in branch state for case 1 and case 2

7 Conclusion and Perspectives

This paper presented a work in progress that combine V2V communications with an infrastructure. We proposed a new cooperation scheme considering multiple situations that reflect the reality of the road facilities, such as technical issues and missing RSUs area. Results have led to better prediction and analysis of data. The evaluations performed by simulation on the highway for the first and the second case showed that RSUs always manage to transform to branches and keep the chain stable. In the other hand when there is issues on some RSUs, the CBL takes over to keep the chain solid. We demonstrated CBL adaptability, cooperation and interoperability. Future work aims to adapt this version of CBL in order to achieve a coordinated and optimal distribution of functions, and services of V2V and V2I communications, in the routing of critical information, required for cooperative driver automation applications. These developments will take into account expected traffic loads and message priority.

References

1. Bilal, S.M., Bernardos, C.J., Guerrero, C.: Position-based routing in vehicular networks: a survey. J. Netw. Comput. Appl. **36**(2), 685–697 (2013). https://doi.org/10.1016/j.jnca.2012.12.023, https://linkinghub.elsevier.com/retrieve/pii/S1084804512002706
2. Chen, J., Mao, G., Li, C., Zafar, A., Zomaya, A.Y.: Throughput of infrastructure-based cooperative vehicular networks. IEEE Trans. Intell. Transp. Syst. **18**(11), 2964–2979 (2017)
3. Fiems, D., Vinel, A.: Connectivity times in vehicular networks. IEEE Commun. Lett. **22**(11), 2270–2273 (2018)
4. Moustafa, H., Zhang, Y.: Vehicular Networks: Techniques, Standards, and Applications, 1st edn. Auerbach Publications, Boca Raton, USA (2009)
5. Nguyen, B.L., Ngo, D.T., Tran, N.H., Vu, H.L.: Combining V2I with V2V communications for service continuity in vehicular networks. In: 2019 IEEE Intelligent Transportation Systems Conference (ITSC), pp. 201–206 (2019)
6. Rivoirard, L., Wahl, M., Sondi, P., Berbineau, M., Gruyer, D.: Chain-branch-leaf: a clustering scheme for vehicular networks using only V2V communications. Ad Hoc Netw. **68**, 70–84 (2018). https://doi.org/10.1016/j.adhoc.2017.10.007, http://www.sciencedirect.com/science/article/pii/S1570870517301798. Advances in Wireless Communication and Networking for Cooperating Autonomous Systems
7. Saleh, H.H., Hasson, S.T.: A survey of routing algorithms in vehicular networks. In: 2019 International Conference on Advanced Science and Engineering (ICOASE), pp. 159–164 (2019)
8. Santa, J., Gómez-Skarmeta, A.F., Sánchez-Artigas, M.: Architecture and evaluation of a unified V2V and V2I communication system based on cellular networks. Comput. Commun. **31**(12), 2850–2861 (2008). https://doi.org/10.1016/j.comcom.2007.12.008, http://www.sciencedirect.com/science/article/pii/S0140366407005191
9. Sathya Narayanan, P., Joice, C.S.: Vehicle-to-vehicle (V2V) communication using routing protocols: a review. In: 2019 International Conference on Smart Structures and Systems (ICSSS), pp. 1–10 (March 2019). https://doi.org/10.1109/ICSSS.2019.8882828
10. Sethi, V., Chand, N.: A destination based routing protocol for context based clusters in VANET. Commun. Netw. **9**(3), 179–191 (2017). https://doi.org/10.4236/cn.2017.93013, http://www.scirp.org/journal/doi.aspx?DOI=10.4236/cn.2017.93013
11. Tripp-Barba, C., Zaldívar-Colado, A., Urquiza-Aguiar, L., Aguilar-Calderón, J.A.: Survey on routing protocols for vehicular ad hoc networks based on multimetrics. Electronics **8**(10), 1177 (2019)
12. Vegni, A.M., Little, T.: Hybrid vehicular communications based on V2V–V2I protocol switching. Int. J. Veh. Inf. Commun. Sys. **2**, 213–231 (2011). https://doi.org/10.1504/IJVICS.2011.044263

Integration of Antennas for Communication System on Complex Platforms

Naveen Kumar[1]([⊠]) [iD], Ozuem Chukwuka[2], and Divitha Seetharamdoo[1,2] [iD]

[1] Institut de Recherche Technologique Railenium, 59300 Famars, France
naveen.kumar@railenium.eu
[2] COSYS, LEOST, IFSTTAR, Universite Gustav Eiffel, Univ Lille,
59650 Villeneuve d'Ascq, France
{ozuem.chukwuka,divitha.seetharamdoo}@univ-eiffel.fr

Abstract. This paper provides an overview of the antenna integration problem with an illustration of antenna integration for the next generation railway communication systems. The influence of integration on the basic antenna parameters is detailed and the challenges and constraints for integration are discussed. State-of-the-art antenna integration schemes are summarised and a novel approach for antenna integration based on the use of metamaterial inclusions and intermodal coupling analysis is proposed.

Keywords: Antenna integration · Railway communication system · Antenna for railway

1 Introduction

A variety of radio network architectures for commercial or military applications use multiple or single antenna systems. For wireless communication in outdoor applications, antenna systems are usually integrated or mounted on complex platforms such as buildings, road/rail infrastructure, or vehicles. It is well-known that antenna system performances are highly influenced by surrounding media and structures. Antennas are however designed for operation in free space or ideally close to a ground plane of given dimensions. In industrial applications, an additional step for antenna integration is required if one is to guarantee the performances of the antenna and more generally the communication system.

Antenna integration can be based on two basic approaches. The first more common one is that the antenna is designed without prior knowledge of the immediate environment in which it will be placed and integration then relies

The authors acknowledge partial funding by the regional project SMARTIES in the framework of the ELSAT 2020 program co-financed by the European Union with the European Regional development fund, the French state and Hauts de France Regional council.

© Springer Nature Switzerland AG 2020
F. Krief et al. (Eds.): Nets4Cars/Nets4Trains/Nets4Aircraft 2020, LNCS 12574, pp. 125–136, 2020.
https://doi.org/10.1007/978-3-030-66030-7_11

solely on electromagnetic (EM) modeling. The objective being to achieve a trade-off where the antenna performances will be generally lower but the main specifications for the radio network architecture will be met. The problem to be modeled is said to be a multi-scale one since the antenna and the environment can have orders of magnitude of difference in electrical dimensions. Simulation time in this context can become prohibitive. This can be handled by hybrid numerical models including full-wave models of the antenna and asymptotic models for the interaction between the antenna and the environment. Or alternatively, semi numerical models are also used based on the measurement results of the antenna radiation performances which are then integrated into an asymptotic model. Irrespective of the choice of the numerical models, a good understanding of the communication system requirements is essential, sorting between the ones which are relevant for antenna specifications and those which should be handled by the digital signal processing blocks. The description of the environment from the electromagnetic point of view is another important input with the identification of predominant obstacles and structures.

The second approach for antenna integration would be a scenario where some prior knowledge of the environment is already available during the design phase of the antenna thus allowing for some optimization before integration. Several techniques such as geometry optimization, selective excitation of the relevant points on the platform [20, 24] use this approach.

The aim of this paper is to provide an overview of the antenna integration problem based on both approaches described above with an illustration of antenna integration for the next generation railway communication systems. The influence of integration on the basic antenna parameters will be detailed and the challenges and constraints for integration will be discussed. Antenna integration concepts and methods generally used will then be described. State-of-the-art approaches as well as novel approaches will be addressed.

2   Challenges and Constraints upon Antenna Integration

In this section, general system specification requirements for antenna integration on complex platforms are presented. As an example, general considerations for the antenna integration in the railway environment are discussed. Few of the European projects for next-generation railway communication system are briefly discussed.

2.1   System Specification Requirements

While integrating antennas on a platform such as vehicles, railways, air-crafts, and ships, there are several system specific requirements for each application which needs to be considered. Some of which are:

Bandwidth Coverage: The bandwidth coverage of an antenna is defined as the frequency range over which the impedance exhibited by the antenna is near to 50 Ω level [1]. As per the requirements of a communication system, the antenna may need to support multiple standards. To satisfy this requirement, the bandwidth of the antenna should be enough to support all the desired standards operating within different frequency bands.

Gain and Directivity: Gain and directivity vary from application to application. In the railway environment, most of the practical antennas show 0 dBi gain in the horizontal plane (zero degrees elevation) while other applications may require higher gain. The degree to which the radiation emitted is concentrated in a single direction is termed Directivity [2].

Polarisation: Antenna polarisation refers to the direction in which the electric field oscillates. Mismatch in the transmitter and receiver polarisation results in degraded signal quality [2]. An antenna with dual polarisation is well suited for most of the applications.

2.2 Example of Antenna Integration for Communication System in Railways

This section discusses various general considerations to be taken care of while integrating the antenna system in railway environment.

General Considerations

Train Rooftop Structure: The structure of the train rooftop can be curved which has an impact on antenna operation. The antenna mounted away from the centre line of the train will exhibit the worst performance due to the obstruction provided by the curvature of the roof [3]. There are several other train rooftop shapes and obstructions such as sunken roof, roof with bars, air-conditioning unit, pantographs, etc. which poses few constraints on the antenna installation.

Positioning: There is a space constraint on the train rooftop and antenna system positioning should be done carefully to avoid obstructions and variations in antenna parameters. The limited space makes it challenging to satisfy all the requirements. Also, the antenna position at some height above the roof is desired but this is constrained by the gauge limit on the train [5].

Separation Between Antenna Systems: When there are several antenna modules present on the roof, interference can occur which should also be taken care of. For antenna systems covering the same frequency band, their recommended spacing should be at least five times the wavelength of the operating frequency [3]. For example, a GSM-R at 900 MHz has a wavelength of approximately 0.33 m, and five times this wavelength is 1.65 m. Therefore, the spacing between the antenna systems operating at GSM-R frequency should be greater than 2 m. The antenna systems can be placed closer if the operating frequency bands are not identical with low risk of interference but this is directly linked to the design of the GSM-R rack, the modem and filtering, presence of diplexer, etc. [3].

Ground Plane Size: Normally, there is a minimum ground plane size required for an antenna system to operate properly. For antennas with radiators of electrical sizes $\lambda/2$ or $\lambda/4$, having a small ground plane size may result in reduced radiation efficiency. The dimensions of the ground plane depend on the operating wavelength (λ) of the antenna [6]. For example, at 900 MHz ($\lambda = 333$ mm) GSM-R band, the recommended ground plane dimensions are 500 mm × 500 mm [4].

Radome Size and Material: To protect the antenna from environmental and electrical factors, a radome is used and it is made up of materials that provide minimal attenuation to transmit/receive electromagnetic signals. The size of the antenna radome depends on the overall size of the antenna system and the assembly method. The most common materials used for radome are ASA (acrylic ester-styrene-acrylonitrile), fiberglass, and amorphous thermoplastic polyetherimide (PEI) [6].

Blocking and Out-of-Band Emissions: There are two types of interference phenomena: blocking and noise in the victim's band from the aggressor [7]. Radio receiver blocking can also be referred to as receiver desensitization and it occurs when strong signals are present and results in the level of lower level signals being reduced i.e. the receiver is desensitized. Good radio receiver blocking performance or receiver desensitization performance is particularly important in the scenarios where several radios of various forms are used near each other. Out of band spurious emission are unwanted emissions immediately outside the channel bandwidth resulting from the modulation process and non-linearity in the transmitter but excluding spurious emissions. To prevent this kind of perturbation it is necessary to add filter to the interfering source or behind the antenna of the receiver. The decoupling between the transmitting and potential victim receiving antenna can also use possible decoupling techniques such as polarisation decoupling [8] or angular selectivity through the use of directive antennas.

Next Generation Railway Communication Systems EU Projects

NGTC Project. The scope of the Next Generation Train Control (NGTC) project was to analyse the similarities and differences as per the requirements of railway systems for both the European Train Control System (ETCS) and Communications-based Train Control (CBTC). The deliverable WP6 "D6.2 Choice of technologies to study" presented the specifications of the communication system [9]. A multi-vector (multi-standard) approach for railway communication system i.e. the use of multiple radio technologies for seamless connection was proposed in NGTC. New standards and communication technologies can be integrated in the multi-vector architecture along with the technologies already in use. It was concluded that LTE should be a common vector for both Mainline and Urban rail which can operate in different bands (Fig. 1).

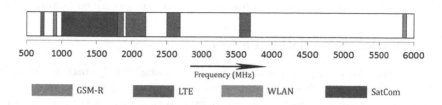

Fig. 1. Proposed NGTC frequency bands

FRMCS Project. Future Rail Mobile Communication System (FRMCS) project was launched by Union Internationale des Chemins de fer (UIC) in 2012 to study the successor of GSM-R [10]. The European Railway Community is working towards identifying and defining the foundation of FRMCS. As it is predicted that the current GSM-R technology will be obsolete by the year 2030, the requirements as per FRMCS system architecture are to provide bearer flexibility, to enable inter-working with external networks such as public communication networks or fixed networks. This is discussed in a technical report 'Study on Future Railway Mobile Communication System (FRMCS)' by 3GPP [10]. The main focus was the requirements of mainline and high-speed domains (Fig. 2).

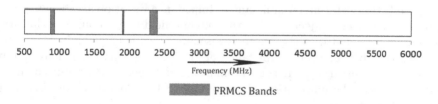

Fig. 2. Proposed FRMCS frequency bands

Shift2Rail Project. As presented and discussed in X2Rail-1 WP3 D3.1 and D3.3, the Adaptable Communication System (ACS) architecture requires bearer (radio access technology) independence and parallel use of bearers [11]. The selection of the bearers depends on the railway scenario such as mainline/high-speed, urban/metro, or regional/freight. The railway environment is different for each case with different user and system requirements and specifications. For instance, the ACS system for mainline/high-speed trains is proposed to use public LTE, dedicated LTE, and Wi-Fi networks. For urban/metro lines, the ACS system is proposed to support LTE and Wi-Fi with an ad hoc mesh approach. For regional/freight, the ACS system is proposed to use Public Land Mobile Network (PLMN) which can be LTE and satellite communication (SatCom) technology.

3 Influence of Integration on Antenna Performances

Most antennas tend to perform well when operating in free space but upon integration, some of their performances are affected by the integration platform. Some effects of integration on the antenna performance are given below.

3.1 Distortion of Radiation Pattern

The radiation pattern of an antenna is one of the characteristics used to define it. For most transport applications, omnidirectional radiation pattern is required but radiation pattern is easily influenced by external factors such as interference from other RF sources, ground reflection, nearby antennas and objects which either reflect or absorb the radiated signal. A good example is an antenna mounted on a large platform such as a ship, aircraft, and a train which have their radiation pattern determined by the host structure and the varying environments. These parameters cannot be defined prior to antenna design since they can be very specific to a type of train (or other vehicles) and because of the cost, certified antennas can generally not be customized for each train or scenario [12].

3.2 Impedance Mismatch

Maximum power transfer between a load and a source is achieved when the impedance is matched such that the reflection loss between the load and the source is reduced [13]. In antennas, the impedance varies considerably with frequency and other external circumstances. Impedance variation also occurs due to the presence of other objects within the antenna field (e.g.. mounting platform) and aging which de-tunes the antenna resonance frequency. Nominal antennas are designed with an input impedance of $50\,\Omega$ and its matching may not be sustained after integration if the antenna was designed and optimized in the free-space hence, the integration platform should be a factor to consider in its design and optimization.

3.3 Coupling Between Antenna and Platforms

Antenna coupling arises due to free space radiations, surface currents, and surface waves. It describes the energy absorbed by an antenna's surroundings during the antenna's operation. It is amplified by the choice of the antenna's feeding mechanism which causes a change in input impedance, reflection coefficient, and radiation pattern [14]. The design of an integrated antenna is therefore a process that involves respecting the strong interaction between an antenna and the components on its mounting platform. The coupling causes an increase in the stored energy of the antenna, re-distributes the antenna's surface current, and changes the input impedance and the radiation pattern [15]. A large ground plane does not necessarily produce a better antenna performance but rather the location of the antenna and its feeding point primarily establishes the antenna's performance since the surface current distributions on all metallic objects have to be taken into account and can distort the radiation pattern.

3.4   Isolation Between Antennas in Multiple Antenna Systems

The increased need for multiple wireless applications requires multiple antenna systems to be fitted within limited space however, when antennas are very close together, the coupling effect is inevitable and cannot be neglected [16] therefore, proper isolation between the antennas is required. Mutual coupling causes an increase in the stored energy of the individual antenna and changes the input impedance and the radiation pattern [15]. To ensure proper isolation, the spacing between antennas must be sufficient enough to avoid blocking issues and spurious emissions. The use of decoupling techniques such as the inclusion of slots [27], the use of bad-gap structures, and metamaterials are also ways to achieve proper isolation [25].

3.5   Increase in Antenna Quality Factor

Antenna Q-factor is dependent on not only the size and shape of the antenna but also on the integration platform since the platform becomes a part of the antenna and increases its electrical size. System specifications limit the design to compact miniaturized antenna with low radiation resistance (due to short radiating length), significant ohmic loss (due to long current path), and large stored energy (due to compact design structure) [17].

The Q-factor is a figure of merit that determines the ability of the antenna to radiate effectively [18], measures the sharpness of the antenna's resonance, and indicates the extent to which the resonator is capable of storing electromagnetic energy at its resonance frequency. It is proportional to the ratio of the energy stored in the antenna to the rate at which the antenna emits radiation. The Q-factor also has a simple relation with the antenna's operating bandwidth approximately given by the reciprocal of the antenna's bandwidth:

$$\text{BW} = \frac{f_0}{Q}. \tag{3.1}$$

The higher the antenna Q, the smaller the impedance bandwidth which indicates the trade-off between the radiation efficiency, the antenna maximum dimension and its bandwidth.

4   State-of-the-Art and Novel Antenna Integration Methods and Concept

In this section, some of the existing approaches to design integrated antennas and an overview of proposed techniques to design and enhance integrated platform is presented.

4.1   Existing Antenna Integration Schemes/Methods

Most antennas are designed based on their free space operation with degraded performances upon integration. One of the major challenges of antenna integration is to enhance the performance of the antenna such that it operates based on the system specification. The physical limitation of an antenna which requires a trade-off between bandwidth, efficiency, and size increase the level of this challenge. Thus, a lot of research works are focused on techniques and methods to enhance the performance of integrated antennas. A summary of some of the implemented techniques for enhancing the performance of integrated antennas and their performances are given in Table 1.

Table 1. Summary of some of the implemented techniques for enhancing the performance of an integrated antenna.

Antenna design	Integration method	Antenna Performance
[21]	**Trial and error**	Antenna width size reduced from 0.9mm to 0.2mm, Bandwidth increased by 12%
[22]	**Geometry optimization**	Dual band achieved, Gain of 6.67 dBi, Bandwidth of 33.54 MHz
[24]	**Use of parasitic elements**	Increased directivity, gain increased by 1.8 dBi and bandwidth of 22.3%
[27]	**Q-factor optimization**	Bandwidth enhancement of 160%
[29]	**Use of characteristic modes theory**	Best positioning of antenna for mobile phone
[32]	**Use of metamaterial**	Radiation efficiency of 89.34% and size ka of 0.497

From Table 1, the choice of an integration method is determined by the parameter to be enhanced however, the theory of characteristic modes and the use of metamaterials which are engineered materials with properties not readily found in nature provide a way to engineer integrated antenna designs with enhanced performance.

4.2   New Antenna Integration Concept

A new concept for the integration of antenna is proposed based on the evaluation of stored energy, the use of metamaterial inclusion, and the analysis of inter-modal coupling. A simple flow chart in Fig. 3 shows the process for the implementation of the concept.

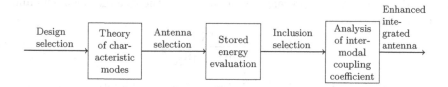

Fig. 3. Flow chart for new antenna integration concept

From Fig. 3, the first step is choosing the integrated system design and having a good knowledge of the system. System requirements such as the frequency of operation, bandwidth, radiation pattern, gain, and allocated antenna space have to be known to ensure that the antenna meets the specified requirement upon integration. Based on the chosen system design, an antenna is selected and analyzed using the theory of characteristic modes to gain insight into its physical behaviour and to evaluate its radiation properties. The theory of characteristic modes are current modes that represent the eigenvectors of a particular weighted eigenvalue equation solved using a generalized impedance matrix of the conductor and it is given as:

$$XJ_n = \lambda_n RJ_n. \tag{4.1}$$

where λ_n is the eigenvalue, J_n is the eigen-current of the n mode, R is the real part and X is the imaginary part of the generalized impedance matrix.

The next step is the evaluation of the quantitative modal stored energy of the antenna element. The modal stored energy provides quantitative insight into the near-field behaviour of the antenna element. It uses the characteristic mode impedance matrix in its evaluation and it is given as [29];
the electric energy (W_e) and magnetic energy (W_m):

$$W_m = \frac{1}{8\omega}I^H X_m I, \tag{4.2}$$

and

$$W_e = \frac{1}{8\omega}I^H X_e I, \tag{4.3}$$

where, ω is the angular frequency, X_m and X_e are the capacitive and inductive component of the impedance matrix.

Similarly, a group of metamaterial inclusions with properties similar to the required antenna property of the system are evaluated for their modal stored energy. The modal stored energy has been shown to provide similar qualitative analysis to the effective parameter classification on metamaterials [30]. From the analysis, the inclusion with enough modal stored energy to compensate for the modal stored energy of the antenna is chosen (i.e. if an antenna stores electric energy, an inclusion with sufficient compensating magnetic energy is selected).

The final step is the analysis of the inter-modal coupling co-efficient. It shows how the antenna and metamaterial inclusion interact. The evaluated coupling is between the modes that represent the behaviour of the different elements and it is given as [32]:

$$| M_{ij} | = \frac{I_i^H X' I_j}{\sqrt{I_i^H X' I_i . I_j^H X' I_j}}, \tag{4.4}$$

where i and j are the two modes being evaluated. The inter-modal coupling provides a guide on how to place the inclusion with respect to the antenna for better performance such that 0.7 is taken as the threshold. The modes which have their inter-modal coupling greater the 0.7 have significant coupling and affect the performance compared to modes which have their values lower than 0.7.

5 Conclusion

Antennas being generally designed to operate in free space, their performances are degraded upon integration on complex platforms. Several basic or more elaborate approaches can be developed for antenna integration with the objective to reach a trade-off whereby the antenna performances though not optimal meet the requirements of the radio communication network. In this paper, the problem of antenna integration has been described through the detailed description of the influence of complex platforms on basic antenna performances such as the radiation pattern, the input impedance and the antenna efficiency or antenna quality factor. The challenges and constraints for antenna integration have then been briefly discussed. A focus on railway platforms through an illustration of antenna performances for the next generation railway communication system has then been proposed. Finally, state-of-the-art antenna integration schemes are summarised and a novel approach for antenna integration based on the use of metamaterial inclusions and intermodal coupling analysis is proposed. Current research trends in the field of antenna integration are described.

References

1. Balanis, C.A.: Antenna Theory. Wiley, New York (1997)
2. Bahl, I.J., Bharta, P.: Microstrip Antennas. Artech House, Massachusetts (USA) (1980)
3. RSSB, NR - GK/GN0602, Guidance on Train Rooftop Antenna Positioning. Accessed 31 Jul 2020
4. Antonics: Installation instruction for train and bus antennas (outdoor). Accessed on 2 Oct 2020

5. Report ITU-R M.2442-0, Current and future usage of railway radio communication systems between train and trackside. Accessed 31 Jul 2020
6. Arya, A.K., et al.: Shark-Fin antenna for railway communications in LTE-R, LTE, and lower 5G frequency bands. Prog. Electromagnet. Res. **167**, 83–94 (2020)
7. Electronic Communications Committee (ECC) report 146. Compatibility between GSM MCBTS and other services operating in the 900 and 1800 MHz frequency bands, pp. 28–46 (2010). Accessed 31 Jul 2020
8. Recommendation ITU-R SM.329-10, Unwanted emissions in the spurious domain. Accessed 5 Oct 2020
9. NGTC, WP6 D6.2: Choice of Technologies to study (2014). Accessed 31 Jul 2020
10. 3GPP: Study on Future Railway Mobile Communication System (FRMCS), Technical report 22.889, Release 17.2.0. Accessed 31 Jul 2020
11. X2Rail-1, Deliverable 3.3: Specification of the Communication System and Guideline for Choice of Technology (2019). Accessed 31 Jul 2020
12. Chen, Y., Wang, C.-F.: Characteristic Modes: Theory and Applications in Antenna Engineering. Wiley, Hoboken (2015)
13. Hwang, S., Hong, S.-Y.: A study of measurement the load impedance mismatch. In: 2011 IEEE MTT-S International Microwave Workshop Series on Intelligent Radio for Future Personal Terminals, pp. 1–2. IEEE (2011)
14. Tunio, I.A., Mahe, Y., Razban, T., Froppier, B.: Study of impedance matching in antenna arrays due to total radiation. In: 2019 13th European Conference on Antennas and Propagation (EuCAP), pp. 1–5. IEEE (2019)
15. Zhao, W.-J., Gan, Y.-B., Li, L.-W., Wang, C.-F.: Effects of an electrically large airborne radome on radiation patterns and input impedance of a dipole array. IEEE Trans. Antennas Propag. **55**(8), 2399–2402 (2007)
16. Diez, M.A.B., Lindenmeier, S.: A highly efficient car2car-multiband rooftop automotive antenna. In: 2015 IEEE International Symposium on Antennas and Propagation and USNC/URSI National Radio Science Meeting, pp. 1606–1607. IEEE (2015)
17. Ma, H., Yang, H.Y.D.: Miniaturized integrated folded helical antennas. In: 2011 IEEE International Symposium on Antennas and Propagation (APSURSI), pp. 753–756. IEEE (2011)
18. Mohammadpour-Aghdam, K., Faraji-Dana, R., Guy, A.E., Vandenbosch, S.R., Gielen, G.G.E.: Physical bound on Q factor for planar antennas. In: 2011 41st European Microwave Conference, pp. 250–252. IEEE (2011)
19. Gustafsson, M., Nordebo, S.: Optimal antenna currents for Q, superdirectivity, and radiation patterns using convex optimization. IEEE Trans. Antennas Propag. **61**(3), 1109–1118 (2012)
20. Chen, Y., Wang, C.-F.: Electrically small UAV antenna design using characteristic modes. IEEE Trans. Antennas Propag. **62**(2), 535–545 (2013)
21. Kibria, S., Islam, M.T., Azim, R.: A heuristic approach to design broadband microstrip patch antenna. In: Conference: IIEEJ Image Electronics and Visual Computing Workshop, vol. 6 (2015)
22. Behera, S.K., Choukiker, Y.: Design and optimization of dual band microstrip antenna using particle swarm optimization technique. J. Infrared, Millimeter Terahertz Waves **31**(11), 1346–1354 (2010)
23. Sahoo, R., Vakula, D.: Gain enhancement of conformal wideband antenna with parasitic elements and low index metamaterial for WiMAX application. AEU-Int. J. Electron. Commun. **105**, 24–35 (2019)

24. Dicandia, F.A., Genovesi, S., Monorchio, A.: Efficient excitation of characteristic modes for radiation pattern control by using a novel balanced inductive coupling element. IEEE Trans. Antennas Propag. **66**(3), 1102–1113 (2018)
25. Alibakhshikenari, M., Khalily, M., Virdee, B.S., See, C.H., Abd-Alhameed, R.A., Limiti, E.: Mutual-coupling isolation using embedded metamaterial EM bandgap decoupling slab for densely packed array antennas. IEEE Access 7, 51827-51840 (2019)
26. Liu, H., Yin, C., Gao, W., Sun, Y.: Optimization and design of wideband antenna based on factor. Int. J. Antennas Propag. **2015**, 971646 (2015)
27. Park, J., Park, J., Choi, J., Kim, Y.-S.: Ground slot with capacitor for high isolation between MIMO antenna. In: 2011 11th Mediterranean Microwave Symposium (MMS), pp. 197–200. IEEE (2011)
28. Gampala, G., Reddy, C.J., Ludick, D., Futter, P.: Systematic design of antennas using the theory of characteristic modes for mobile phone applications. In: 2014 IEEE Antennas and Propagation Society International Symposium (APSURSI), pp. 1421–1422. IEEE (2014)
29. Capek, M., Jelinek, L.: Optimal composition of modal currents for minimal quality factor Q. IEEE Trans. Antennas Propag. **64**(12), 5230–5242 (2016)
30. Chukwuka, O., Seetharamdoo, D., Rabah, M.H.: Stored energy of arbitrary metamaterial inclusions. J. Phys. D Appl. Phys. 53(23), 235501 (2020)
31. Erentok, A., Ziolkowski, R.W.: Metamaterial-inspired efficient electrically small antennas. IEEE Trans. Antennas Propag. **56**(3), 691–707 (2008)
32. Lin, J.-F., Chu, Q.-X.: Extending bandwidth of antennas with coupling theory for characteristic modes. IEEE Access **5**, 22262–22271 (2017)

5G for Remote Driving of Trains

Yamen Alsaba[1]([⊠])(iD), Marion Berbineau[1,2](iD), Iyad Dayoub[1,3], Emilie Masson[1],
Gemma Morral Adell[4], and Eric Robert[5]

[1] Railenium, Valenciennes, France
`yamen.alsaba@railenium.eu`
[2] COSYS, University Gustave Eiffel, 59650 Villeneuve d'Ascq, France
`marion.berbineau@uni-eiffel.fr`
[3] UPHF, Valenciennes, France
`iyad.dayoub@uphf.fr`
[4] SNCF, Saint-Denis, France
`gemma.morral-adell@sncf.fr`
[5] Thales GT, Paris, France
`eric.robert@thalesgroup.com`

Abstract. Automatic Train Operation (ATO) is a new growing market in the railways sector since 2019. Several railways operators such as SNCF, DB, SBB and so on have launched deep transformation in their infrastructures and rolling stock in order to enter in digital era. One of this game changers is upgrading to autonomous train on existing or new infrastructure. Since autonomous train means the absence of train driver, there is a big need of uplinked information to supervise autonomous trains from the ground. This includes the need of remotely driving the train if it encounters a problem, *e.g.* a non-recognised obstacle, an infrastructure breakdown. Remote driving will be a new operation mode in the railways sector that will rely on a well-designed radio link provided by 5G. This paper presents preliminary results on test tracks with Long Term Evolution (LTE) and a simulation based comparison between LTE and 5G at physical layer using Non orthogonal Multiple Access.

Keywords: Autonomous trains · Remote driving · 5G · OFDM · NOMA

1 Introduction

Full automation of trains will allow increasing drastically infrastructure capacity, optimizing train operations in general and also speed of the trains. Safety, security and passenger service issues are also targeted namely punctuality, train according to demand, *etc.,* Driverless system already exists in the urban segment with full automation of train operation on dedicated lines. The next challenge, is now to generalize automation to other railway segment such as freight, regional

© Springer Nature Switzerland AG 2020
F. Krief et al. (Eds.): Nets4Cars/Nets4Trains/Nets4Aircraft 2020, LNCS 12574, pp. 137–147, 2020.
https://doi.org/10.1007/978-3-030-66030-7_12

and main lines with possibly mix of traffic between trains with driver and driver-less trains. In this context, a mandatory brick relies on the remote driving of trains.

The demonstration[1] and development of such a brick is the aim of the TC-Rail project, a partnership formed by SNCF, Thales, Actia Telecom, CNES and Railenium, that will demonstrate the possibility of driving a locomotive safely from a remote location, without a driver in the train cabin, with a level of safety similar to that obtained in presence of a driver in the train. This project constitutes the first proof of concept for telecontrol of a train without European Railway Management System (ERTMS) infrastructure and at maximum target speed of 100 km/h. It is foreseen to remove the main technical obstacles that could prevent such exploitation.

As the driver is no longer in the cabin, video of what the train perceives in front of it associated with other perception information is transmitted to a distant site where is the driver, in what so called "the eyes of the train". The train-to-ground transmission link will therefore have to be very high data rate with a high quality of service so that the remote driver can have a vision similar to that which he would have if he were in the cabin of the train. Consequently, remote driving is based on three major technological blocks: a good perception system able to combine video with other information (audio, localization, *etc.*), a high data rate, robust, reliable and ultra-low latency radio communication uplink between the train and the remote site and a remote driving Human Machine Interface (HMI) with ergonomics suitable for a new job position in railways sector, *i.e.* remote train driver. There are three main applications for remote driving of trains:

- the management of sectors between yard and the client's site called "last kilometers" to reduce prolonged periods of transportation and waiting time for the drivers;
- the management of technical routes between maintenance centers and stations;
- the recovering from an autonomous train (failing or not).

In this paper we focus on the wireless link of the remote driving of the train. The rest of the paper is organized as follows: Sect. 1 gives a brief state of the art related to wireless communication for railways. Section 2 summarises the results obtained during the preliminary experiments performed with 4G/ LTE. In Sect. 3, we propose a comparison between LTE and 5G at physical layer using Non Orthogonal Multiple Access (NOMA) in the case of two trains in the cell. Finally we conclude and give perspectives.

2   Wireless Communications for Railways

GSM-R is used in the European railway sector for the control and command of high speed trains. Based on GSM phase2+ system, its date of obsolescence is

---

[1] TC-RAIL demo: https://www.sncf.com/fr/groupe/newsroom/teleconduite-train-autonome [Last accessed 12th July 2020].

predicted by 2030. To anticipate, a new system called Future Railway Mobile Communication System (FRMCS) is under development and preliminary specifications have been published [8]. The most important and mandatory characteristics of this new system are: Internet Protocol (IP) based communications, bearer agnostic, flexibility and resilience to technological evolution. FRMCS should satisfy all the needs for existing critical communications but also new ones related to driverless trains, virtual coupling and decoupling of trains, and communications with sensors along the tracks. In addition, non-critical applications such as real time video calls, augmented reality data communication, and wireless internet on-train for passengers, should be supported [11]. The Long Term Evolution (LTE) system has been particularly studied [6,9] as a serious candidate to replace GSM-R associated with other radio access technologies (RAT). However, the fact that FRMCS requires higher data rate and higher bandwidths due to real time HD video transmission for remote driving of train for example, has pushed researchers and industry to envision the 5G wireless communication system as another alternative [1,12]. Furthermore, in the European Shift2rail program, prototypes of a new Adaptable Communication System (ACS) are under development by industry [3]. The aim is to combine different RAT *e.g.,* 4G, 5G, Wi-Fi and Satellite communications that will cooperate to provide the required communication needs of the different safety and non safety related railway applications.

3   Preliminary Experiments on the Tracks

In the framework of the TC-Rail project, an LTE infrastructure in Time Division Duplex (TDD) mode was deployed specifically on a small area (around 4 km) covering a portion of a french line in Paris region in order to evaluate the performance of this dedicated technology for the remote driving of the train. It was deployed using eNodeB products from Nokia at 2.6 GHz with 20 MHz bandwidth. The masts were located at 15 m above the ground level and near the tracks. The preliminary tests were done in Single Input Single Output (SISO) configuration. The maximal transmitted power was 43 dBm and the antennas offered a gain of 16 dB. The radio coverage was performed by SNCF Réseau teams along the tracks in order to optimize connectivity along the trip. The measurements were done using a non GBR (Guaranteed Bit Rate) bearer with a QCI (QoS Class Identifier) equal to 7. The results showed an average data rate of 7.7 Mbits/s in uplink in the covered area. This is very satisfying as the minimal requirement was 2 Mbps for video. The round trip latency was 60 ms in average. Figure 1 shows the train used for the demonstrator equipped with cameras, antennas and modem, and the remote driver cabin developed in the project.

4   5G and LTE Comparison

4.1   Context

Under the umbrella of the 5G and beyond wireless communication systems, many enabling technologies have emerged recently that offers different improve-

Remote driving cabin   Testing train on the tracks

Fig. 1. The TC-Rail experimentation

ments to 4G systems [2]. Among them, a first enhancement concerns the high system throughput offered by the Non-Orthogonal Multiple Access technology (NOMA). In multiple users scenarios, the users access the radio network by sharing the available time and frequency resources. Conventionally, users will be allocated different time and frequency resources in an orthogonal manner such as in the Time Division Multiple Access (TDMA) and the Frequency Division Multiple Access (FDMA) techniques. Recently, NOMA technology [7] has gained a widespread interest due to its accompanied gains in the overall system throughput. NOMA technique allows users to share the same time and frequency resources by adopting a superposition coding schemes at the transmitter and a successive interference cancellation schemes at the receiver. This proved to bring critical improvements in terms of the achieved sumrate of the corresponding users at the cost of additional interference components that needs to be considered within the transceiver design process.

NOMA has been recognized as the potential multiple access scheme for future communication systems. By virtue of exploiting power domain, NOMA can serve multiple users at the same time, frequency, and code resources yielding higher spectral efficiency. NOMA communication system implementation involves two major processes namely Superposition Coding (SC) and Successive Interference Cancellation (SIC) at the base station and users terminals, respectively. NOMA users are distinguished according to their channel status, wherein users are allocated with portion of power inversely proportional to their channel condition. To decode their own messages, NOMA users suppress the information messages of all weaker users, while considering the information of the stronger users as interference.

Most of the literature on NOMA based communication systems has considered Perfect SIC (PSIC) process, *i.e.* an accurate knowledge of all weaker users information messages is available at the each user's terminal. However, this assumption is not practical in the TC-Rail project as it implies that the user should perfectly estimate both the amplitude of all weaker users waveform

[5]. Moreover, this task becomes extremely challenging in doubly selective channels such those encountered for vehicular and railway wireless communication systems. A few literature can be found on imperfect SIC based NOMA system. NOMA versus OMA based systems' performance comparison has been carried out in the literature for different scenarios. NOMA superiority over OMA is proved in terms of users fairness [10], multi-user capacity [15], beamforming aspects [4], and cell-edge user data rate [14]. Numerical simulations illustrate that NOMA scheme provides higher data-rate, higher spectral efficiency, lower latency. However, NOMA users suffer from inter-user interference.

To be compliant with the 3GPP 5G Phase 2 (release 16) [16] that adopts NOMA as the potential multiple access candidate for the 5G systems, NOMA has been adopted as the multiple access scheme for the TC-Rail project. It is worth mentioning that Orthogonal Frequency Division Multiple Access (OFDMA) has been adopted in the LTE and 3GPP standard release 8 as the multiple access method.

In order to illustrate the gain provided by the proposed 5G-based communication systems, a comparison with LTE-based system is carried out at the physical layer only, where no higher layers techniques are involved. As the 5G physical implementation is not realized yet, and important parameters such as carrier frequency and bandwidth are not identified especially in the railway system, the TC-Rail implementation configuration and physical parameters are adopted to perform the comparison. Table 1 illustrates the adopted setup configuration in the comparison.

Table 1. TC-rail setup configuration parameters

Parameter	Value
Carrier Frequency	2585 MHz
Bandwidth	20 MHz
Transmit Power	20 W
Antenna Gain	16.5 dBi
Number of OFDM Subcarriers	1200
OFDM Subcarrier Spacing	15 kHz
Trains Velocity	100 km/h
Trains number	2
Channel Model and Doppler	Vehicular A, Jakes
Monte-Carlo Simulation Realization Number	1000

The physical layer technologies in the LTE setup are 3GPP release 8 compliant, wherein the OFDMA, OFDM, turbo coding are the technologies used for the multiple access, waveforms and channel coding blocks respectively. OFDM is adopted for both LTE and 5G communication systems. However, the OFDM parameters in terms of number of subcarriers, subcarriers spacing, symbol and CP length are different in the 5G than its values in the LTE, as the bandwidth in the 5G is 100 MHz for operating frequencies below 6 GHz and 400 MHz at 28 GHz and above where the bandwidth is 20 MHz in the LTE. As we consider the TC-Rail LTE-based setup and for the sake of fairness, the OFDM parameters are kept the same in the LTE and 5G systems. Furthermore, the same MIMO (Multiple Input Multiple Output) scheme is used for LTE and 5G systems to guarantee the comparison to be fair as choosing different MIMO schemes will change radically the system performance in terms of throughput and Bit error rate (BER). Table 2 summarizes the technology used for both LTE and 5G in the comparison.

Table 2. 5G and LTE technologies

Technology	LTE	5G
Multiple Access	OFDMA TDD	NOMA
Waveform	OFDM	OFDM
MIMO	2 * 2 Alamouti	2 * 2 Alamouti
Channel Coding	Turbo Coding	LDPC

The simulation involves two served trains at the same time, a train with good channel condition (center train) and the second one with poor channel condition (edge train). The comparison between the LTE and 5G is carried out in terms of sum rate (the sum of the both trains rate) and BER with considering the simulation parameters and technologies illustrated in Tables 1 and 2.

4.2   System Model

We consider a communication system, wherein a base station is communicating with two moving users at the center and the edge of the cell. Due to the mobility of the users, doubly selective fading channel model is adopted. The transmitted users' messages are first mapped into a 2-dimensional space "a time frequency space", then transformed into the signal space via the synthesis function $g_{m,k}(t)$. Hence, the transmitted signal can be expressed as follows:

$$s(t) = \sum_{k=0}^{K-1} \sum_{m=0}^{M-1} g_{m,k}(t) x_{m,k} \tag{1}$$

where $x_{m,k}$ is the transmitted message at the mth subcarrier and the kth time domain symbol . K denotes the number of time domain symbols and M is the number of subcarriers of the whole transmission block. The synthesis function $g_{m,k}(t)$ that maps $x_{m,k}$ into the signal space can be written as follows:

$$g_{m,k}(t) = p_{tx}(t - kT)e^{j2\pi mF(t-kT)} \tag{2}$$

where $p_{tx}(t)$ is the pulse shape, also known as the prototype filter. This pulse shape will determine the energy distribution (in time and frequency domains) of the transmitted symbol. T is the symbol duration while F is the subcarrier spacing. Hence, we can read Eq. 2 as follows: $g_{m,k}(t)$ *is considered as the prototype filter $p_{tx}(t)$ with translation of kT and modulation of mF.*

After conducting the sampling process, Eq. (1) be represented in matrix form $s = Gx$ as [13], where

$$G = [g_{1,1}g_{2,1}...g_{M,1}g_{1,2}...g_{M,K}] \tag{3}$$

$$x = [x_{1,1}x_{2,1}...x_{M,1}x_{1,2}...x_{M,K}]^T \tag{4}$$

By sampling $g_{m,k}(t)$ in Eq. (2), the samples are grouped in one vector $g_{m,k} \in \mathbb{C}^{N \times 1}$ where $g_{m,k} = G(:, mk)$. N denotes the number of samples of the whole transmission block.

In OFDM-based NOMA techniques, super-positioned coding is applied to send edge and cell users symbols while sharing the same time and frequency resources. In other words, at the mth subcarrier and the kth time symbol, the sent message is written as follows:

$$x_{m,k} = \sqrt{\alpha}\text{dedge}_{m,k} + \sqrt{1 - \alpha}\text{dcenter}_{m,k} \tag{5}$$

$\text{dedge}_{m,k}, \text{dcenter}_{m,k} \in \mathbb{C}$ are the transmitted symbols of the edge and the center user, respectively. $d_{m,k} \in \mathbb{R}$ is the possible special case e.g., Pulse Amplitude Modulation (PAM). α and $1 - \alpha$ are the power allocation factor for NOMA edge and center user respectively and hence the transmitted power is normalized; i.e, $E\left[|x_{m,k}|^2\right] = 1$.

In the OFDM-based OMA case, different time and frequency resources are allocated to the center and edge users, where

$$x_{m,k} = \begin{cases} \text{dedge}_{m,k}, (m, k) \in \Omega_{edge} \\ \text{dcenter}_{m,k}, (m, k) \in \Omega_{center} \end{cases} \tag{6}$$

We consider a fair distribution of resources among users, *i.e.* $|\Omega_{edge}| = |\Omega_{center}| = MK/2$. Where $|\Omega|$ indicates the number of elements in the set Ω.

At users terminals, the demodulated signal can be written as follows:

$$y = \underbrace{QHG}_{STM} x + Q\eta \tag{7}$$

where STM $= QHG$ is the corresponding System Transmission Matrix. The non-diagonal elements of this STM represents the interference components, while the desired signal dwells its diagonal elements. In the NOMA case, inter-user interference exists even in the diagonal elements. However, at the center user, SIC is implemented to remove the effects of the edge user interference.

4.3 Sum Rate

The sum rate, which represents the overall data rate at both edge and center users, is written as follows: $R_{\text{sum}} = R^{edge} + R^{center}$ where R^{edge}, R^{center} express the data rate of the edge and the center user, respectively.

NOMA Case: we assume that each time frequency resource has the same data rate. Hence, the data rate at user $u \in$ {edge, center} is given as:

$$R^u = \gamma \frac{M}{T} \log_2 \left(1 + \text{SINR}^u\right) \tag{8}$$

In Quadrature Amplitude Modulation (QAM) based waveforms and for OFDM, we give $\gamma = 1$. In order to calculate the SINR of the ith symbol, we start by writing the ith row of the corresponding STM as follows

$$\boldsymbol{D}(i,:) = \boldsymbol{Q}(i,:)\boldsymbol{HG} = \left(\boldsymbol{G}^H \sum_{l=0}^{L-1} diag\left(\boldsymbol{q}_{i,l}^H\right) \boldsymbol{h}_l^H \right)^H \tag{9}$$

where $diag(\boldsymbol{x})$ is the diagonal matrix of the vector $\boldsymbol{x}$. We calculate the covariance matrix $\boldsymbol{C} = E\left[\boldsymbol{D}(i,:)^H \boldsymbol{D}(i,:)\right]$ as:

$$\boldsymbol{C} = \boldsymbol{G}^H \left(\sum_{l=0}^{L-1} \boldsymbol{R}_{q_l} \odot \boldsymbol{R}_{h_l} \right) \boldsymbol{G} \qquad \text{where} \qquad \boldsymbol{R}_{q_l} = \boldsymbol{q}_{i,l}^H \boldsymbol{q}_{i,l} \tag{10}$$

At the Edge User: we first need to calculate the power of the useful signal $P_{edge} = \alpha \boldsymbol{C}(i,i)$, the power of the inter-user interference $P_{\text{Inter}} = (1-\alpha)tr\{\boldsymbol{C}\}$, the power of the intra-user interference $P_{Intra} = \alpha\left(tr\{\boldsymbol{C}\} - \boldsymbol{C}(i,i)\right)$ and hence:

$$\text{SINR}^{\text{edge}} = \frac{P_{\text{edge}}}{P_{\text{Intra}} + P_{\text{Inter}} + P_n} \tag{11}$$

where P_n is the noise power.

At the Center User: the SIC process will eliminate the inter user interference component, we write $P_{\text{center}} = (1-\alpha)\boldsymbol{C}(i,i)$ and $P_{\text{Intra}} = (1-\alpha)\left(tr\{\boldsymbol{C}\} - \boldsymbol{C}(i,i)\right)$, and hence:

$$\text{SINR}^{\text{center}} = \frac{P_{\text{center}}}{P_{\text{Intra}} + P_n} \tag{12}$$

OMA Case: in the OMA case, users won't share same time and frequency resources. By assuming fair distribution of resources among users, the bit rate at each user is given as:

$$R^{OMA} = \gamma \frac{M}{2T} \log_2 \left(1 + \text{SINR}^{OMA}\right) \tag{13}$$

where the prelog factor of $1/2$ in the rate equation is due to the fair resource allocation between the two users. This implies also that $P_n^{\text{OMA}} = (1/2)P_n^{\text{NOMA}}$.

4.4   Simulation Results

Figure 2a illustrates the sumrate of the proposed 5G communication system and LTE for different waveforms. The rate is almost doubled in the 5G case with two trains due to the non-orthogonal resource allocation in 5G NOMA while the trains need to share the time and frequency resources in LTE. However, NOMA users suffer from inter-user interference that makes the gain in sumrate between 5G and LTE nonlinear. The curves shown in Fig. 2b represents the BER performance for different multi-carrier waveforms in LTE and 5G communication systems, namely OFDM, Filter Bank Multi Carrier (FBMC), Filtered OFDM (FOFDM) and Weighted Overlap and Add (WOLA). The BER of all waveforms in the 5G is better than that of the LTE. This is due to the fact that non-orthogonal resources allocation in 5G is more robust toward channel impairments especially in the railway environment, where the orthogonality doesn't hold in the selective fading channel resulting from the mobility. Figure 3 draws a 3D representation of the system sumrate in LTE and 5G system as a function of both trains' velocity. We can notice from the figure that the 5G system maintains its superiority over LTE even in high speed regime. The sumrate in 5G varies with speed between 180 and 160 Mbps at the highest speed for both trains, however the sumrate in the LTE case is between 100 and 80 Mbps. Hence, the 5G system is more robust against speed and the resulting non orthogonality in the channel.

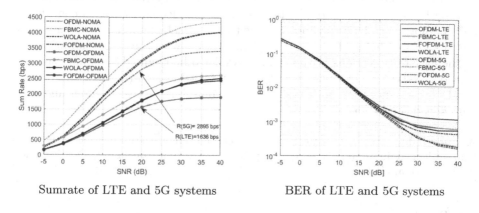

Sumrate of LTE and 5G systems   BER of LTE and 5G systems

Fig. 2. Sumrate and BER results for LTE and 5G

5   Conclusion and Perspectives

Trains are entering the era of full automation thanks to sensors and wireless communications shifting control functions from the human driver to computers. Driverless systems already exist for metro and dedicated lines. The full automation of trains in the context of existing lines with the possibility to cross other non automatic trains is very complex. To reach this challenge, a mandatory brick is the remote control of a driverless train from a distant site thanks to radio transmission. This will allow telecontrol of the train anywhere at any time for example for specific maneuver in stations or marshalling yards or in case of

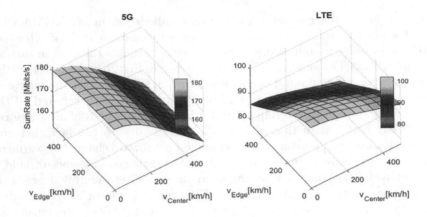

Fig. 3. Sumrate of LTE and 5G systems

failure of the driverless system. The TC-Rail project aims to bring a proof of concept of the remote control of the train. In this paper we have briefly presented the evolution of the wireless communication systems for trains and the first performance results for the train-to-ground video transmission considering LTE deployment along the line. Thanks to numerical simulations, we have compared LTE and 5G performances at physical layer with the same characteristics in the case of two trains in the cell and we have highlighted the importance to consider NOMA techniques associated with OFDM and MIMO to guarantee a good performances for both trains even in doubly selective channel and with high speed condition.

Acknowledgements. This work has been carried out in the framework of the TC-Rail project co-financed by a public and private consortium (Railenium, SNCF, Thales, Actia Telecom, CNES).

References

1. Ai, B., et al.: Future railway services-oriented mobile communications network. IEEE Commun. Mag. **53**(10), 78–85 (2015)
2. Akyildiz, I.F., Nie, S., Lin, S.C., Chandrasekaran, M.: 5G roadmap: 10 key enabling technologies. Comput. Netw. **106**, 17–48 (2016)
3. Allen, B., Eschbach, B., Mikulandra, M.: Defining an adaptable communications system for all railways. In: proceedings of the 7th Transport Research Arena TRA 2018 (TRA) (2018)
4. Alsaba, Y., et al.: Full-duplex cooperative non-orthogonal multiple access with beamforming and energy harvesting. IEEE Access **6**, 19726–19738 (2018)
5. Andrews, J.G., et al.: Optimum power control for successive interference cancellation with imperfect channel estimation. IEEE Trans. Wirel. Commun. **2**(2), 375–383 (2003)

6. Brunel, L., Bonneville, H., Charaf, A.: Throughput performance of 3GPP LTE system in railway environment. In: Pirovano, A., et al. (eds.) International Workshop on Communication Technologies for Vehicles, vol. 10222, pp. 60–71. Springer, Cham (2017). https://doi.org/10.1007/978-3-319-56880-5_7
7. Cai, Y., Qin, Z., Cui, F., Li, G.Y., McCann, J.A.: Modulation and multiple access for 5G networks. IEEE Commun. Surv. Tutorials **20**(1), 629–646 (2018). https://doi.org/10.1109/COMST.2017.2766698
8. FRMCS Functional Working Group: Future Railway Mobile Communication System, User Requirements Specification, FU-7100 (2019)
9. He, R., et al.: High-speed railway communications: from GSM-R to LTE-R. IEEE Veh. Technol. Mag. **11**(3), 49–58 (2016)
10. Li, A., et al.: Investigation on low complexity power assignment method and performance gain of non-orthogonal multiple access systems. IEICE Trans. Fundam. **97**(1), 57–68 (2014)
11. Moreno, J., Riera, J.M., de Haro, L., Rodriguez, C.: A survey on future railway radio communications services: challenges and opportunities. IEEE Commun. Mag. **53**(10), 62–68 (2015). https://doi.org/10.1109/MCOM.2015.7295465
12. Mottier, D.: How 5G Technologies Could Benefit to the Railway Sector: Challenges and Opportunities. Mitsubishi Electric R&D Centre Europe, France (2018)
13. Nissel, R., et al.: Filter bank multicarrier modulation schemes for future mobile communications. IEEE J. Sel. Areas Commun. **35**(8), 1768–1782 (2017)
14. Saito, Y., et al.: Non-orthogonal multiple access (NOMA) for cellular future radio access. In: 2013 IEEE 77th Vehicular Technology Conference (VTC Spring), pp. 1–5. IEEE (2013)
15. Weingarten, H., et al.: The capacity region of the Gaussian multiple-input multiple-output broadcast channel. IEEE Trans. Inf. Theory **52**(9), 3936–3964 (2006)
16. Yuan, Y., Yuan, Z., Tian, L.: 5G non-orthogonal multiple access study in 3GPP. IEEE Commun. Mag. **58**(7), 90–96 (2020)

Sensing the Health of the Catenary-Pantograph Contact on Railway Vehicles with Radio Receivers: Early Results

Juan Moreno[1,2(✉)], Julián Martín Jarillo[1], and Sonsoles García-Albertos[1]

[1] Área de Ingeniería, Metro de Madrid S.A, Madrid, Spain
juan.moreno@metromadrid.es
[2] Departamento de Ingeniería Audiovisual Y Comunicaciones, Universidad Politécnica de Madrid, Madrid, Spain

Abstract. Overhead lines or catenaries are the most common method to supply electric energy to trains, at least in modern railway lines. Electric trains collect energy using a pantograph which is in physical contact with the catenary. However, this sliding contact is not perfect because of many factors: vertical displacements, wear of the contact strip, aerodynamic effects, geometry defects, etc. These imperfections may cause sparks and electric arcs which could seriously damage the pantograph, the catenary and increase the operational costs of the railway line. The usual approach to know the condition of this contact is installing video cameras in the top of the train to determine where, when and why sparks and arcs happen. Given that both sparks and arcs cause a significant EM interference, in this paper we propose a methodology to sense the health of the catenary-pantograph contact using radio receivers tuned in the frequencies where this interference appears. The objective of this measurement campaign is not to perform an academic characterization of the physical phenomenon but to begin working on a practical condition-based maintenance system. Moreover, some early results of this work are provided based on measurements from a Metro de Madrid train in Line 6 whose voltage is 600 V DC.

Keywords: Catenary-pantograph · Channel measurement · Channel modelling · Condition-based maintenance · EM interference

1 Introduction

Ideally, in electric trains catenary and pantograph are attached in a perfect contact, letting the current flow from the wayside to the train and vice versa in case regenerative braking is feasible. Actually, reality is more complex and this contact is not perfect due to vertical displacements, imperfections in the contact strip, aerodynamic effects, etc. These imperfections in the contact usually lead to sparks and, in the worst-case scenario, electric arcs. Both of them but specially arcs are easy to identify because of the emitted light that is associated to them. The problem is very relevant for both railway operators and infrastructure managers because arcs and sparks lead to an excessive wear

© Springer Nature Switzerland AG 2020
F. Krief et al. (Eds.): Nets4Cars/Nets4Trains/Nets4Aircraft 2020, LNCS 12574, pp. 148–156, 2020.
https://doi.org/10.1007/978-3-030-66030-7_13

in the contact strip of the pantograph, a loss of electric potential in vehicle engines, as well as damage in the catenary and also in the electrical equipment of substations and trains. Finally, we should account as well the reputational impact on the public image of the network operator of the presence of electric arcs and sparks that can be seen by passengers. For all the above, it is of the outmost importance to suppress all the potential causes for both arcs and sparks in the catenary-pantograph contact. However, this is one of the hardest-to-fix problems in railway engineering, because this contact is affected by a large number of parameters (both dynamic and static) from the catenary and the pantograph as well. As an example, we can look at the force applied by the pantograph spring to the catenary: if it is very high, the wear on the contact of the pantograph will be very high, leading to a increase in the maintenance costs; on the contrary, if it is loosen, there will be frequent gaps which lead to electric arcs. Therefore, a balance is needed and, moreover, a time-variant balance because contact strips get some wear as they operate. All these effects are also relevant when the catenary is rigid instead of the traditional one. In this case, the rigid catenary leads to higher wear in the contact strip of the pantograph.

Consequently, it is very important for railway operators to assess the condition of the contact, being able to understand where, when and why arcs and sparks appear, in order to apply the corrective or preventive measures. The traditional approach has always been using optic detectors [1] and, more recently, video cameras installed on the top of the train. Indeed, the European Standard [2] for the characterization of this contact refers only to optical sensors but the contents of this standard are applicable to other methods as well.

The main drawback for both optical and video-related methods is that they require to be installed in the top of the train and more or less close to the pantograph and in line-of-sight conditions as well. The advantages are many, but this drawback implies higher installation costs as well as safety issues for the maintenance staff. Moreover, in some railway operators (like Metro de Madrid) it is forbidden to have wires from the top of the train to the driver's cabin, in order to avoid high-voltage electric contact.

Therefore, the focus of this paper is to provide the very early results of a study on the feasibility of using radio receivers to assess the condition of the catenary-pantograph contact. The physical phenomenon that relates EM emission and electric arcs has been studied exhaustively in the past and also measured by other research groups, both in DC [3] and AC [4], characterized in both cases as human-made interference. However, in these works the objective was to characterize interferences with communication systems like GSM-R [3] but not to characterize the health of the catenary-pantograph contact.

The contribution of this paper is to provide some early results of the first stages of the design and validation of an experimental condition-based maintenance system focused on assessing the health of the catenary-pantograph contact using radio receivers instead of optical or video devices. This study was performed in Line 6 of Metro de Madrid on a line with a DC supply voltage of 600 V.

The structure of this paper is the following: in Sect. 2 the environment where measurements were done is described as well as the physics behind the catenary-pantograph interaction; in Sect. 3 we explain the setup for the measurements; early results obtained in this measurement campaign are presented in Sect. 4 and, finally, conclusions are provided in Sect. 5.

2 Environment

Electric traction is the most favorable type of power supply for railways from both an environmental and economic perspective; indeed, in the case of urban mass transit and high-speed trains it is the only possible type of traction [5].

In electrified railways, there are two main tribology contacts: wheel-rail contact and pantograph-wire contact. The first one is characterized by high stresses on the contact zone and relative rotational movement plus pseudo-sliding between surfaces. Meanwhile, pantograph-wire contact is the most common interface between overhead line system and rolling stock (there are other constructive solutions to supply electrical energy, such as the third rail) and is characterized by an ideally full-sliding relative movement and high current density circulating through the contact.

Historically, characterizing pantograph-wire contact has been challenging because it is so complicated; in fact, there are many unsolved matters [6] about it due to the nature of the contact itself and the number of external variables on which it depends: amount of the collecting current, velocity of trains, catenary type and its installation accuracy, condition of the contact wire surface, and others [6]. Moreover, the repeatability of results is very low because the conditions change on every run; many times, sensorized trains are test trains and not commercial ones, which provide results not realistic for the latter; as well as many other aspects that do not help to the obtention of suitable predictive models.

Electrified tracks are costly to maintain, so, therefore, any improvement in the cost figures like CBM strategies is more than welcome [7]. There are many components in the railway traction power systems, from interface with utility distribution network to contacts with trains, and they are physically located along the rail line; all of these components reliability is vital to the quality of train services [8].

Metro de Madrid has been using electric traction to move its rolling stock since the first section of Line 1 was inaugurated in 1919. From the first moment, the electrical energy was supplied from an overhead line, which offers important advantages from the point of view of the electrical risk, and through a sliding contact formed by the overhead line and the current collector device of the vehicle. Main technical characteristics of early railway electrification system in Metro de Madrid were initially as follows: 600 V DC, tram catenary, bow current collector mechanically spring loaded, cooper-cooper contact, maximum commercial speed of 55 km/h. Throughout this century, the configuration of the system has been gradually evolving as technical requirements have increased and more advantageous technical solutions have emerged, although in certain areas of the Metro de Madrid network there are still reminiscences of that early installation. Some of the upgrades in Metro de Madrid are as follows: 1500 V DC, compensated catenary, rigid catenary, single arm pantograph mechanically air-spring loaded, cooper-graphite contact and a maximum commercial speed of 110 km/h. All these advances have been focused on improving performance, reliability, availability, maintainability and safety.

This preliminary study has been carried out on Line 6 of Metro de Madrid. which is very important and representative within Metro de Madrid network for several reasons:

- 23.5 km long circular line, all of it on double track and fully underground.
- It has 28 stations distributed separated no more than 1.4 km. As the trains make a stop at all stations, the starting and braking processes (high energy demand) are very frequent.
- From an operational point of view, it is a line that interconnects almost all the other ones and, therefore, it is the one that supports the most passenger and rolling stock traffic.
- The signalling system installed on this line (Communications-Based Train Control, CBTC) allows for a very short interval between trains, reaching 150 s at rush hour.
- Maintains the legacy supply voltage at 600 V, although all the catenary is already rigid in the whole line.
- There are two rolling stock series: 5000 and 8000 series, both in 6-car configurations. Type 5000 has three pantographs while type 8000 has two pantographs, in both cases equipped with double graphite slider. Therefore, even though the total maximum current figure is similar, the current per pantograph is 50% higher in the case of type 8000, reaching in this last case a current of approximately 1800 A per pantograph.
- The longitudinal profile of the line is very demanding, with gradients of up to 50‰, which carries high and usual current requirements, both in the traction phase and in regenerative braking.

In Fig. 1 a depiction of electric current, slope and speed for one trip between two of its station is provided.

3 Measurement Setup

Given that the objective is to characterize the interference emissions from the catenary-pantograph contact, we installed three different receivers plus a video camera onboard plus the associated antennas. First of all, a Tektronix MDO3054 oscilloscope in order to have good time-resolution; secondly, a Rohde&Schwarz portable spectrum analyzer model FSH13, and a software-defined radio evaluation board. We placed three antennas on the top of the train, 2 m away from the contact area between the pantograph and the catenary (See Fig. 2), as well as the video camera plus one antenna in the passenger area of the train. The objective for this antenna inside the train is to study the feasibility of having the sensors there instead of on the top of the train. Two of the three antennas used for the measurements are well-adapted for the band 460–676 MHz whereas the third one is suitable for the 0.67–12 GHz [9] where it has a VSWR (Voltage Standing Wave Ratio) shorter than 2. The camera is a GoPro 3 and the purpose of this device is to record all the sparks and electric arcs that happened in the tests in order to see the correlation with the radio measurements taken with the three receivers. Both the oscilloscope and the spectrum analyzer were connected to a LAN and each one was controlled by a different laptop. The software-defined radio was connected directly (via USB) to another laptop. All three receivers were controlled using MATLAB.

The oscilloscope's trigger was set just above the noise level in order to be able to detect low-energy arcs if needed. The sampling rate was set at 2.5 GS/s.

In order to have information about train location, speed, catenary voltage, electric current, etc., we retrieved the train logs from the data recorder of the train. All installation

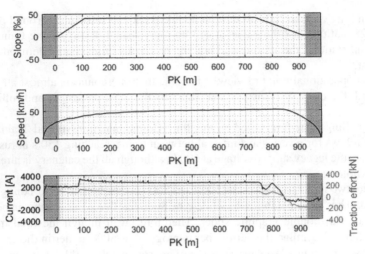

Fig. 1. Record of slope, speed, current and effort of an 8000 train between the Puerta del Ángel and Alto de Extremadura stations on line 6 of the Madrid Metro.

in the trains were removed at the end of the measurement campaign. Measurements were performed with all the instrumentation onboard the train. No equipment was placed on the wayside. In Fig. 3 is depicted the overall measurement setup.

On the other hand, given that these trains have a current limitation in the vicinity of the station (up to 1000 A per pantograph) and we wanted to experience as much arcs as possible, we removed this software limitation during the tests (which were performed during the night, out of the commercial service) in order to not limit the usual current figures, which can go up to 1800 A per pantograph.

The objectives for this first measurement campaign were the following:

1. See the correlation between arcs and sparks and EM interference in radio bands.
2. Identify suitable frequency bands to sense the catenary-pantograph contact.
3. Check the feasibility of installing a receiver in the passenger area of the train and not in the top of the train.
4. Assess the performance of a low-cost receiver for this task.
5. Measure the arc duration in order to meet the requirements of the standard [2].

In this paper we provide some results for objectives 1 and 2. More results will be provided in the future. Moreover, in the future we have planned to do more measurements with a more capable oscilloscope and using a real-time spectrum analyzer in order to be even more sure about the results. However, the objective of this measurement campaign is not to perform an academic characterization of the physical phenomenon (which was already done [3,4]) but to begin working on a practical condition-based maintenance system.

(a)   **(b)**

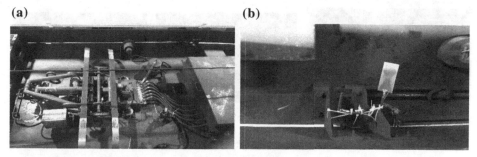

Fig. 2. Measurement setup on the top of the train. In the figure (a), pantograph with its contact strips are shown as well as the whole system. The video camera is in the bottom right and antennas in the top right. Installed antennas on the top of the train are shown in figure (b).

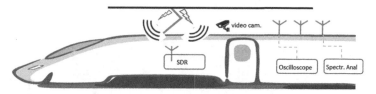

Fig. 3. Schematic of the measurement setup.

4   Results

4.1   Generation of EM Interference Related to Arcs and Sparks

To perform this analysis, we compared video recordings retrieved from the GoPro camera placed on the top of the train and measurements obtained with the oscilloscope and the spectrum analyzer.

The most important outcome of this test is that the spectra related to arcs and sparks really differ from each other. Arcs occupy a very wide bandwidth but sparks are more limited. Power is also more limited for sparks. In Fig. 4 we can see both the pictures of an electric arc and some minor sparks together with their associated spectrum. We have focused the measurements on the frequency band that ranges from 460 MHz to 676 MHz, in order to avoid receiving power from train-to-ground communications systems installed on line 6. Previously, we checked that there were no potential transmissions on this band.

This difference between both power and spectrum between arcs and sparks is good news because it eases the implementation of a condition-based monitoring system, that, at least could be able to differentiate between both effects, which is something important as well.

Figure 4 measurements were obtained from 2 s of measurements with the "max hold" function activated and a sweep time for the whole band of 20 ms, which means 100 sweeps over the 460–676 MHz band. This setup is not convenient to estimate the arc duration but could be appropriate to identify suitable frequencies to detect both arcs and sparks. Each one of the effects is depicted on a video snapshot in Fig. 4.

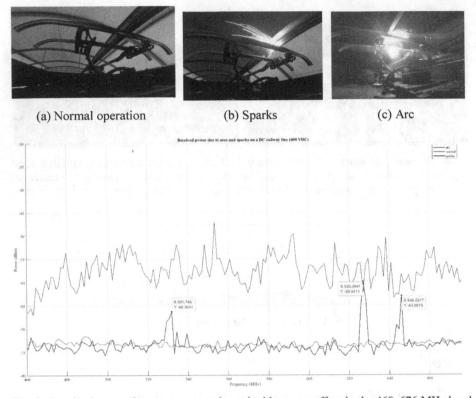

(a) Normal operation   (b) Sparks   (c) Arc

Fig. 4. Received power due to an arc, sparks and without any effect in the 460–676 MHz band on a railway electric line (600 V_DC).

4.2 Preliminary Frequency Bands

As we can see in Fig. 4, the 450–676 MHz band provides a good framework to begin the classification of effects. The presence of an arc is remarkable in the whole band (−57.57 dBm in average, which is +15.82 dB of excess power over the baseline scenario with no arcs and no sparks) so the screening between arcs and sparks should be done in bands where sparks are not present. This means that more measurements should be taken in order to identify frequencies that fulfill this requirement. In these preliminary measurements we found sparks' footprints in 531.75 MHz, 626.98 and 646.03 MHz. We had peaks with 6, 13 and 10 dB over the mean power of the no-arc-no-spark measurements which is −73.38 dBm.

In general terms, the spectrum of an arc and some sparks is really different, which is good news for the monitoring system. However, if we want to work with a receiver with a narrower bandwidth we should be able to do this screening based on some particular bands and not on the whole band. Therefore, a deeper analysis should be done.

5 Conclusions

This line of research has one final objective, which is the development of a cost-effective and easy-to-install device for the monitoring of catenary-pantograph interaction, which identifies and characterizes the scenarios that may degrade catenary-pantograph contact, such as electric arcs and sparks. The major advantage of this device will be based on the fact that no video camera will be needed on the top of the train because the sensor is a radio receiver [10].

In this first measurement campaign some important results have been obtained: the spectral differences between arcs and sparks, something very useful for our purpose and the identification of some suitable frequencies for the emissions due to arcs and sparks. Future work will consist on more measurements in the already identified frequencies.

However, it is noteworthy that for the European Standard [2] there are only arcs, we can see two different types of effects: arcs and sparks, each of them with its own footprint.

Finally, the link between the health of the catenary-pantograph contact and the obtained results is that EM emissions may appear when there is no contact between the pantograph and the catenary or it is a low-quality one. This loss of contact could be due to excessive wear in the contact strip of the pantograph, in the wire or in both.

Acknowledgements. Authors want to express gratitude to both Marion Berbineau and Divitha Seetharamdoo from the University Gustave Eiffel (formerly IFSTTAR) for their useful comments and discussion and also for lending us a wideband antenna which proved to be very useful in the measurements.

References

1. CN 105403242. "Locomotive pantograph-catenary hard point photoelectric vibration comprehensive detection and GPS positioning method and system"
2. EN 50317:2012. "Railway applications. Current collection systems. Requirements for and validation of measurements of the dynamic interaction between pantograph and overhead contact line"
3. Mariscotti, A., Deniau, V.: "On the characterization of pantograph arc transients on GSM-R antenna". In: 17th Symposium IMEKO TC 4, 3rd Symposium IMEKO TC 19 and 15th IWADC Work-shop Instrumentation for the ICT Era (2010)
4. Shuangle, Z., et al.: "Measurement and analysis method of electromagnetic signals for DC arcing fault". In: 4th International Conference on Electric Power Equipment—Switching Technology (2017)
5. Kiessling, F., Puschmann, R., Schmieder, A., Schneider, E.: Contact Lines for Electric Railways: Planning, Design, Implementation, Maintenance. John Wiley & Sons, Germany (2018)
6. Beagles, A., Fletcher, D., Peffers, M., Mak, P., Lowe. C.: "Validation of a new model for railway overhead line dynamics". In: Proceedings of the Institution of Civil Engineers—Transport, vol. 169, Issue 5, October, pp. 339–349 (2016)
7. "Railway Handbook 2015. Energy consumption and CO2 emissions". In: UIC International Union of Railways. UIC Homepage. https://uic.org/IMG/pdf/iea-uic_2015-2.pdf

8. Chi, Y.L., Ferreira, L., Ho, T.K., Leung, K., Siu, L.K.: "Evaluation of maintenance schedules on railway traction power systems". In: Proceedings of the Institution of Mechanical Engineers Part F Journal of Rail and Rapid Transit, June 2006
9. Hassanein Rabah, M., Seetharamdoo, D., Addaci, R., Berbineau, M.: Novel miniature extremely-wide-band antenna with stable radiation pattern for spectrum sensing applications. IEEE Antennas Wirel. Propag. Lett. **14**, 1634–1638 (2015)
10. Moreno García-Loygorri, J., Martín Jarillo, J.: "Monitoring device for monitoring catenary-pantograph interaction in railway vehicles", EP3667337

Freight Telematics Systems: An Intelligent Wagon

Roberto C. Ramirez$^{(\boxtimes)}$, Iker Moya$^{(\boxtimes)}$, Imanol Puy$^{(\boxtimes)}$, Unai Alvarado$^{(\boxtimes)}$, Iñigo Adin$^{(\boxtimes)}$, and Jaizki Mendizabal$^{(\boxtimes)}$

CEIT and Tecnun, University of Navarra, Manuel de Lardizabal 15, 20018 San Sebastian, Spain
{rramirezm,imoya,ipuy,ualvarado,iadin,jmendizabal}@ceit.es

Abstract. In order to reach the EU's objectives with regards to developing rail freight in the future, an evolution of the freight train is required. For that, telematics technologies play a crucial role as an enabler for the intelligent freight train. This paper shows different freight train topologies and communications technologies. Moreover, representative use cases enable the intelligent train that has connectivity capabilities such as condition monitoring for train and cargo. Furthermore, an example of intelligent freight wagon architecture is shown.

Keywords: Railway communications · Freight train · Telematics · Monitoring · Intelligent wagon

1 Introduction

There is no doubt the importance of the train for the transport of passengers in the European Union (EU) as well as its constant growth and improvement, but not in freight transportation. The railway still has a lot to improve specifically to be a more attractive option for merchandises transportation against road transportation. Actually, and despite the advantages in technologies for rail freight transport, it has serious limiting factors to disincentive its use, such as high installation and maintenance costs, poor payload-deadweight ratios, lack of integration of freight data, transit times, lack of standardization in their elements, or logistics complexity.

EU's strategy towards a competitive and resource-efficient transport system is described in Transport White Paper 2011. There are set long-term objectives to develop rail freight: A 50% shift of medium distance intercity passenger and freight journeys from road to rail and waterborne transport by 2050 [1]. Therefore, intending to reach these ambitious objectives, freight infrastructures and services need to be upgraded, developing and adapting technologies to improve competitiveness and reliability.

The overwhelming challenges require collaborative efforts from the public and private sectors of the EU members, and the Shift2Rail initiative was created to attend the matter. This initiative sets a specific Innovation Programme 5 (IP5) focused on Technologies for Sustainable & Attractive European Rail Freight. Specifically, the 'Freight Electrification, Brake and Telematics' (TD 5.1) aims to improve strategic areas of rail

© Springer Nature Switzerland AG 2020
F. Krief et al. (Eds.): Nets4Cars/Nets4Trains/Nets4Aircraft 2020, LNCS 12574, pp. 157–165, 2020.
https://doi.org/10.1007/978-3-030-66030-7_14

transport by developing key components such as condition-based maintenance of loco-motives and wagons, and wagon monitoring systems and telematics, as well as automatic coupling of wagons [2].

There are several projects in the IP5 with different objectives and partners. FR8RAIL project was aimed to work on the "Development of Functional Requirements for Sustain-able and Attractive European Rail" to achieve, among others, 100% availability of rail freight transportation information to the logistic chain information system [3]. FR8RAIL II is a continuation of this project and it includes challenging technological improve-ments such as new automatic coupler, modernization in telematics and electrification, improved methods to planning traffic operations, real-time network management, among others related to future freight wagon design and operation [4].

The telematics technologies (including HW, SW and algorithms), developed in this project may act as enablers to provide essential input information for different appli-cations such as condition-based and predictive maintenance, logistic services, traffic management, real-time network management and intelligent gate terminals. The telem-atics modules comprise a wagon OnBoard Unit (wOBU), different modules of a wagon and cargo monitoring system for maintenance and logistic purposes, systems for onboard and wayside communication.

The freight trains may have many possible configurations as train composition lengths and wagon styles. Therefore, wOBU's design should consider modular and adaptable options for various applications and settings.

This paper presents different wireless communications topologies and technologies for onboard monitoring systems in rail freight, some typical use cases, and propose a basic configuration and functions for an Intelligent Freight Wagon.

2 Freight Telematics System

Terms like digital, smart or intelligent railway, in a general and simplified view, refer to the same concept, a railway equipped with proper infrastructure to monitoring and connect the whole system to improve its operational efficiency [5–7]. From the previous definition, the Freight Telematics System (FTS) is a subsystem in a smart railway infras-tructure endow with the capacity to continue, remote and real-time monitoring significant elements of the freight train such as the loco and wagons, their position and performance, environment variables, or infrastructure condition. These systems are based on sensor networks, wired or wireless depending on the specific application, connected to a base or hub to put the data accessible in the cloud or some proprietary server. Nowadays, the leading technologies for sensor networks are the Wireless Sensor Network (WSN) and Internet of Things (IoT). These are variety of topologies and communication protocols for the sensor networks.

2.1 Communication Network Topologies

Specifically, in train application, the integration of the sensor networks requires commu-nications technologies that are adaptable to the linear network topology of a train. Some typical configurations are: a direct-wired connection (Fig. 1a); a wireless radio link to a hub in the locomotive (Fig. 1b); a node-to-node communication architecture centralized in the locomotive hub (Fig. 1c); and a fourth option is a direct link between each node and a remote, internet-connected base hub (Fig. 1d) [6].

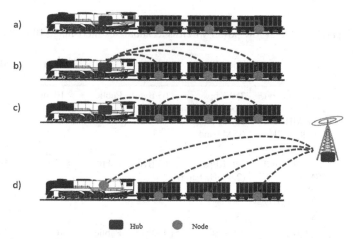

Fig. 1. Freight train communication topologies [6].

The choice of the appropriate topology to deploy could be some variation of the mentioned ones or even mixtures. Mainly, the characteristics and objectives of the primary application, the availability of electric power and mechanical requirements, safety regulations in communications and infrastructure, among others, should be taken into account. Communication systems deployed in freight trains may consider that, in most cases, wagons are not electrified. Hereafter any electronic system must include its power supply like a battery, power harvesting or generation techniques. The selected topology, but also the communication technologies, will determine the implementation, operation, and further maintenance, costs as well the benefits. A conscience cost-benefit evaluation should be done to ensure efficiency in the investment to improve competitiveness.

2.2 Communication Technologies

The required communication technologies for an FTS deployment include those that interconnect intra-wagon sensors to a wOBU and those that establish "train-to-ground", or between wagons and loco, communications. Direct-wired connectivity is in many cases avoided but is an option for intra-wagon communication. This option is considered where the problem of electrification has the priority. Wired connectivity is also robust for communications with proven protocols like CAN or RS485.

Nowadays, there is a wide range of communication technologies and protocols available for a Wireless Sensor Network (WSN) in an FTS deployment. Several relevant research studies surveyed and delivered the comparison of the most promising low-power wireless technologies, in terms of availability and performances [7, 8]. Following tables show the performance of different techniques for short-range and large-range respectively.

Short-range options in Table 1 can be used to connect sensors to wOBU, or interwagon communications, but also for wagon to wagon, or intra-train interactions. Long-range ones in Table 2 are suitable for intra-train and train-to-ground communications.

Table 1. Comparison table of low-power wireless technologies short-range 10–1000 m [9, 10].

Name	Freq.	Data rate	Packet size	Use	Latency	Max range
6LoWPAN	2,4 GHz band, ISM band (868 MHz EU, 908/916 MHz USA)	250 Kbps (2,4 GHz band) 20–40 Kbps (ISM band)	63 Bytes	Public	10 ms	1–75 m
Thread	2,4 GHz band, ISM band (868 MHz EU, 908/916 MHz USA)	250 Kbps (2,4 GHz band)	63 Bytes	Public	100 ms	10–100 m
Bluetooth	2,4 GHz	1 Mbps	100 Bytes	Public	10 ms	10–100 m
ANT/ANT+	2450, 2457 MHz	20 Kbps	8 Bytes	Unlicensed	10 ms	30–100 m
Z-wave	ISM band (868 MHz EU, 908/916 MHz USA)	9,6 Kbps	64 Bytes	Public	200 ms	20–150 m
802.11.a/b/g/n/ac	ISM band (868 MHz EU, 908/916 MHz USA)	11–1000 Mbps	64–512 Bytes	Public	1–10 ms	10–250 m
Enhanced ShockBurst (ESB)	2,4 GHz	1–2 Mbps	252–255 Bytes	Public	10 ms	25–500 m
802.11ah	2,4/3,7/5,0 GHz	0,65–234 Mbps	64–512 Bytes	Public	20–100 ms	100–1000 m
ZigBee	2,4 GHz band, ISM band (868 MHz EU, 908/916 MHz USA)	250 Kbps (2,4 GHz band) 20–40 Kbps (ISM band)	128 Bytes	Public	10 ms	100–1000 m

Additional standard long-range wireless technologies like GSM-R and TETRA were excluded in the comparison because they are in the way to be replaced for LTE-R and 5G technologies in train-to-ground communications.

Table 2. Comparison table of low-power wireless technologies long-range up to 50 km [9, 10].

Name	Freq.	Data rate	Packet size	Use	Latency	Range
802.11p	2,4/3,7/5,0 GHz	6–108 Mbps	–	Unlicensed	40–200 ms	50–3000 m
NB-IoT	GSM/LTE	250 Kbps	1600 Bytes	Licensed	1,6–10 s	10 km
LoRaWAN	2,4 GHz band, ISM band (868 MHz EU, 908/916 MHz USA)	0,3–50 Kbps	15 Bytes	Public	4–120 s	20 km
Sigfox	2,4 GHz band, ISM band (868 MHz EU, 908/916 MHz USA)	0,1–1 Kbps	12 Bytes	Licensed	1,6–10 s	50 km
Symphony link	2,4 GHz band, ISM band (868 MHz EU, 908/916 MHz USA)	10–250 Kbps	–	Unlicensed	100 ms–120 s	50 km
WiMAX	2,4 GHz ISM band 2,4–2,7 GHz Lic. 5,8 GHz Unlic. 10,5 GHz Lic.	6–376 Mbps	–	Public/Licensed	50 ms	1–50 km

3   Use Cases Enabled by the Freight Telematics Systems

The freight train wireless communication backbone is a crucial enabler of several different applications. For that, a list of Use Cases (UC) have been defined, and a methodology to analyze the wOBU system operational scenarios with that aim of defining the high-level architecture has been chosen. Some uses cases are described [9]:

Continuous Condition Monitoring. This use case results from the need for predictive maintenance and real-time condition information. Collecting data directly from the train and wagons, through an automated onboard monitoring system, can provide mass data to enable the use of suitable big data solutions. Predictive modelling of maintenance tasks can be enabled, reducing and hence improves reliability and safety.

A wOBU, as part of a Wagon Monitoring System (WMS), act as a sink node to collect data from source nodes in the form of autonomous sensors on the wagon. The wOBU, in this case, allows data pre-processing, storage, and transmission to the locomotive and wayside. Onboard and wayside condition monitoring can be used to derive real-time safety information in the form of pre-warning measures and a later stage for predictive maintenance.

Cargo Monitoring System. There are many companies and technological tools to track and monitoring cargo containers remotely, but this information is not shared, or complemented, with the train information. This UC studies the Cargo Status Tracking and Logistics Planning. In an automatized scenario, the goods managers need to have information about the cargo status and its location in real-time to improve the logistics planning on the fly.

A wOBU, as part of a Cargo Monitoring System (CMS), can enable cargo logistics applications to solve the cargo status-monitoring problem allowing real-time access to data about the wOBU and the cargo status.

This UC has to provide solutions to several needs like composition computerization, cargo movement, or predictive cargo logistics, among others. Composition Computerization allows the customization of the locomotive settings per train composition on the fly. This process requires performing a cargo status diagnosis and the system must be able to detect cargo failures like cargo movement or cargo break down. Cargo Logistics has to implement the logistics workflow to produce historical data to improve logistics planning and allow the good managers to access this data.

Onboard Positioning. In the current freight environment, positioning services are included to enable other applications. An intelligent wagon can provide its position for operational purposes, logistics together with CMS, for monitoring infrastructure together with WMS. This information could be available in real-time for the corresponding stakeholders. Two positioning strategies are foreseen: stand-alone wagon positioning and collaborative positioning of the train, where the loco would help to improve the wagon position estimation accuracy. This UC provides solutions to several needs, like composition computerization, and the functions of CMS and WMS.

Wayside and Onboard Monitoring Data Integration. Wayside train monitoring solutions, such as Hot Axle Bearing Detectors, are already present in the market from several years. These systems are mainly used for safety purpose, e.g., to prevent derailment or a few cases for infrastructure maintenance related issues. There is still a great potential to use the same information, enriched with the one obtained directly from onboard monitoring systems, for other purposes, such as wagon maintenance logistics and safety issues of dangerous freight.

Wayside monitoring systems are installed at certain specific points along a line and belong to the Infrastructure Manager. The information obtained by these systems is a single type, representing the state of the train during its passage at the monitoring point. Onboard monitoring systems, on the other hand, perform continuous monitoring on specific parameters and these systems belong to the fleet operator, wagon owner, or the company in charge of maintenance. These systems are complementary, being the set of monitoring parameters probably overlapping, but for sure not the same, and the characteristics of the information collected, e.g., accuracy and completeness, different. By integrating the information obtained by both types of systems, a complete vision of the wagons and load current situation is obtained.

4 Wagon Monitoring System

Due to the complexity in adapting new technological solutions in rail freight, because of the vast configuration options for different applications, the needed investment, and also safety regulations and certifications, among other challenges, an appropriate approach to develop an FTS is to propose a modular system. With this modularisation, the owners, operators and regulator entities may choose the optimal configuration for the required application and available budget, as well to design strategies to add capabilities to the system.

A proposal for a basic Intelligent Freight Wagon (b-IFW) equipped with a basic FTS, which has minimum operational capabilities to consider it intelligent, must suppose some Use Cases and common operational scenarios (Fig. 2). For this proposal, the Continuous Condition Monitoring is the main challenge to solve, and typical operational scenarios like non-electrified wagons, train composition deprived of interwagon and loco connectivity, lack of intelligent wagons in the train composition, the existing intelligent wagons operating independently, operation in zones with unstable or non-existent connection to the 2G/3G/LTE network and GPS signal.

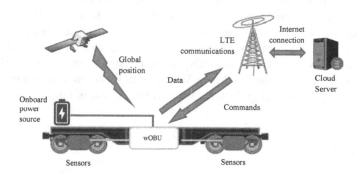

Fig. 2. A b-IFW with the WMS.

From the previous considerations, some starting requirements have been defined: low-power-consumption electronics; power supply for extended autonomy; adaptability to use several wired or wireless sensors; a central unit to collect, pre-process and store the data from the sensors; wireless wagon-to-ground communication capability; GNSS connectivity and dead-reckoning positioning. Besides, the system can be considered intelligent if it is capable of pre-processing or processing data and, as a result, executes specific routines. Different intelligence levels can be reached depending on the complexity in the data computation and the taken actions. A basic intelligent algorithm should verify the data sensors are in a pre-programmed range and, if data is out of range, send alarms. It also had to be able to package the sensor's data, with time and position stamps, to transfer it to ground and store it onboard as a backup. A different approach, with all computing data made in a ground server after the data transfer, may result in a conventional telematics system with deprived of intelligence if communication fails.

A b-IFW (Fig. 2) should include a wOBU as a central unit with the capacity to receive GNSS signal for positioning, short-range wireless connectivity with sensors in the wagon, bidirectional long-range connectivity for train-to-ground communications, and a battery to assure its autonomy from months to years.

In the matter of intra-wagon communications, the sensors have wired connectivity with the wOBU to optimize power consumption. The wOBU design, thinking in modularity as a priority, is able to have wireless communication and be configurable to link with sensors in the most common short-range protocols, even with wired connections, and those have to be self-powered with batteries for long-last autonomy.

A monitoring system, depending on the number of sensors, their sampling rate, and operation mode, may generate significant amounts of data, not a problem for a big data algorithm, but a big challenge for a telematics system. The generated data has to be transmitted to a hub or other node, and wireless communications are by far the most power-consuming process in the system when the link needs to be on permanently, thence the importance to optimize the data transfer. An effective way to drastically reduce the data size to be transmitted is sending only alarms or event detections but, in many cases, this is not suitable for the significance of the data. Hence, an efficient data compression algorithm is a convenient option for shrinking data to transfer and optimize transmission time.

The present configuration could ensure a basic level of operability for all the aftermentioned use cases. Continuous Condition Monitoring can be achieved by sending data sensors continuously, periodically, event-triggered, or out-of-range alarms from wOBU to interwagon linkage or directly to ground. The wOBU will be capable of Onboard Positioning with GNSS, and dead-reckoning if satellite signals are unstable or lost. This configuration also endows the Intelligent Wagon with short-range communications to Wayside and Cargo Monitoring Systems for data integration in upgraded or advanced use cases.

5 Conclusions

Monitoring systems in freight trains may have many design considerations and particular challenges for every specific application. Modular design, with standard communication protocols, will be crucial for an efficient implementation in rail freight.

In general, no matter the application or configuration, any intelligent onboard telematics system has to use some wireless communication link. Appropriate short and long-range communication technologies must be selected for specific configurations and applications.

These systems, to be considered intelligent, must be able to pre-process collected data before transmission and take actions accordingly.

Acknowledgements. The authors acknowledge the European Commission and the Shift2Rail JU, which support the FR8RAIL II project in terms of funding and coordination.

References

1. European Commission. Mobility and Transport. White Paper 2011. https://ec.europa.eu/transport/themes/strategies/2011_white_paper_en (2020). Accessed 22 Jan 2020

2. Shift2Rail. Innovation Programme 5. https://shift2rail.org/research-development/ip5/ (2020). Accessed 22 Jan 2020

3. Mendizabal, J., Goya, J., Alvarado, U., Bergstrand, J., Ekmark, A.: FR8RAIL: Development of functional requirements for sustainable and attractive European Rail Freight. In: World Congress on Railway Research (2019)

4. Shift2Rail. FR8RAIL II. https://projects.shift2rail.org/s2r_ip5_n.aspx?p=FR8RAIL%20ii# (2020). Accessed 22 Jan 2020

5. Hodge, V., O'Keefe, S., Weeks, M., Moulds, A.: Wireless sensor networks for condition monitoring in the railway industry: A survey. IEEE Trans. Intell. Transp. Syst. **16**(3), 1088–1106 (2015)

6. Bernal, E., Spiryagin, M., Cole, C.: Onboard condition monitoring sensors, systems and techniques for freight railway vehicles: A review. IEEE Sens. J. **19**(1), 4–24 (2019)

7. Fraga-Lamas, P., Fernández-Caramés, T.M., Castedo, L.: Towards the internet of smart trains: A review on industrial IoT-Connected railways. Sensors **17**, 1457 (2017)

8. Mahlknecht, S., Madani, S.: On architecture of low power wireless sensor networks for container tracking and monitoring applications. In: IEEE International Conference on Industrial Informatics, pp. 353–358 (2007)

9. Mendizabal, J., Ramirez, R., Goya, J., Batista, D., Parrilla, F.: Technologies evaluation for freight train's wireless backbone, freight train wireless communication backbone architecture. In: World Congress on Railway Research (2019)

10. Parrilla, F., et al.: Technologies evaluation for freight train's wireless backbone, communication technologies for vehicles. In: Nets4Cars/Nets4Trains/Nets4Aircraft 2018. Lecture Notes in Computer Science, vol. 10796, pp. 79–91 (2018)

NEWNECTAR: A New gEneration of Adaptable Wireless Sensor NEtwork for Way Side objeCTs in rAilway enviRonments

Dereje Mechal Molla[1]([✉]), Hakim Badis[1]([✉]), Laurent George[1]([✉]),
and Marion Berbineau[2]([✉])

[1] LIGM, ESIEE Paris, University Gustave Eiffel, CNRS,
77454 Marne-la-Vallée, France
{dereje.molla,laurent.george}@esiee.fr, hakim.badis@univ-eiffel.fr
[2] COSYS, Université Gustave Eiffel, Villeneuve d'Ascq, France
marion.berbineau@univ-eiffel.fr

Abstract. Efficient data collection from railway environment is crucial for railway infrastructure monitoring. Due to the various type of data to be collected from the environment, a large number of heterogeneous sensors are installed at different places on the railway infrastructure. These sensors are equipped with low-power wireless communication transceivers and grouped into Wireless Sensor Network (WSN) domains. Each WSN domain is configured to have one or multiple sink nodes (static or mobile, carried by vehicles such as trains or drones) responsible for collecting data and forwarding them outside the WSN to a cloud server. As the number of deployed WSN domains and sensor nodes rises with a high degree of heterogeneity, the tasks of data gathering, resource optimization and Quality of Service (QoS)-based service deployment become complex and highly challenging. In this paper, we propose a new generation of WSN for adaptive data collection and forwarding, called NEWNECTAR, based on the combination of both Software Defined Radio (SDR) and Software Defined Network (SDN) technologies at the sink node. NEWNECTAR defines a universal sink node thanks to the use of a programmable transceiver in forms of a General Purpose Processor (GPP)-based SDR platform, which enables the support of multiple wireless communication technologies in a single interface. Additionally, an SDN support is added to the NEWNECTAR to efficiently control the traffic forwarding from sink nodes to the cloud server and enhance its QoS profile (bandwidth, latency, reliability, *etc.*). Based on the proposed architecture, theoretical performance analysis of GPP-based SDR platform has been performed and its performance has been tested with varied train speeds. The result indicates that GPP-based SDR platform can collect information for trains having speeds upto 300 km/h.

Keywords: Wireless Sensor Networks · Railway environment monitoring · SDR · SDN · Universal sink node

© Springer Nature Switzerland AG 2020
F. Krief et al. (Eds.): Nets4Cars/Nets4Trains/Nets4Aircraft 2020, LNCS 12574, pp. 166–178, 2020.
https://doi.org/10.1007/978-3-030-66030-7_15

1 Introduction

The railway sector plays a critical role in economic and social development of any region in the world. It offers an efficient and sustainable transport mode to carry numerous passengers and goods on a predetermined fixed route and schedule. It is the second transport mode after road, but before air and maritime transport. According to the passenger transport statistics [1], in 2017, more than 9.6 billion passengers travelled on national railway networks in the European Union (EU). This is considerably larger than the air and maritime passengers, where the same year has registered 1 billion air passengers at EU level and 415 million maritime embarking and disembarking in EU ports. However, while road transport is still the principal mode of transport with passengers due to its greater mobility and flexibility, it is much more polluting than rail transport [2].

The infrastructure of the rail network is a complex system that aims to offer high quality rail services. It include several elements such as trains, railway lines, passenger stations, structures (bridges, tunnels, building, *etc.*), signals, level crossings, *etc.* Railway infrastructure monitoring is a crucial and vital task for transport safety, infrastructure sustainability and infrastructure adaptability or flexibility to existing and emerging needs. It requests the collection of various data related to meteorology, lineside vegetation, structures and vehicles behaviours and aging, energy consumption, maintenance and diagnosis, property management (energy consumption, structures aging, trolleys management, *etc.*), exploitation and operation, customer services, *etc.* As a consequence, Wireless Sensor Networks (WSN) are now widely deployed to capture and collect autonomously distributed information [3,4]. The sensed data is then delivered to a cloud server and processed in order to extract relevant and targeted information that will allow defining criteria on which decision-making process of different stakeholders will be based at operational levels of exploitation.

In railway environments, the transmission of collected/sensed data towards a global information system (cloud server) constitutes a big challenge regarding the complexity and size of this type of environment, the radio spectrum scarcity and the drastic electromagnetic rules and regulations. Each WSN domain in the railway environment consists of a set of sensor nodes and a sink node that can be static or mobile. The sensors may be gathered in several independent domains of WSN. As of today, the wireless technologies and network architectures considered for WSN domains are very heterogeneous in terms of the used wireless communication technologies and capability of sensor nodes in processing, memory, accuracy and energy consumption. The heterogeneity in WSN domains significantly increases the complexity of sink nodes reuse to interact with different WSN domains, data forwarding to the cloud server and satisfying QoS requirements of tele-monitoring services. To deal with these challenges, we propose a new generation of WSN for adaptive data collection and forwarding based on software defined approaches: Software Defined Radio (SDR) at physical layer and Software Defined Network (SDN) at network layer. It includes a universal sink node to collect data across heterogeneous WSN domains, a centralized SDN controller to remotely configure the routing policy and traffic control of sink nodes, and sensor nodes (end devices and domain heads) that remain unchanged.

The paper is organized as follows: Sect. 2 will present background and related works. Section 3 will detail the chosen adaptable WSN architecture based on SDR and SDN. Section 4 will show performance analysis of SDR platforms in the railway setting. We will conclude and give perspective in Sect. 5.

2   WSNs for Railway Infrastructure Monitoring

Maintenance of the global railway system is crucial to guarantee perfect operation of the different entities of the railway system, namely tracks, signalling, rolling stock, facilities (bridges, tunnels...), catenary, electrical devices, *etc.* Optimisation and efficiency of the railway system depends on real time monitoring of the different entities. In [4], Table II and Table III summarized the fixed and moving objects monitored in the Railway systems and give a good vision of the huge amount of data to be collected and forwarded autonomously to the cloud server. P. Fraga-Lamas *et al.* [5] presented a large summary related to advanced services for the Internet of Things (IoT)-connected railways. Figure 1 illustrates a use case showing several types of sensors placed at different locations of the railway and wayside environment.

The development of networking and wireless technologies has open the door to the deployment of various type of WSNs in the railway sector, allowing important numbers of distributed sensors to be networked to constantly monitor fixed and moving objects in the railway systems. The wireless sensor nodes can be installed everywhere and organized in different domains and based on different wireless technologies. Deploying these varied type of wireless technologies poses challenges such as resource optimization, QoS, scalability, energy consumption, *etc.* [6,7]. In this context, we have proposed a new generation of low-power and resource-constrained WSN for adaptive data collection and forwarding based on software defined approaches.

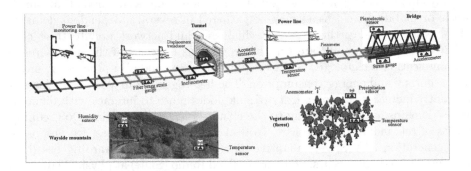

Fig. 1. Railway infrastructure and wireless sensor nodes.

3   NEWNECTAR Architecture

The data collection in heterogeneous WSN domains and data forwarding to an external cloud server tasks raise several challenges such as sink nodes' control, data traffic management, routing policy configuration, energy efficiency and spectrum scarcity. To cope with these challenges and form a WSN domain out of independently deployed WSNs with heterogeneous wireless communication technologies, we propose to develop a New gEneration of adaptable Wireless sensor NEtwork for way side objeCTs in rAilway enviRonments (NEWNECTAR). It is an adaptive data collection and forwarding strategy based on software defined approaches both at the physical and higher layers. Figure 2 illustrates a general view of the proposed NEWNECTAR architecture. At the physical layer, it defines a universal sink node using GPP-based SDR platform able to interact with several WSN nodes through its reconfiguration capability. At higher level, SDN technique is added to the architecture to demonstrate reconfigurability and adaptability features at network level when needed for example in case of specific event in some part of the network (see Sect. 3.2 for discussion about SDN).

As shown in Fig. 2, the universal mobile sink (SDR platform) on a moving train collects data from WSN domain heads or directly from sensor end-devices until it gets to a data upload zone to upload collected data to the cloud server. Group of fixed sensor nodes, each node equipped with one or more sensors and a radio transceiver, in the railway infrastructure form the WSN domain. The universal mobile sink node, capable of supporting multiple wireless technologies, reconfigures itself to the radio transceiver of the target WSN domain. Indeed,

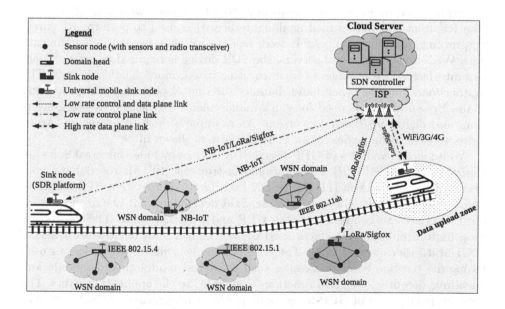

Fig. 2. Proposed NEWNECTAR architecture.

in NEWNECTAR, the advantage of fixed route of railway transport system and scheduled timetable of trains are considered to enable reconfiguration of the SDR platform towards the desired wireless technology. In addition to the universal mobile sink node used to collect and forward data, NEWNECTAR considers the use of long-range wireless technologies to enhance the reliability of the WSN. Using long-range wireless technologies, WSN nodes can directly forward collected data from WSN domains to the cloud server. It is also worth mentioning that, the architecture tries to fulfill some of the fifth generation (5G) cellular network technology requirements such as by supporting large number of WSN nodes and covering all WSN domains in the railway line. Moreover, employing low power wide area cellular network technologies in the proposed NEWNECTAR architecture offers reduction of network energy usage, which is one of the main requirements of 5G technology.

3.1   Universal Sink Node

To gather sensed data in WSN domains and forward to an external cloud server, a universal sink node carried by a train is used. This sink node is equipped with GPP-based SDR platform which is defined as a re-configurable and programmable radio communication system where hardware components are implemented in software on a generic microprocessor rather than hardware [8]. It is capable of supporting multiple wireless technologies by executing separate software program for each wireless technology. It is assembled by combining an SDR device with baseband processing (GPP) platform through a suitable communication interface. The SDR device is a programmable device constructed by integrating one or more radio frequency (RF) front-ends with a motherboard. The RF front-end (also called as daughterboard) is used to perform RF filtering, mixing, amplification, *etc.* Indeed, as the sink node needs to communicate with WSN nodes and cloud servers, the SDR device is required to have at least two interfaces. This is achieved by integrating two or more daughterboards. The motherboard, on the other hand, handles the digital part of signal processing chain. Specifically, it is used for clock management, digital and analog conversion, and digital up/down conversion. An example of how to aggregate two or more wireless technologies on an SDR platform is shown in [9].

Well known examples of GPP-based SDR devices include Universal Software Radio Peripheral (USRP) from National Instrument [10], Microsoft Sora from Microsoft Research Asia [11], LimeSDR from Lime Microsystems [12], HackRF One from Great Scott Gadgets [13], *etc.* SDR devices support one or more standard interfaces to connect with the GPP and exchange data. The most common high throughput interfaces used by well known SDR devices are USB3.0, 10Gigabit Ethernet, and PCIe. The GPP is a single or multi-core processor used to handle the baseband processing such as digital modulation/demodulation, encoding/decoding, *etc.*, and functions from MAC to the application layers. The general architecture of GPP-based SDR platform integrating all the three components and with two transceiver daughterboards is shown in Fig. 3.

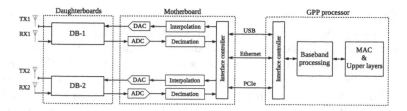

Fig. 3. GPP-based SDR platform block diagram.

The universal sink node, in one of its interfaces, uses low-rate short and long range wireless communication technologies to communicate with WSN nodes (sensor end-devices and domain heads). Examples of low rate, short range technologies include IEEE 802.15.1, IEEE 802.15.4, nRF24, *etc.*, and long range technologies such as NB-IoT, LoRa, Sigfox, *etc.*, as indicated in Fig. 2. Whereas, to communicate with the cloud server a high-power, high rate wireless communication technologies are used on another interface. This is due to the fact that the universal sink node, as it is responsible to collect, process and store sensed data from several sensor nodes, is required to support higher rate and higher radio range WSN technologies. Typical examples of such technologies include IEEE 802.11x (WiFi), LTE, *etc.* In addition to the universal sink node, other static sink nodes that wish to forward sensed data directly to cloud server use low-power long range wireless technologies.

3.2   Data Forwarding Control

Elements of WSN (or part of the WSN) domains in the railway infrastructure such as domain heads, sink nodes or communication links could get endangered due to mobility, wind, flooding, *etc.* When such events occur, efficient forwarding of data from the sink nodes to the external cloud server becomes a problem unless the network can dynamically adapt to these changes. In order to adapt the WSN to these changes, components of the WSN should be controlled and reconfigured dynamically to switch into an appropriate alternate wireless interface. One of the approach to control the data forwarding decision is to use Software Defined Networking (SDN) solution. Various researchers have studied the development of SDN solution to WSNs [6,14,15]. SDN is a network paradigm characterized by its ability to control, change and manage the behavior of a network and network devices in a dynamic manner. To achieve this, the control plane is moved off the network devices to an external controller. By this way, the controller can configure and send the forwarding rules over the control plane to the network devices via an SDN protocol. An example of well known SDN protocol for use in WSN infrastructure include Sensor Openflow [6].

In NEWNECTAR architecture, only universal sink nodes integrate the SDN technology as they are responsible for forwarding data (data plane). Since the universal sink nodes are implemented using GPP-based SDR platform, the SDN solution will be incorporated to the deployed SDR platform. Thus, a centralized

SDN controller can dynamically and remotely (from cloud server) configure the routing rules of the sink nodes through a dedicated Light SDN protocol. In order to provide a reliable on-demand control between the sink nodes and the SDN controller to transmit small amounts of control packets, the SDN protocol is performed over long range and low power/rate wireless technologies such as NB-IoT, LoRa, Sigfox, *etc.* On the other hand, high rate wireless technologies such as IEEE802.11x, LTE, *etc.*, are used for data forwarding to meet the QoS traffic requirements. This is illustrated in Fig. 2 with separate links for control and data plane.

4   Data Collection Using GPP-Based SDR Platform

The speed of trains and the short distance covered by short-range wireless technologies raises a concern on how GPP-based SDR platforms can perform to collect data in railway based WSNs. The main question on this aspect is, will the SDR platform collect data from WSN nodes before the train goes out of the communication range of the WSN node? To illustrate this, we first discuss how data collection can be performed in railway environment monitoring using SDR platforms as sink node of the WSN. Then, we present latency analysis and numerical result to show the performance of SDR platforms in railways.

4.1   Data Collection and Performance Analysis of SDR Platforms

To collect data using GPP-based SDR platforms, the sink node need to connect with WSN node (sensor node or domain head). This is performed by handshake procedure similar to the procedure followed between legacy wireless technologies. Two modes of handshake can be considered: beacon enabled and non-beacon enabled (or Ad-hoc) mode. The first step, in beacon enabled mode, is to send a request for pairing (pairing request in BLE, beacon in IEEE 802.15.4, IEEE 802.11ah and LoRa), and then perform association and/or authentication, key distribution, *etc.*, depending on the protocol. Finally, exchange the data and close the connection. In non-beacon enabled mode, the SDR platform directly requests the data (data request in IEEE 802.15.4 and IEEE 802.11ah, and Get data in nRF24) and close the connection. In both cases, we assume the SDR platform switches to the intended WSN technology before entering the coverage range of WSN nodes using Global Positioning System (GPS) location or time-scheduling [16]. Moreover, in beacon enabled mode, we consider beacons are already prepared and stored in the SDR platform to reduce the latency introduced due to packet generation during the pairing phase. Figure 4 illustrates these procedures.

We define the time the sink node takes to collect data from the WSN nodes as the latency of the SDR platform. It is the total time spent in performing each step during the handshake process as indicated in Fig. 4. The latency of GPP-based SDR platform can be computed using Fig. 3 where performing a single step (sending/receiving a packet) in the handshake process will undergo

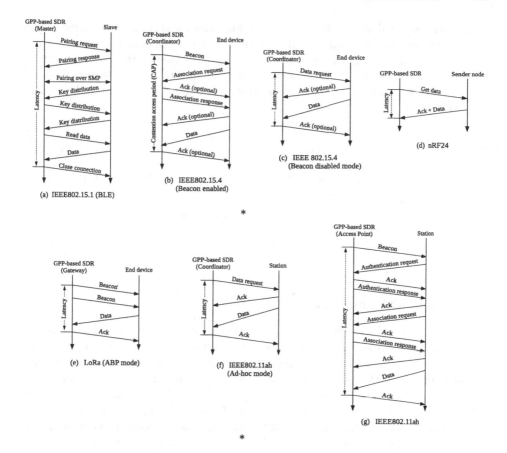

Fig. 4. Handshake between SDR platform and selected wireless technologies.

generating/consuming a packet and transmitting/receiving the packet through an interface to/from the SDR device. Consequently, the latency in GPP-based SDR platform can be given by the sum of the latencies at the GPP processor, used interface and SDR device, for TX and RX path separately. The total latency, then, becomes the sum of all the latencies (including TX and RX latencies) due to each step of the handshake process.

The wireless technologies have limited coverage range (from less than 100 meters to several kilometers) [17]. This imposes a limit on the time required for a moving train to perform all the operations (launching the target wireless technology and performing the handshake). Considering constant train speed for Urban, Inter-City and High Speed trains, ideal coverage by the universal sink node and WSN transceivers and free space path loss, we can determine the time a passing train will be in communication range with a particular WSN node, as illustrated in Table 1. Please note that the coverage range of NB-IoT, LTE-M, EC-GSM-IoT, LoRa and Sigfox given by their respective specification is different for urban and rural areas. Hence, the time for Urban and Inter-city railway types for these technologies is computed with their Urban area coverage and for High Speed their rural area coverage is used. Indeed, in reality the communication coverage range and hence the time are affected due to several factors such as by the speed of train, frequency of the wireless technology, Doppler fading, path loss, *etc.* [18].

Table 1. Time (in seconds) a train can be in communication range with WSN node.

Railway type	Max. speed (km/h)	BLE	802.15.4	nRF24	802.11ah	NB-IoT	LTE-M	EC-GSM-IoT	LoRa	Sigfox
Urban	80	9	9	8	90	90	450	450	450	900
Inter-city	180	4	4	4	40	40	200	200	200	400
High speed	300	2.4	2.4	2.4	24	240	360	360	480	960

4.2   Numerical Result and Discussion

To compute the single step (in the handshake process) latency of GPP-based SDR platforms, numerical analysis has been performed at each part of the platform. For the SDR device and interface, theoretical minimal latencies are computed using the SDR buffer size and ADC/DAC clock rate, and possible high performance interface speed, respectively. However, for the GPP latency, we conducted experimental test on Intel x86_64 Core i7 microprocessor as the GPP processor. It is configured as having 8 cores running 3.3 GHz clock speed; and Ubuntu 18.04.2 LTS and Linux 5.3.0–45 generic operating system. Selected wireless technologies are tested based on their implementation on GNU Radio [19] by different authors. For IEEE 802.15.1 from [20], IEEE 802.15.4 from [21], nRF24 from [22], IEEE 802.11ah from [23], and LoRa from [24]. The test measurements are performed using `perf-stat` tool [25]. We then compute the total minimal latency using all the steps performed to collect data from the respective wireless technology. Please note that, the propagation time from sink node to the WSN nodes is assumed to be negligible (in the order of few hundred nanoseconds). The total latency of GPP-based SDR platform for selected wireless technology is depicted in Table 2.

Table 2 illustrates the performance of GPP-based SDR platform with respect to latency. From the table we see that the latency at the GPP processor is much larger than the latency at the SDR device and interface. This implies large portion of the total latency is contributed due to the baseband and MAC processing by the GPP processor. To minimize the effect of this processing, we checked two cases by removing some steps from the pairing procedure (such as disabling beacons, authentication, association, *etc.*) and taking an assumption that the baseband and MAC functions are handled by Field Programmable Gate Array (FPGA) inside the SDR device or other hardware accelerators such as Graphics Processing Unit (GPUs) and Digital Signal Processors (DSPs). The effect

Table 2. Minimal latency of GPP-based SDR platform.

Wireless technology	Comm.Interface	SDR device	TX/RX	Min. latency (ms) SDR device	Interface	GPP processor	Min. Total latency (ms) With GPP	Without GPP	Railway support (with GPP) Urban	Inter-city	High speed
IEEE 802.15.1	USB2.0	HackRF	TX	$183x10^{-6}$	$17x10^{-3}$	210.51	1052.64	0.086	✓	✓	✓
			RX	6.55	$17x10^{-3}$	207.72	1071.44	32.84			
	10Gig.Eth	USRP-X3x0	TX	$7.5x10^{-6}$	$2.5x10^{-3}$	210.51	1052.56	0.01	✓	✓	✓
			RX	4.47	$2.5x10^{-3}$	207.72	1060.96	22.36			
	USB3.0	USRP-B2x0	TX	$48.8x10^{-6}$	$3.2x10^{-3}$	210.51	1052.56	0.02	✓	✓	✓
			RX	3.28	$3.2x10^{-3}$	207.72	1055.02	16.42			
	PCIe-x8	Sora	TX	$75x10^{-6}$	$1x10^{-3}$	210.51	1052.55	0.005	✓	✓	✓
			RX	0.95	$1x10^{-3}$	207.72	1043.35	4.75			
	PCIe-x4	LimeSDR	TX	$9.37x10^{-6}$	$2.1x10^{-3}$	210.51	1052.56	0.01	✓	✓	✓
			RX	0.04	$2.1x10^{-3}$	207.72	1038.81	0.21			
IEEE 802.15.4 (Beacon enabled)	USB2.0	HackRF	TX	$183x10^{-6}$	$17x10^{-3}$	226.56	906.31	0.068	✓	✓	✓
			RX	6.55	$17x10^{-3}$	224.69	693.77	19.70			
	10Gig.Eth	USRP-X3x0	TX	$7.5x10^{-6}$	$2.5x10^{-3}$	226.56	906.25	0.01	✓	✓	✓
			RX	4.47	$2.5x10^{-3}$	224.69	687.48	13.42			
	USB3.0	USRP-B2x0	TX	$48.8x10^{-6}$	$3.2x10^{-3}$	226.56	906.25	0.013	✓	✓	✓
			RX	3.28	$3.2x10^{-3}$	224.69	683.92	9.85			
	PCIe-x8	Sora	TX	$75x10^{-6}$	$1x10^{-3}$	226.56	906.24	0.0043	✓		✓
			RX	0.95	$1x10^{-3}$	224.69	676.92	2.85			
	PCIe-x4	LimeSDR	TX	$9.37x10^{-6}$	$2.1x10^{-3}$	226.56	906.25	0.0084	✓	✓	✓
			RX	0.04	$2.1x10^{-3}$	224.69	674.19	0.13			
IEEE 802.15.4 (Beacon disabled)	USB2.0	HackRF	TX	$183x10^{-6}$	$17x10^{-3}$	226.56	453.15	0.0344	✓	✓	✓
			RX	6.55	$17x10^{-3}$	224.69	462.51	13.134			
	10Gig.Eth	USRP-X3x0	TX	$7.5x10^{-6}$	$2.5x10^{-3}$	226.56	453.12	0.005	✓	✓	✓
			RX	4.47	$2.5x10^{-3}$	224.69	458.33	8.945			
	USB3.0	USRP-B2x0	TX	$48.8x10^{-6}$	$3.2x10^{-3}$	226.56	453.13	0.0065	✓	✓	✓
			RX	3.28	$3.2x10^{-3}$	224.69	455.95	6.566			
	PCIe-x8	Sora	TX	$75x10^{-6}$	$1x10^{-3}$	226.56	453.12	0.0022	✓	✓	✓
			RX	0.95	$1x10^{-3}$	224.69	451.28	1.902			
	PCIe-x4	LimeSDR	TX	$9.37x10^{-6}$	$2.1x10^{-3}$	226.56	453.12	0.0042	✓	✓	✓
			RX	0.04	$2.1x10^{-3}$	224.69	449.46	0.084			
nRF24	USB2.0	HackRF	TX	$183x10^{-6}$	$17x10^{-3}$	205.26	205.28	0.017	✓	✓	✓
			RX	6.55	$17x10^{-3}$	235.94	242.51	6.567			
	10Gig.Eth	USRP-X3x0	TX	$7.5x10^{-6}$	$2.5x10^{-3}$	205.26	205.26	0.0025	✓	✓	✓
			RX	4.47	$2.5x10^{-3}$	235.94	240.41	4.472			
	USB3.0	USRP-B2x0	TX	$48.8x10^{-6}$	$3.2x10^{-3}$	205.26	205.26	0.0032	✓	✓	✓
			RX	3.28	$3.2x10^{-3}$	235.94	239.22	3.283			
	PCIe-x8	Sora	TX	$75x10^{-6}$	$1x10^{-3}$	205.26	205.26	0.0011	✓	✓	✓
			RX	0.95	$1x10^{-3}$	235.94	236.89	0.951			
	PCIe-x4	LimeSDR	TX	$9.37x10^{-6}$	$2.1x10^{-3}$	205.26	205.26	0.0021	✓	✓	✓
			RX	0.04	$2.1x10^{-3}$	235.94	235.98	0.0421			
IEEE 802.11ah	USB2.0	HackRF	TX	$183x10^{-6}$	$17x10^{-3}$	356.89	2141.44	0.1031	✓	✓	✓
			RX	6.55	$17x10^{-3}$	349.90	1782.33	32.835			
	10Gig.Eth	USRP-X3x0	TX	$7.5x10^{-6}$	$2.5x10^{-3}$	356.89	2141.35	0.015	✓	✓	✓
			RX	4.47	$2.5x10^{-3}$	349.90	1771.86	22.363			
	USB3.0	USRP-B2x0	TX	$48.8x10^{-6}$	$3.2x10^{-3}$	356.89	2141.36	0.0195	✓	✓	✓
			RX	3.28	$3.2x10^{-3}$	349.90	1765.92	16.416			
	PCIe-x8	Sora	TX	$75x10^{-6}$	$1x10^{-3}$	356.89	2141.35	0.0065	✓	✓	✓
			RX	0.95	$1x10^{-3}$	349.90	1754.25	4.755			
	PCIe-x4	LimeSDR	TX	$9.37x10^{-6}$	$2.1x10^{-3}$	356.89	2141.35	0.0126	✓	✓	✓
			RX	0.04	$2.1x10^{-3}$	349.90	1749.71	0.2105			
IEEE 802.11ah (Ad-hoc mode)	USB2.0	HackRF	TX	$183x10^{-6}$	$17x10^{-3}$	356.89	713.81	0.0344	✓	✓	✓
			RX	6.55	$17x10^{-3}$	349.90	712.93	13.134			
	10Gig.Eth	USRP-X3x0	TX	$7.5x10^{-6}$	$2.5x10^{-3}$	356.89	713.78	0.0050	✓	✓	✓
			RX	4.47	$2.5x10^{-3}$	349.90	708.74	8.945			
	USB3.0	USRP-B2x0	TX	$48.8x10^{-6}$	$3.2x10^{-3}$	356.89	713.78	0.0065	✓	✓	✓
			RX	3.28	$3.2x10^{-3}$	349.90	706.36	6.566			
	PCIe-x8	Sora	TX	$75x10^{-6}$	$1x10^{-3}$	356.89	713.78	0.0022	✓	✓	✓
			RX	0.95	$1x10^{-3}$	349.90	701.70	1.902			
	PCIe-x4	LimeSDR	TX	$9.37x10^{-6}$	$2.1x10^{-3}$	356.89	713.78	0.0042	✓	✓	✓
			RX	0.04	$2.1x10^{-3}$	349.90	699.88	0.0842			
LoRa	USB2.0	HackRF	TX	$183x10^{-6}$	$17x10^{-3}$	260.98	782.99	0.0515	✓	✓	✓
			RX	6.55	$17x10^{-3}$	142.65	149.22	6.567			
	10Gig.Eth	USRP-X3x0	TX	$7.5x10^{-6}$	$2.5x10^{-3}$	260.98	782.95	0.0075	✓	✓	✓
			RX	4.47	$2.5x10^{-3}$	142.65	147.12	4.473			
	USB3.0	USRP-B2x0	TX	$48.8x10^{-6}$	$3.2x10^{-3}$	260.98	782.95	0.0097	✓	✓	✓
			RX	3.28	$3.2x10^{-3}$	142.65	145.93	3.283			
	PCIe-x8	Sora	TX	$75x10^{-6}$	$1x10^{-3}$	260.98	782.94	0.0032	✓	✓	✓
			RX	0.95	$1x10^{-3}$	142.65	143.60	0.951			
	PCIe-x4	LimeSDR	TX	$9.37x10^{-6}$	$2.1x10^{-3}$	260.98	782.95	0.0063	✓	✓	✓
			RX	0.04	$2.1x10^{-3}$	142.65	142.69	0.0421			

of the first case is shown by the latency reduction in IEEE 802.15.4 (beacon disabled) and IEEE 802.11ah (Ad-hoc mode). It has resulted in a latency reduction, respectively, by around 42% and 63%. The second case is illustrated by the result in the table under 'Without GPP' column. The result shows that more than 98% of the latency can be removed from the latency 'With GPP'. However, the processing in hardware accelerators will add very small extra latency. The table also presents whether the performance of GPP-based SDR platforms satisfy the time requirement of the three railways while in communication with WSN nodes, see Table 1. From our result we see that all the considered wireless technologies can transmit their data (or SDR platforms can receive transmitted data) before the train goes out of communication range.

5   Conclusions and Perspectives

This paper proposed a new generation of low-power and resource-constrained WSN architecture, called NEWNECTAR, for adaptive data collection and forwarding in railway environments based on SDR and SDN approaches. A universal mobile sink node is defined in the NEWNECTAR architecture using GPP-based SDR platform to gather data from heterogeneous WSN domains. It uses low rate low power wireless technologies and high rate/power technologies, respectively, to communicate with WSN domains and cloud server. Moreover, to make the architecture more reliable, long range, low rate/power wireless technologies are included to directly forward sensed data from WSN domains to the cloud server. In order to configure and control the universal sink node, SDN solution is proposed where an SDN controller from the cloud server communicates with the SDR platform using SDN protocol through long range low power wireless technologies. As the core element in the NEWNECTAR architecture is the SDR platform, we have presented a theoretical performance analysis, in terms of latency, considering its communication with selected wireless technologies. The obtained numerical result shows that the SDR platform can collect data from WSN domains with train speeds upto 300 km/h. We have also shown that the latency performance can be improved, on average, by half, by removing some steps in the handshake procedure without affecting the data collection process.

For future work, we plan to develop a demonstrator for our NEWNECTAR architecture. Furthermore, we plan to use NFV framework to enhance the reconfigurability and adaptability features of the architecture. This can be shortly described as, since the SDR platform is required to implement several wireless technologies, we propose to use virtual machines (VM) running a single GPP processor dedicated to each wireless technology. Each VM can, then, be scheduled through a hypervisor to launch the target wireless technology.

In the proposed NEWNECTAR architecture, the SDR platforms are assumed to switch to the necessary wireless technology just before entering the communication range of the installed WSN based on location and/or time-schedule. However, this solution can be further enhanced by making the SDR platform detect the type of wireless technology used by WSN domains and launch the target technology. This can be achieved by enabling cognitive radio capabilities such as spectrum detection and adaptable radio access technologies (RAT) on the SDR platform.

References

1. Passenger transport statistics. https://ec.europa.eu/eurostat/statistics-explained/pdfscache/1132.pdf. Accessed Aug 2020
2. Environment sustainability of rail transportation. Available: http://www.railwaysignalling.eu/wp-content/uploads/2014/06/Environmental_Sustainability_of_Rail_transportation__.pdf. Accessed Aug 2020
3. Aboelela, E., Edberg, W., Papakonstantinou, C., Vokkarane, V.: Wireless sensor network based model for secure railway operations. In: 2006 IEEE International Performance Computing and Communications Conference, pp. 6–628 (2006)
4. Hodge, V.J., O'Keefe, S., Weeks, M., Moulds, A.: Wireless sensor networks for condition monitoring in the railway industry: a survey. IEEE Trans. Intell. Transp. Syst. **16**(3), 1088–1106 (2015)
5. Fraga-Lamas, T., Fernández-Caramés, M., Castedo, L.: Towards the internet of smart trains: a review on industrial IOT-connected railways. Sensors **17**, 1–44 (2017)
6. Luo, T., Tan, H., Quek, T.Q.S.: Sensor openflow: Enabling software-defined wireless sensor networks. IEEE Commun. Lett. **16**(11), 1896–1899 (2012)
7. De Gante, A., Aslan, M., Matrawy, A.: Smart wireless sensor network management based on software-defined networking. In: 27th Biennial Symposium on Communications QBSC 2014, pp. 71–75 (2014)
8. Dillinger, M., Madani, K., Alonistioti, N.: Software Defined Radio: Architectures, Systems and Functions. John Wiley & Sons, New Jersey (2005)
9. Molla, D.M., Badis, H., Desta, A.A., George, L., Berbineau, M.: SDR-based reliable and resilient wireless network for disaster rescue operations. In: 2019 International Conference on Information and Communication Technologies for Disaster Management (ICT-DM), pp. 1–7 (2019)
10. Universal software radio peripheral (USRP). https://www.ni.com/fr-fr.html. Accessed Aug 2020
11. Tan, K., Liu, H., Zhang, J., Zhang, Y., Fang, J., Voelker, G.M.: Sora: high-performance software radio using general-purpose multi-core processors. Commun. ACM **54**(1), 99–107 (2011). https://doi.org/10.1145/1866739.1866760
12. Software defined radio - lime microsystems. Accessed Aug 2020. https://limemicro.com/
13. Software defined radio - hackRF one. https://greatscottgadgets.com/hackrf/one/. Accessed Aug 2020
14. Galluccio, L., Milardo, S., Morabito, G., Palazzo, S.: SDN-WISE: design, prototyping and experimentation of a stateful SDN solution for WIreless SEnsor networks. In: 2015 IEEE Conference on Computer Communications (INFOCOM), pp. 513–521. IEEE (2015)
15. Jacobsson, M., Orfanidis, C.: Using software-defined networking principles for wireless sensor networks. In: SNCNW 2015, May 28–29. Karlstad, Sweden (2015)
16. Cañete, E., Chen, J., Díaz, M., Llopis, L., Reyna, A., Rubio, B.: Using wireless sensor networks and trains as data mules to monitor slab track infrastructures. Sensors (Switzerland) **15**(7), 15:101–15:126 (2015)

17. Lee, J., Su, Y., Shen, C.: A comparative study of wireless protocols: Bluetooth, UWB, ZIGBEE, and Wi-Fi. In: IECON 2007 33rd Annual Conference of the IEEE Industrial Electronics Society, pp. 46–51 (2007)
18. Briso-Rodríguez, C., Guan, K., Xuefeng, Y., Kürner, T.: Wireless communications in smart rail transportation systems. Wirel. Commun. Mobile Comput. **2017**, 1–11 (2017)
19. Gnu radio. https://www.gnuradio.org/. Accessed Aug 2020
20. Scapy radio with GNU radio for bleutooth. https://bitbucket.org/cybertools/scapy-radio/src/default/. Accessed Aug 2020
21. Bloessl, B., Leitner, C., Dressler, F., Sommer, C.: A GNU Radio-based IEEE 802.15. 4 Testbed. 12. Gi/Itg FachgesprÄCh Sensornetze, p. 37 (2013)
22. nrf24-sniffer. https://wiki.bitcraze.io/misc:hacks:hackrf#sniffing_nrf24_with_gnu_radio_and_hackrf. Accessed Aug 2020
23. Bloessl, B., Segata, M., Sommer, C., Dressler, F.: An IEEE 802.11a/g/p OFDM receiver for GNU radio, p. 9 (2013)
24. GNU radio OOT module implementing LORA. https://github.com/BastilleResearch/gr-lora. Accessed Aug 2020
25. Linux kernel profiling with perf. https://perf.wiki.kernel.org/index.php/Tutorial. Accessed Aug 2020

Air

Allowing People to Communicate After a Disaster Using FANETs

Frédéric Guinand[1,2](✉) , François Guérin[3] , and Pawel Lubniewski[2]

[1] Normandy Univ, UNIHAVRE, LITIS Lab, Rouen, France
`frederic.guinand@univ-lehavre.fr`
[2] Cardinal Stefan Wyszynski University in Warsaw, Warsaw, Poland
`{f.guinand,p.lubniewski}@uksw.edu.pl`
[3] Normandy Univ, UNIHAVRE, GREAH Lab, Le Havre, France
`francois.guerin@univ-lehavre.fr`

Abstract. When a disaster occurs, during a long period of time people suffer to have no means to communicate with their relatives. The presented work aims at proposing a solution composed of a ground station located nearby the damaged area coupled with a swarm of drones. The ground station plays the role of a gateway between cellular networks, that are still up but out of reach of people, with drones that carry messages from and to people located in the disastered region. We analyze the possibility of deploying drones with fixed positions and a more flexible solution allowing drones to move but at the cost of intermittent communications, allowing only sms-like messages. We show that using the same number of drones, allowing drones to move improves dramatically the coverage of people with respect to a FANET in which drones stay at a fixed position. We also show that even for a very restricted number of drones, for reasonable communication ranges, almost all the people benefit from an important average connected time.

Keywords: Flying ad hoc networks · Disaster · Intermittent communication network · Coverage · Swarm of drones · UAV

1 Introduction

In the two last reports of IPCC[1] many clues show that Global Warming entails meteorological events more and more sudden and strong like hurricanes, forest fires and floods. Most often, communication networks become out of order during periods ranging from few days to several weeks. This is especially true when the events are floods (Hurricane Katrina in 2005 for instance or very recently in South of France (Vesubie and Roya Valleys)) because the accesses are cut off for a long period of time. The deployment of equipments for restoring cellphones networks usually requires from several days up to weeks since electricity is often

---

Supported by SolarFarm Project.
[1] Intergovernmental Panel on Climate Change.

F. Krief et al. (Eds.): Nets4Cars/Nets4Trains/Nets4Aircraft 2020, LNCS 12574, pp. 181–193, 2020.
https://doi.org/10.1007/978-3-030-66030-7_16

missing as well as safe infrastructures (roads) for moving to the right places and because first aid teams have logically the priority for accessing the damaged zones.

If the conditions during such meteorological events are not favorable to the deployment of medium sizes drones, usually after some hours such machines can safely fly in the sky above the concerned areas. In addition, after a first overview of the region, the damaged zones are usually identified and geographically bounded (GPS points for instance).

In most works dealing with communication networks recovery using drones, the primary goal of the temporary network is to support rescue teams. However, as reported by testimonies of people living these catastrophes, communicating as soon as possible with their relatives is one of their priorities. One possibility for offering people living in these areas a way of communicating with people living outside consists in building a temporary and infrastructureless network able to relay messages between these two populations. The connectivity constraint of such a network may be relaxed since the communication between people located inside and outside the damaged area can be intermittent (like sms). Moreover, as energy consumption for hovering or for moving have same magnitude, moving drones scenarios can be considered as alternative solutions to a full-time connected network.

The network considered in this work is composed of a ground station, acting as a gateway with cellular phone networks still up, and drones able to communicate with each other, with the gateway and with people. As a first attempt to address this problem we consider that drones are randomly distributed over the area. The main goal of this preliminary work is to determine the impact of some swarm's characteristics on messages delivery and area coverage. The number of uavs, communication range (people-drone and drone-drone) and drones' moving behavior are discussed and simulations results are analyzed.

2   Related Works

The problem of communication networks recovery in case of disaster have received much attention these last decades [3,6], and many works have also been dedicated to the possibility of building ad hoc networks using drones [1].

In order to obtain a clear view of the disaster area, [5] propose to build a network of camera embedded by drones. The goal of the work consists in computing the best position of the drones such as to maintain the connectivity of the communication network while ensuring a correct coverage of the area. For solving the problem the author model it as an ILP problem for which a solution is computed offline. Unlike this centralized approach, Maza and his colleagues propose a real-time solution for deploying UAVs and sensors for disaster management. However, the focus is mainly on task allocation and cooperation between drones rather than communications problems that are not explicitly taken into account [4]. More recently, in [7] the proposed solution brings into play two types of drones. Rescue drones, performing tasks directly related to the actions of the rescue teams, and relay drones for maintaining the connectivity between rescue drones and a gateway located outside of the damaged area. The problem addressed is the minimization of the number of relay drones for guaranteeing the connectivity of the network composed by the gateway and the rescue drones.

3   Problem, Model and Algorithm

The problem can be expressed as the deployment of a swarm of drones within an area defined by a set of GPS positions. Without loss of generality we consider a square area of dimensions $L \times L$ with the gateway located at one corner.

The swarm has to self-organize such that messages can be sent from people-to-drone and routed from drone-to-drone and from drone-to-gateway to be delivered outside of the area. Conversely, incoming messages should be routed from the gateway to people. Technical issues at the level of the gateway are out of the scope of this work and will not be discussed further as well as technologies used for drone-to-drone and drone-to-gateway communications. We only assume that drone-to-drone and drone-to-gateway communication range is equal to r_{d2d}. It is supposed that each drone can serve as an access point to which people can connect to. Communication range to and from these access points is equal to r_{d2p}. People are supposed to be uniformly and randomly distributed over the area and their number is equal to $m = \delta \times L \times L$ where δ is the density of people in the considered region.

The general algorithm executed by every drone is reported in Algorithm 1. In a first phase, each drone starts by an initialization phase: gets the limits of the area, its initial position, a destination in the area, and a set of waypoints or a shape defining the mobility pattern. Note that apart from the limits of the area, the destination can be randomly chosen as well as the waypoints or the mobility pattern. It then takes off and moves toward this point. Once arrived, it starts the access point. The UAV then iterates on three tasks: (i) accept connections from people (ii) manage messages and (iii) move according to the chosen mobility pattern and get its current position while moving.

Messages are managed by different tasks processed simultaneously by each drone D:

1. reception of messages sent by people connected to D,
2. emission of a message containing D's position to neighbors drones,
3. reception of people's messages routed by neighbor drones
4. routing of people's messages to neighbors closer to the gateway than D, or directly to the gateway if such a connection exists.

When a drone reaches its position and starts an access point. People in the communication range of this drone establish a connection with the access point. Messages are then emitted from them to the drone. In the same time, using another communication channel, drones emit some messages containing their initial position (dest) to their neighbors. Note that, since drones are moving, the neighborhood of each of them may change all the time. During its movement, a

---

Algorithm 1: Generic Algorithm executed by every drone

---

1 AreaLimits[] ← getAreaLimits()
2 initialPosition ← getPosition()
3 dest ← chooseDest(AreaLimits)
4 pattern ← getMobilityPattern()
5 takeOff
6 moveTo(dest)
7 openAccessPoint
8 **while** *batteryLevel > critical value* **do**
9 $\quad$ acceptConnections
10 $\quad$ messagesManagement()
11 $\quad$ myPosition ← moveTo(pattern)
12 moveTo(initialPosition)
13 landing

---

drone can route people's messages to another drone if the initial position of this latter is closer to the gateway. Finally, when directly connected to the gateway, a drone delivers all the carried messages.

Remark: we only consider messages going from people to the gateway and not messages coming from the gateway to people. Note however that messages from a person to the gateway can be stamped by both the phone number of the person and the GPS position of the drone to which the person was connected. Thus, when a message, coming from outside, in destination to a given phone number arrives to the gateway, it recovers the GPS position corresponding to the phone number and the mechanism used for outgoing messages can be applied for routing the message to the intended person.

We study first, in Sect. 4.1, the likelihood for the network, formed by the gateway and drones, to be connected, as well as the percentage of people located in the communication range of drones in the case where drones remain at a static position in the air.

In a second part, we consider our solution, defined by two parameters: the number of drones and the mobility pattern. For a set of fixed values of δ, L, r_{d2d} and r_{d2p} we measure the percentage of people connected to the drones and the average delay for their messages to reach the gateway.

4   Simulations and Analysis

In this section we investigate the impact of the mobility on the coverage of people by drones. All simulation were performed using GraphStream[2], a dynamic graphs library [2].

---

[2] graphstream-project.org.

4.1 Without Mobility

First remark that if drones remain at fixed positions, in order to fulfill the requirements (routing messages from people to the gateway), the drones network (including the gateway) has to be connected and all the people have to be connected to a drone. As illustrated by Fig. 1 covering all the people is a big challenge if uavs are randomly distributed over the area.

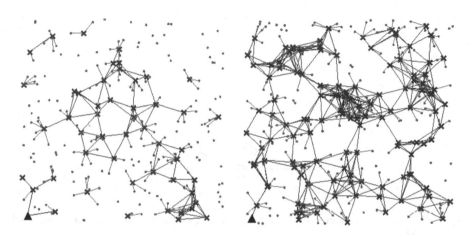

Fig. 1. Two networks obtained for fixed drones' positions, randomly chosen. Parameter values: $r_{p2d} = 80, L = 1000$ and $r_{2d2} = 150$. On the left side $n = 50$ and $n = 120$ on the right side. Crosses are drones, points are people, the antenna is represented by a black triangle at the bottom left corner of the area.

If uavs are randomly distributed over the area, if $S = \frac{\pi r^2}{L^2}$ denotes the surface covered by one drone (with r the communication range and L^2 the surface of the area), then for n drones, the probability of the network to be connected is approximately $e^{-\alpha}$ where $\alpha = n \times e^{n \times S}$.

From Fig. 2 we can argue that if drones are randomly distributed over the area and if the communication range of the drones is approximately one fifth of the size of the damage area, about 200 drones are needed by square kilometer for ensuring the connectivity.

If drones are not randomly distributed over the area (supposed to be a square), if the communication range is r and the length of one side is L, then the minimum number of drones needed for covering the area while maintaining the connectivity of the network is equal to: $(\frac{L}{r} + 1)^2$.

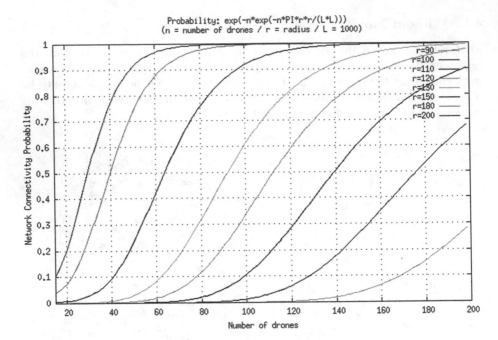

Fig. 2. Network connectivity probability according to the number of drones and their communication range.

Thus for an area of $4\,\text{km}^2$ if the communication range of drones are around $200\,\text{m}$, the number of drones required for that task is 120. Figure 3 represents this minimum number for various values of r, the communication range, and L the size of the area.

In order to reduce the number of drones necessary for answering the initial question, our approach consists in allowing drones to move around their initial position such as to cover a larger area. The direct consequence of this choice is that anytime connectivity can no longer be guaranteed. In the context of this study where only sms-like messages are routed within the network this choice does not prevent message delivery but may entail an additional delay. The next sections attempt to measure the impact of the number of drones and of the mobility on the coverage of the people, the average people to drone connected time and on the delay of messages delivery.

4.2 With Mobility

The mobility pattern considered in this section is a circle. Each drone randomly chooses the center of a virtual circle located at a distance between $r_{d2d}/2$ and r_{d2d}. It may happen that the center of the virtual center is located outside of the area of interest. It then moves along this circle while its battery level is greater than a given critical level. Each person can only connect to one drone at

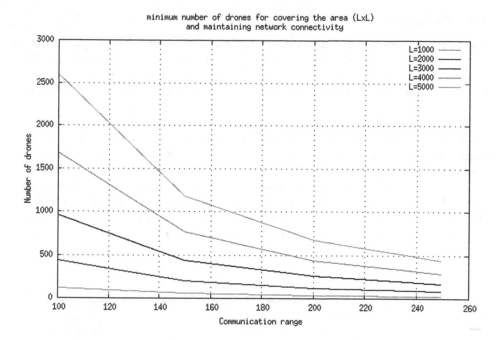

Fig. 3. Minimum number of drones required for maintaining network connectivity and guaranteeing the coverage of the area.

a time. For the simulations we set some parameters: the number of people is set to 200, the area is a square of size 1000 × 1000 and we set the drone-to-drone communication range to $r_{d2d} = 150$. We study the impact of the number of drones and of the people-to-drone communication range (r_{p2d}) on:

- the percentage of people covered by the swarm
- the percentage of time during which people are connected to drones
- the number of messages that successfully reach the gateway
- the average delay for a message to reach the gateway

Note that: (i) each person emits only one message, (ii) no message is lost and (iii) during one time step, a message can cross more than one link between drones.

Each point of the figures in the following sections and paragraphs corresponds to a set of fixed parameters and results from 100 runs.

4.3   Coverage

The coverage does not depend on drone-to-drone communication range, but only on the number of drones, on the distribution of people in the area and on the people-to-drone communication range. Each run is performed with a different random uniform distribution of people in the area. On Fig. 4 simulation results are reported.

The addition of the mobility dramatically decreases the number of required drones for ensuring the connectivity of people with respect to a scenario for which drones hover over a fixed position. If people-to-drone communication range is equal to 150 then as few as 20 drones are enough for covering more than 95% of people. This number should be compared when the drones of the swarm remain at fixed positions in the air. In order to obtain the same coverage value, keeping the same $r_{p2d} = 80$ value, at least 200 drones have to be deployed in the swarm. Note also that with 10 drones and a communication range limited to 50 more than 50% of people are reached.

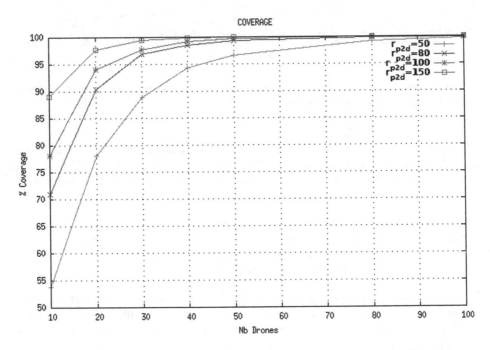

Fig. 4. Percentage of people covered by the swarm according to the number of drones (x axis) and to people-to-drone communication range.

4.4   Connection Time

The second measure focuses on the average people-to-drone connected time. If the solution without mobility ensure a constant connection between any connected person to the network, it is no longer guaranteed when drones are moving. However the average time during which each person can be connected to one drone increases up to more than 80% when using 40 drones with $r_{p2d} = 150$. In comparison with the static scenario (drones hover over a fixed position), using five times less drones (40 instead of 200), can achieve a QoS up to 4/5 of the optimum (permanent connection). In addition, as the mobility pattern is a circle, connections are periodically re-established.

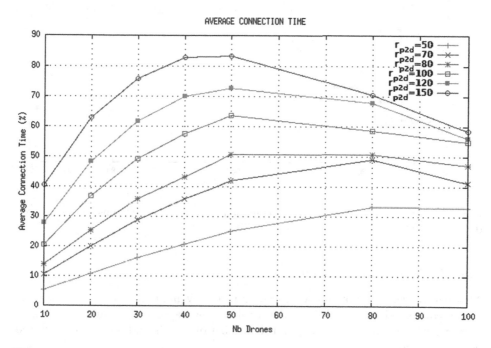

Fig. 5. Percentage of time during which people are connected to drones, according to the number of drones (x axis) and to people-to-drone communication range.

One point is currently not well understood, the average connection time seems to decrease when the number of drones increases. We plot in Fig. 6 the variation of the average connection time for the 100 runs with respect to the number of drones when $r_{p2d} = 150$ (distributions are sorted). The result is quite surprising and we are currently working for explaining this phenomenon.

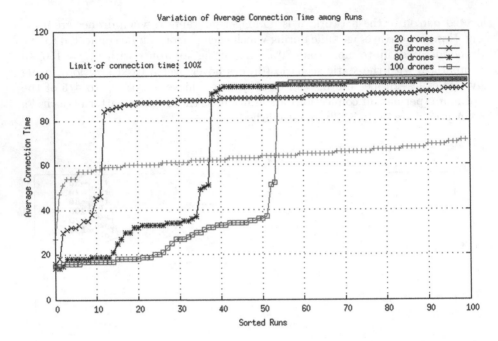

Fig. 6. Distribution of the average connection time for the 100 runs performed for different number of drones and for $r_{p2d} = 150$.

4.5 Delivered Messages and Delay

Message delivery is not always successful, it may happen that the gateway is never connected to any drone. The table below reports the number of times this situation occurs depending on the number of drones and on people-to-drone communication range.

#drones/r_{p2d}	50	70	80	90	100	120	150
10	44	43	36	33	36	38	34
20	16	18	9	18	13	17	11
30	5	4	3	6	4	6	11
40	1	3	3	1	1	2	7
50	0	0	2	0	1	1	1
80	0	0	0	0	0	0	0
100	0	0	0	0	0	0	0

When the gateway is intermittently connected to some drones, some messages are delivered. Figure 7 represents the average number of delivered messages according to the number of drones and people-to-drone communication range.

As illustrated by the graphics, the impact of r_{p2d} is negligible, only the number of drones matters. Additional experiments should be performed in order to measure the impact of r_{d2d} on the same metrics. These results suggest that even if almost all people are connected (20 drones and $r_{p2d} = 150$), the network is not connected and there exist probably several connected components that never connect with each other, a kind of archipelago of isolated groups of connected people.

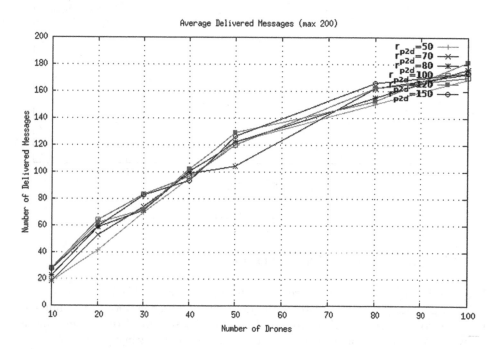

Fig. 7. Number of delivered messages with respect to the number of drones and people-to-drone communication range.

The last proposed measure concerns the delay for routing messages from the source (people) to the gateway. The form of the curve can be explained by relying on connectivity. When the network is poorly connected, even along time, only the messages coming from the people and thus drones which positions are close to the gateway are delivered. For such messages, the delay is short. When the connectivity is better at the network level, more messages are delivered, coming from drones located farther from the gateway, entailing an increase in the delay. But the intermittent connectivity between groups entails also some delays which are partially removed when the number of drones increases. This last point explains the decrease of the value of the average delay when the number of drones increases.

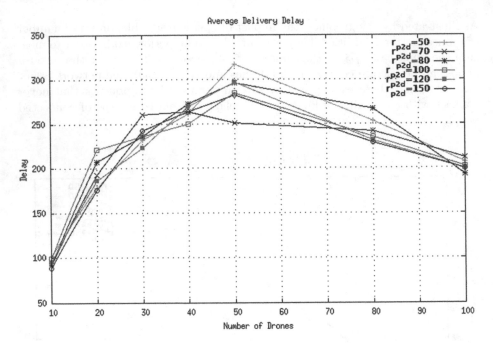

Fig. 8. Average delivery delay of messages.

5   Conclusion and Perspectives

When a disaster occurs in some regions with limited access, like mountains, deep valleys, or poorly connected areas, the deployment of a temporary communication network composed of a ground station and a swarm of drones may be a relevant solution for offering people a way of communicating with their relatives. However, covering the whole damaged area may require a large number of drones. We have shown that if we allow drones to move over this area instead of hovering over a fixed position, the required UAVs number is much smaller. But this economy comes at the cost of intermittent communications, preventing people to use real time streaming applications.

The solution envisioned relies on a randomly distribution of drones over the area. While this distribution is not optimized it gives some ideas for covering an unknown area with a restricted number of UAVs. One weakness of such a distribution is that in some cases, the gateway is never connected to any drone and thus no message is delivered.

The solution may be improved in many ways and deserves further investigations. The first point that could be improved is the choice of a random location in the area as the initial drones' positions. We may envisioned a new version in which drones are communicating with each other in order to avoid closeness or too large distances. But this can only be done during the first phase of the deployment, not studied in this work, when drones are moving from the ground station to their assigned position, since their number is too small for ensuring the connectivity of the network once in place.

The second point refers to the balance between the number of drones and the average people-to-drone connected time or the percentage of connected people (for a given value of r_{p2d}). This problem deserves a further study when the mobility pattern is a parameter. Some questions can be raised about the performances of different mobility patterns, in terms of average connected time, elapsed time between two connections, percentage of people connected, or message delivery delays.

References

1. Bekmezci, İ., Sahingoz, O.K., Temel, Ş.: Flying ad-hoc networks (FANETs): a survey. Ad Hoc Netw. **11**(3), 1254–1270 (2013). https://doi.org/10.1016/j.adhoc.2012.12.004
2. Dutot, A., Guinand, F., Olivier, D., Pigné, Y.: GraphStream: a tool for bridging the gap between complex systems and dynamic graphs. In: Alaoui, A., Bertelle, C. (eds.) Proceedings of Emergent Properties in Natural and Artificial Complex Systems. Satellite Conference within the 4th European Conference on Complex Systems (ECCS 2007), 4–5 October 2007, Dresden, Germany, pp. 63–72 (2007)
3. Franzolini, J., Guinand, F., Olivier, D.: Mobile ad hoc network designed to communicate during crisis. In: Report EUR 26719 EN - Proceedings of the 43rd ESReDA Seminar: Land use Planning and Risk-Informed Decision Making. 22–23 October 2014, Rouen (France), pp. 387–402 (2014)
4. Maza, I., Caballero, F., Capitán, J., de Dios, J.R.M., Ollero, A.: Experimental results in multi-UAV coordination for disaster management and civil security applications. J. Intell. Robot. Syst. **61**(1–4), 563–585 (2010). https://doi.org/10.1007/s10846-010-9497-5
5. Quaritsch, M., Kruggl, K., Wischounig-Strucl, D., Bhattacharya, S., Shah, M., Rinner, B.: Networked UAVs as aerial sensor network for disaster management applications. e & i Elektrotechnik und Informationstechnik **127**(3), 56–63 (2010). https://doi.org/10.1007/s00502-010-0717-2
6. Reina, D.G., Askalani, M., Toral, S.L., Barrero, F., Asimakopoulou, E., Bessis, N.: A survey on multihop ad hoc networks for disaster response scenarios. Int. J. Distrib. Sens. Netw. **2015**, 1–16 (2015). https://doi.org/10.1155/2015/647037
7. Yang, T., Foh, C.H., Heliot, F., Leow, C.Y., Chatzimisios, P.: Self-organization drone-based unmanned aerial vehicles (UAV) networks. In: ICC 2019–2019 IEEE International Conference on Communications (ICC). IEEE (2019). https://doi.org/10.1109/icc.2019.8761876

Remote ID and Vehicle-to-Vehicle Communications for Unmanned Aircraft System Traffic Management

Ethan Murrell, Zach Walker, Eric King, and Kamesh Namuduri$^{(\boxtimes)}$

University of North Texas, Denton, TX, USA
Kamesh.namuduri@unt.edu

Abstract. This article presents the results of experiments on vehicle-to-vehicle (V2V) communications between two Unmanned Aircraft Systems (UASs) and a ground control station conducted in conjunction with UAS Traffic Management (UTM) Technology Capability Level Four (TCL-4) flight tests. For V2V implementation, two UASs were equipped with Dedicated Short-Range Communication (DSRC) radios and experiments were conducted to assess the functionality, capabilities, and limitations of DSRC-based V2V communications. Remote ID is implemented using Globally Unique Flight Identifier (GUFI) assigned to each UAS by the UAS Service Supplier (USS). This article also summarizes the critical issues and recommendations to address them.

Keywords: Vehicle-to-vehicle communications · Unmanned Aircraft Systems · Remote indetifiation

1 Introduction and Concepts

A V2V communication system provides a direct means of communication between two aircraft and more generally among multiple aircraft. If every vehicle is equipped with a radio, then V2V communications can be extended to create an ad hoc network with UASs as nodes. In general, V2V communications is useful for real-time information sharing among the aircraft. In the context of UTM, there are two primary benefits of V2V communications: 1) Collision Avoidance or Deconfliction between UASs and 2) Beyond Radio Line of Sight (BRLoS) communications between any pair of UASs. In order for implementation, each aircraft first needs to be identifiable with a unique ID and a unique IP address. Standards for Remote ID were recently published by ASTM International (formerly known as American Society for Testing and Materials) and Federal Aviation Administration (FAA). Remote ID is the ability of a UAS in flight to provide identification information that can be received by other parties [1]. As the Remote ID specification matures, it serves as the primary means of identification of a UAS in flight. During the TCL-4 flight tests, GUFI assigned to each UAS by the USS was used as Remote ID.

© Springer Nature Switzerland AG 2020
F. Krief et al. (Eds.): Nets4Cars/Nets4Trains/Nets4Aircraft 2020, LNCS 12574, pp. 194–202, 2020.
https://doi.org/10.1007/978-3-030-66030-7_17

1.1 V2V Communication Strategies

Table 1. General comparison of the three modes of V2V communications

V2V communication strategy	Latency	Area of coverage
SATCOM	Large	Large
Cellular Network	Medium	Medium
Direct air-to-air	Small	Small

Fig. 1. A conceptual view of V2V communications. Options for direct communications between UASs include WiFi and DSRC among others.

V2V communications can be established in three ways: using satellite communications (SATCOM), cellular Networks (using D2D option in 3GPP, for example), or direct air-to-air communications using WiFi or DSRC without any infrastructure support. Each has its own advantages and disadvantages. In general terms, latency for round-trip communications between a UAS and its ground control station (GCS) and area of coverage greatly vary for the three modes of communications (see Table 1). The complementary capabilities of the three methods suggest that one can make use of all three means of V2V communications as backup to one another. For example, the PLANET Terminal, a commercial product from ATMOSPHERE Inc., enables mobile communication on the ground and in the air, using Iridium satellite network and terrestrial cellular networks (LTE) [2] (Fig. 2).

2 Challenges in Establishing Direct V2V Communications Between Aircraft Systems

A direct approach to V2V communications (as depicted in Fig. 1) without any supporting infrastructure is attractive because of the minimal latency it offers compared to the other

Fig. 2. Matrice equipped with a DSRC radio from Unex, Raspberry PI, and a GPS unit. The radio was affixed to the bottom of the aircraft's frame.

two options. However, it also comes with a big challenge: the impact of high mobility. While high mobility impacts Cellular- and Satellite-based V2V communication also, they are easier to address with the supporting infrastructure. The impact of mobility on direct V2V communication is significant and it includes (1) Doppler shift at physical-layer level and (2) frequent loss of connectivity at network-layer level. In order to address these challenges, there is a need for developing accurate air-to-air (A2A) channel models. Although there are few theoretical A2A models available in the literature, there is a need for experimentally validated models under different settings such as urban and suburban as well as under various environmental conditions [7, 8]. The Doppler shift on A2A communication is large as opposed to terrestrial V2V communications due to high mobility and becomes even larger when mmWave carrier frequencies are used. Further, a simple rotation of the aircraft might affect the LoS between the transmitter and receiver causing loss of connection. Unless these issues are addressed, it is difficult to rely solely on direct means of V2V communications without any supporting infrastructure. Although, V2V communication strategies were proposed using WiFi and D2D option within 3GPP, they haven't been rigorously evaluated under adverse conditions such as high mobility. Further, none of the V2V communication strategies have been tested for scalability. Current literature consists of results from isolated experiments with limited number (often with just two or three) UASs under free-space conditions. Thus, even today, V2V communication remains as an open problem for fundamental research and development, particularly in topics such as A2A channel models.

2.1 Our Contributions

The contributions of this paper are primarily experimental. The novelty is in terms of setting the context, feasibility study, and identifying the challenges surrounding direct V2V communications. The flight tests were conducted in downtown Corpus Christi, Texas. DSRC radios, typically used for automobiles, were used to design the V2V communication system. These radios were equipped with omni-directional antennas. The UASs were flown in the suburban setting consisting of buildings typically present in any downtown area. Experiments were conducted multiple times in order to test the feasibility of direct V2V communications. A simple V2V communication protocol for information sharing is designed. The protocol makes use of Remote ID implemented in its basic form. Visualization plots showcase the experimental results. General conclusions derived from experimental observations are summarized. While this paper didn't address the theoretical aspects discussed in the previous section, the results presented here highlight these challenges in V2V communications for UASs when tested in real world context.

3 Direct V2V Communication System Design

Messages shared between two UASs primarily include UAS identification, telemetry information including current Global Positioning System (GPS) coordinates, heading, acceleration, distress status, at the very least. Sharing telemetry information between aircraft allows for implementation of collision avoidance strategies in the airspace. As each UAS receives telemetry information from its neighbors, it can determine potential conflicts that may arise, and avoid such conflicts by implementing established deconfliction strategies. A deconfliction strategy may also consider telemetry and other relevant information received from the other aircraft such as the battery status, distress level (if any) that could affect the aircraft's mobility. A predetermined algorithm would then determine the best course of deconfliction while taking the surrounding environment into account as well, avoiding any additional obstacles that may be present, to allow the aircraft to continue their separate flight plans.

A V2V system should be able to record aircraft interactions to allow for analysis of how deconflictions take place and if there are any anomalies or new problems that need to be addressed. One major concern would be deconfliction with an aircraft that is not equipped with a compatible V2V system, or no V2V system at all. Another use of V2V system would be relaying or forwarding telemetry packets from any UAS that it is currently communicating with to its GCS while the other aircraft is out of range from its GCS or USS. This would allow USS operators to be aware of more vehicles at any given time while they are performing their normal operations.

3.1 Platform and Hardware

The hardware used V2V communications during UTM TCL4 flight testing included a radio, a single board processing unit, and a GPS module. The radio selected for each of the aircraft was the Unex OBU-201U. These are DSRC radios with a frequency band from 5.850–5.925 GHz and +20 dBm power output. The radios can be programmed to function as translators from User Datagram Protocol (UDP) data packets to Wave Short Message (WSM) or vice versa. They will automatically convert and forward any messages received via ethernet to the single board computer equipped on the aircraft. The main advantage of the DSRC radios is the dedicated frequency band for V2V communication that cuts out almost any external interference for the transmitted signal. This would be advantageous for allowing the development of a more robust communication system. The radios are also originally used for V2V and vehicle to infrastructure (V2X) communication in automobiles, meaning that they are already built to withstand the high and low temperatures that an aircraft equipped with a V2V system would be operating in.

The single-board computer selected was the Raspberry Pi 3B+ (Pi) [3], which comes preloaded with an operating system that includes the Python programming language and common libraries along with other basic programs. The Pi handles all computational tasks required by the V2V system utilizing a Quad-core 64-bit processor form arm that has been clocked at a speed of 1.4 GHz and communicates to the DSRC radio via an ethernet connection at speeds up to 300 Mbps, all contained in a footprint of 3.370 in. × 2.224 in. The included HDMI input port and four USB ports allowed for direct monitoring of the system and to make any necessary changes quickly [4]. The PI also includes WiFi capabilities, allowing for additional Python modules to be added as they were needed throughout the software development process. All telemetry information would ideally be pulled directly from the flight controller for the aircraft. The flight controllers used for the Tarot aircraft used in the TCL4 testing were the Pixhawk Cubes that provide two standard telemetry output ports along with other ports that can be configured to different functions such as GPS or telemetry. The flexibility of the Raspberry Pi 3B+ allowed a connection to be made directly with the flight controller via serial communication connecting to the Pi using some of the general-purpose input/output (GPIO) pins. The telemetry data pulled from the Pixhawk is easily manipulated utilizing a specific library for pulling the data that is available for Python. However, integration with the Pixhawk did not occur due to restrictions imposed on aircraft integration by the TCL4 project management. Specifically, any external interfaces to the controller are not recommended during TCL4. Instead, an additional parasite GPS module was used as a workaround. The advantage of using this module includes the ability to simulate navigation loss to trigger a distress status without aircraft performing the test flights without GPS. We were also able to set the time on the Pi based on the data received from the GPS module, ensuring that both aircraft had synced timestamps.

3.2 Software

A Raspberry Pi is used to run a Python script on both vehicles to coordinate communication between the radio as well as to obtain telemetry information from the GPS module. The script establishes a server-client interaction with the Pi and the radio. Python is a robust, high-level programming language that focuses on being readable and boasts a large library of modules that can be downloaded to achieve almost any task required of programmers. Its many libraries include detailed documentation that facilitated quick integration and implementation of new protocols within a code, which was very helpful for developing the script used to pull telemetry from the aircraft and communicate to the neighboring aircraft.

A middleware called uCoupler was used as the interface between DSRC radio and Raspberry Pi. This script was provided as part of the software development kit when the radios were purchased and enables the radios to act as a message forwarder. This means that any message received by the radio, either from the Pi or another radio, is automatically forwarded the opposite way. The uCoupler script translates the UDP packet containing all the telemetry data from the Pi into a wave short message (WSM) packet to transmit to the other radios. When a radio receives the WSM packet, it translates it back to UDP format and forwards it to the Pi. The uCoupler script requires the IP address for the Pi's ethernet port to be statically defined at the start of the python script. It forwards the received WSM messages to a specific IP address. This enables the communication link via the ethernet connection from the Pi to the DSRC radio.

The method used for interfacing with the Pixhawk involves pulling telemetry data off the Pixhawk 4 (PX4) flight controller. The PX4 takes in the information provided by the sensors and can be configured to send and receive information through MAVLink. MAVLink is a messaging protocol used for communicating with drones and their onboard components. The RPI interfaces with the PX4 through the UART (Universal Asynchronous Receiver/Transmitter) communication ports which are then used to send requests to pull information from the PX4. Dronekit was chosen so that their application programming interface (API) that interacts with MAVLink could be used. Dronekit provides access to a vehicle's telemetry data and enables mission management commands that allow for autonomous input [5]. A few drawbacks inherent to Dronekit are that the API is still under development so the program does not utilize the full functionality of MAVLink and the API currently supports Python 2.7. For access to more customization and control integrating with the MAVLink proxy is recommended. This would also allow us to pull time from the PX4, rather than setting it based on the external GPS module.

3.3 Integration with Aircraft

The integration with the aircraft only required few small modifications. The radio was affixed to the bottom of the aircraft's frame, below the batteries. This was similar to how NASA had integrated the radio to their Tarot aircraft [9]. This configuration provided the best LoS to the ground station while also avoiding any interference from the rotors of the aircraft and from the other modules installed on the top side of the frame. The Raspberry Pi 3B+ was installed on the top side of the aircraft without taking space from any other module due to its small footprint. The ethernet connection was fed through the frame along with the power distribution cord. Power for both the board and Pi were pulled directly from the aircraft's batteries, converting the DC voltage to 12 V AC for the radio and 5 V AC for the Pi.

```
msg = {
        "vehicle":source,
        "Lat": Lat,
        "Lon": Lon,
        "alt": alt,
        "time":"{}".format(now),
        "Distress": status,
        "sentCount":sentCount,
        "source":source
        }
```

Fig. 3. V2V message format

3.4 Message Structure

The message structure remains consistent throughout the operation of the aircraft with the values for each transmitted packet updated prior to being forwarded to the DSRC radio from the Pi. Figure 3 shows the V2V message format for each packet sent. The 'vehicle' and 'source' fields are the same when the packet is sent from the originating aircraft, however each aircraft will automatically forward any packet that it receives to account for any instance that an aircraft within its range is out of range of the GCS. The GCS Pi then compares the 'vehicle' and 'source' fields to determine if the message has been forwarded and uses the 'sentCount' to check if the packet contains to most recent telemetry data and logs the information as necessary. Timestamp for each packet is pulled from the Pi itself, and then run through a simple script to format the data according to specifications from NASA. Our 'Distress' value is currently based solely on the GPS signal. Loss of GPS, simulated or actual, will result in the value being changed. The GPS information ('Lon' for longitude, 'Lat' for latitude, and 'alt' for altitude) is queried every time a packet is constructed. If the 'Distress' value is currently true but the query receives good data, the 'Distress' value is reset, and the incident is logged separately.

4 Experiments and Results

The testing consisted of five different scenarios. Each scenario was tested under different urban conditions. In these experiments, the takeoff and landing zones and locations varied along with the distance. When the drones were within the effective range of the DSRC radios V2V communication took place with high throughput. Our results show that the packet ratio had a high variance due to differences in each scenario testing environment like the takeoff/landing zone, LoS, etc. Time delay presented itself as a new issue with the new configuration change. The GPS module does not pull the accurate time down to the second and is not a robust way to input system time. As a result, one system will lag up to 1 s behind and skew the time delay. A real-time clock module will allow a more accurate track of time upon an initial synchronization.

The plots shown in Fig. 4 and Fig. 5 provide a visual representation of the GPS data collected by each aircraft from other aircraft equipped with a V2V system when in range. The gaps in the flight paths indicate the areas where the aircraft were out of communication range from each other during the given scenario.

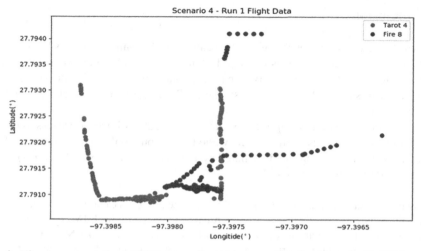

Fig. 4. Visual representation of GPS data collected by two aircraft equipped with V2V system

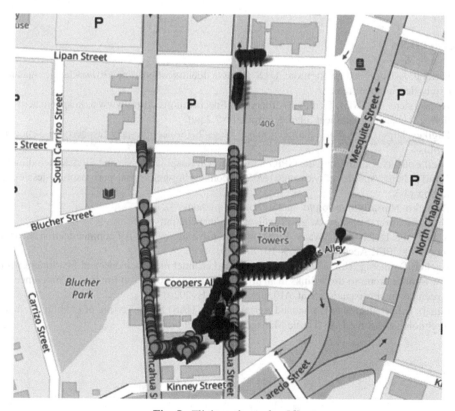

Fig. 5. Flight path overlay [6]

5 Conclusions

This article presented the results of experiments on V2V communications between two UASs and GCS. Each UAS was equipped with a DSRC radio and experiments were conducted to assess the functionality, capabilities, and limitations of DSRC-based V2V communication system. Results suggest that DSRC radio is a viable choice for V2V communications.

Due to time constraints imposed by the project, data collection process was very limited and measurements such as latency and throughput couldn't be completed. Synchronization of time among the distributed systems (for e.g. between GPS units) posed a challenge during data analysis.

Acknowledgements. The authors thank NASA and Lone Star UAS Centre of Excellence, Texas A&M University for providing with an opportunity to engage in the UTM TCL-4 flight test operations. Kamesh Namuduri is a Professor of Electrical Engineering at UNT. Ethan Murrell, Zach Walker, and Eric King are currently pursuing graduate studies in the Department of Electrical Engineering at UNT.

References

1. Federal Aviation Administration. UAS Remote Identification. https://www.faa.gov/uas/res earch_development/remod/
2. Atmosphere, PLANET Terminal – Technical Specifications. http://www.atmosphere.aero/sta tic/media/uploads/datasheet_planet_terminal_v2.2.pdf
3. Digikey. https://www.digikey.com/en/maker/blogs/2018/meet-the-new-raspberry-pi-3-model-b-plus
4. Spell Foundry, Configuring the GPIO Serial Port On Raspbian Jessie and Stretch Including Pi 3 and 4. https://spellfoundry.com/2016/05/29/configuring-gpio-serial-port-raspbian-jessie-inc luding-pi-3/
5. Dronekit. https://github.com/dronekit/dronekit-python
6. GPS Visualizer. https://www.gpsvisualizer.com/map?output_home
7. Yan, C., Fu, L., Zhang, J., Wang, J.: A comprehensive survey on UAV communication channel modeling. IEEE Access **7**, 107769–107792 (2019)
8. Becker, D., Fiebig, U.-C., Schalk, L.: Wideband channel measurements and first findings for low altitude drone-to-drone links in an urban scenario. In: 2020 14th European Conference on Antennas and Propagation (EuCAP), pp. 1–5. IEEE (2020)
9. Glaab, L.J., et al.: Small Unmanned Aerial System (UAS) Flight Testing of Enabling Vehicle Technologies for the UAS Traffic Management Project (2018)

A Unified Smart Mobility System Integrating Terrestrial, Aerial and Marine Intelligent Vehicles

Chahrazed Ksouri[1,2]([✉]), Imen Jemili[3]([✉]), Mohamed Mosbah[1]([✉]), and Abdelfettah Belghith[4]

[1] Uni Bordeaux, CNRS, Bordeaux INP, LaBRI, UMR 5800, 33400 Talence, France
chahrazedksouri@gmail.com, mohamed.mosbah@labri.fr
[2] National School of Engineers of Sfax, Sfax, Tunisia
[3] Faculty of Sciences of Bizerte, University of Carthage, Tunis, Tunisia
imen.jmili@fsb-u.carthage.tn
[4] College of Computer and Information Sciences, King Saud University, Riyadh, Saudi Arabia
abelghith@ksu.edu.sa

Abstract. Smart City is a new concept that relies on digital technologies in order to interact more effectively with its citizens, create new business opportunities and reduce operational costs and resource consumption, while respecting environmental factors and sustainability objectives. Transport of goods and people is at the heart of Smart City activities and influences all other aspects, including economy, tourism, health care, and so on. Great progress has been made in this area, which has led to the emergence of the Smart Mobility concept. However, the current vision of this concept does not adequately reflect the status of the advances perceived by the transportation field. In fact, it is limited only to the on road transportation. Moreover, as the concept of Mobility as a Service (MaaS) is becoming more and more important, a common management of all the means of transportation is required. In this paper, we propose a more general vision of the Smart Mobility ecosystem, while specifying standardization bodies for cellular communication technologies for each domain and the directions of future research work towards a consistent deployment of such a wider vision. In future Smart Cities, a multi-modal service of mobility may combine not only classical means of road transportation, such as cars, bikes, buses, but also air transportation means like drones or marine transportation systems. Based on current technologies and standards, we present in this work a comparison between these technologies and discuss the main issues and challenges to have a unified integrated Smart Mobility system.

Keywords: Smart Mobility · IoV · ITS · VANETs · UAVs · UAM · FANETs · UMVs · SANETs · C-V2X · 5G

© Springer Nature Switzerland AG 2020
F. Krief et al. (Eds.): Nets4Cars/Nets4Trains/Nets4Aircraft 2020, LNCS 12574, pp. 203–214, 2020.
https://doi.org/10.1007/978-3-030-66030-7_18

1   Introduction

Advances in fields such as Information and Communication Technologies (ICT), automation and artificial intelligence have powered major technological revolutions in the transportation domain such as the invention of electric vehicles [1], autonomous cars [2], connected vehicles [3], unmanned aerial [4] and marine [5] vehicles, etc.

Being responsible for a quarter of global CO2 emissions [6] and 10% of the accident ratio mortality in the world [7], not to mention the problems associated with frequent traffic jams, the transportation field leads to economic, human and environmental losses. The ultimate goal is to make this filed more safe and sustainable, while providing users with comfort and advertising services. The convergence of smart solutions brought in the different transport sectors has led to the emergence of Smart Mobility (SM) concept. In the literature, SM is described as being the combination of smart technologies with mobility solutions, resulting in smart governance for sustainable, technology-driven and citizen-oriented mobility [8]. Actually, intelligent Transportation Systems (ITS) and, more recently, Internet of Vehicles (IoV) have attracted a lot of attention from academic and industrial research as building blocks of the Smart Mobility ecosystem. ITS are described as being the incorporation of information and communications technology into transport infrastructures and vehicles [9], while IoV results from the integration of Vehicular Ad-Hoc Networks (VANETs), a terrestrial networking paradigm, with Internet connection, in order to enable vehicles to exchange information with their surrounds (vehicles, roads, human and sensor) [10–12]. In the literature, studies and researches focus mainly on the terrestrial domain. Therefore, the vehicular environment is restricted only to the terrestrial domain, especially cars as well as other transport modes such bus and train, and the current SM vision only involves terrestrial urban mobility. In fact, Car-to-Everything communications are the most developed ones. Nonetheless, the European Telecommunications Standards Institute (ETSI) specified that the deployment of the ITS and the provision of corresponding services are not limited to the road transport sector only, but includes other domains such as railways, aviation and maritime as well [9]. With the continuous proliferation of applications and services related to aerial and marine vehicles, their integration into mobility solutions is more than necessary and consolidating the cooperation between them is mandatory. Whereof, to foster the development of more innovative, sustainable, safe and green mobility solutions, a SM ecosystem that includes all vehicles types and promote their cooperation, is required. The main contributions of this document are:

- We propose a broader vision of Smart Mobility (ITS and IoV), in line with recent technological advances, while specifying the different mobility domains; namely terrestrial, aerial and marin.
- We specify for the different mobility domains the corresponding initiatives towards cellular based ecosystem.
- We discuss open research issues and future trends relative to the new vision of Smart Mobility.

The rest of the paper is structured as follows. Section 2 explicitly describes our vision of Smart Mobility ecosystem. We present, in Sect. 3, the cellular communication technologies standardization bodies for the different Smart Mobility domains. Then, an insight on open research issues that need to be addressed to enable the achievement of the envisioned SM ecosystem is carried out in Sect. 4. Finally, we conclude the paper in Sect. 5.

2   Smart Mobility

Heretofore, Smart Mobility is perceived as a concept that integrates pervasive intelligence with transportation solutions in order to offer a safer and more efficient on road traffic. However, ITS and IoV concepts, hence Smart Mobility, should not be restricted to the terrestrial domain.

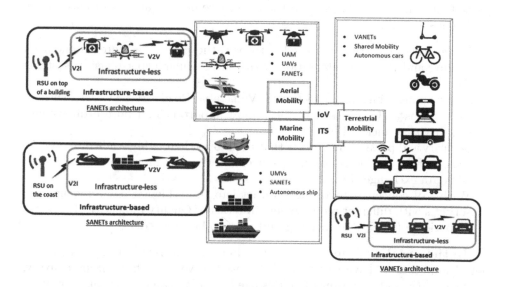

Fig. 1. Smart Mobility ecosystem

For example, transport accidents are not limited to road and highway but affect all transport mode. In a city like Venice (Italy) where boats are the main transport mode, equipping them with technologies to avoid collisions would be beneficial to preserve lives. Besides, Urban Aerial Mobility (UAM), a new concept resulting from the emergence and deployment of novel aerial vehicles such as delivery and medical drones, has emerged. One of the main advantages of adopting aerial vehicles solutions is to lighten the road traffic by relaying on in-sky travel. Moreover, enabling cooperation between the vehicles of the different domains offers a more efficient transportation options. As stated in Fig. 1, we propose a Smart Mobility ecosystem that is structured around three domains, namely terrestrial, aerial and marine:

The terrestrial domain includes all means of transport ranging from two-wheeled commuters (electric scooters, bicycles and bikes), bus, cars (ordinary, electrical, connected and autonomous), transport truck to rail. New services such as carpooling and shared mobility (electric scooters and electric and ordinary cars and bicycles) have revolutionized the urban mobility perception, by making available, at a city scale, energy efficient and environmentally friendly transport solutions. Vehicular Ad-Hoc Networks (VANETs) refer to the most important terrestrial networking paradigm, enabling the communication among vehicles and Road Side Units (RSUs) placed along the roads in order to improve road safety and provide travellers comfort [13]. Several communications-related applications, which we refer to by Cooperative-ITS are proposed [14]. For instance, platooning, which describes vehicles on the road with some common interests that can cooperatively form a platoon-based driving pattern, in which a vehicle follows another one and maintains a small and nearly constant distance to the preceding vehicle [15]. Along with the emergence of innovative solutions, major challenges are arising:

- Large scale field trials are needed to pave the path to a more autonomous driving and a better integration with the vehicular cyber-physical systems [16].
- The response time and detection of Vulnerable Road Users (VRUs), such as pedestrians and cyclists, is of the utmost importance for both ordinary and self-driving vehicles [17].
- Security and privacy are aspects that need to be thoroughly studied to prevent from attacks conducted against connected and autonomous cars and to secure the data exchange [18].
- With IoV concept integrating Internet into the vehicular environment, new services with different requirements in terms of Quality of Service (QoS) and Experience (QeE) are emerging and must to be satisfied.

In the aerial domain, in addition to drones commercialization, many urban aerial applications have emerged these past few years such as drone delivery, medical drone and taxi drone; In cities like Dubai, we can even speak about taxi drone stations [19]. In north Latin American countries, Voom, an on-demand helicopter booking platform connecting travellers with air taxi companies, is already operational [20]; it enables travellers to fly over terrestrial traffic quickly and easily. The convergence of this set of innovative transport solutions has led to the emergence of a new concept, Urban Air Mobility (UAM). UAM can contribute significantly to a multi-modal mobility system and help to build more liveable cities [21], we can cite efforts of AirBus [21] to build a sustainable global mobility system by exploiting the airspace to expand existing ground transport network into the sky. In the air sector, the networking paradigm Flying Ad hoc Networks (FANETs) is attracting a lot of attention. In these networks, the communicating nodes are UAVs (Unmanned Aerial Vehicles) [4], which are characterized by low capital cost, fast deployment and large area coverage. To enable urban transport expanding in the sky, more efforts are still needed:

- The integration of UAM solutions with existing urban infrastructure and the study of those required (helipad, taxi drone station) must be investigated to enable UAM operations scaling in cities [22].
- Further researches are needed to define mobility models that depict the movements of autonomous aerial vehicles in a specified area with high 3D mobility [23].
- On the near future the aerial domain of cities will see an overcrowding, then, measures must be taken to insure regulation in the air by establishing traffic laws. In fact, regulations concerning the management of commercial UAV are already developed, while those related to transportation services still in process [24].
- While energy and computational capacity do not represent a major drawback in the terrestrial domain, more researchers must be conducted to solve these problems in the aerial sector [25].

The Marine domain includes many vehicle types: UMVs (Unmanned Marine Vehicles) at the surface and underwater, gondola, cargo ship (ordinary and autonomous), cruise ships. Similar to other domains, the maritime transportation is evolving with the proliferation of the new communication and computational features and many researchers are being conducted to upgrade the maritime industry. For instance, Rolls-Royce is developing unmanned cargo ships that can be remotely controlled by captains using a virtual-reality recreation of a vessel's bridge [26]. SANET, (Ship Adhoc Network) is a networking paradigm that is being considered as a cost efficiently alternative for satellite marine communication [5]. In fact, it enables ship-to-ship direct communications to exchange information, hence reduces the use of expansive satellites. Besides, the deployment of marine Internet, employing cellular links for data transmission from marine user equipment on a ship to a cellular base station [27] and wireless multi-hop network communication for ships with embedded systems [28], is being investigated. With the technological developments in the maritime domain, some challenges are arising:

- In order to bring Internet to the sea, investments must be made to expand the coast infrastructure to ensure a wider coverage area [27, 28].
- The continued unfolding of digitalization of ships must be handled by analyzing current and emerging cybersecurity threats and vulnerabilities [29].
- While the development of autonomous ships is gathering momentum, there are still legitimate concerns about the safety, security and reliability of autonomous ships operation, in addition, the regulatory scoping must be further revised to cover this recently added technology [30].

Terrestrial, aerial and marine inter-urban mobility is fully developed and the underlying sectors namely routes planning, transport logistics, traffic control and legislative are well specified. However, in urban areas only terrestrial and marine (in city such Venice) mobility is defined. In addition to being a transport mode of the future, which will alleviates some of the on road congestion, aerial vehicles have the potential to play a prominent role in the terrestrial mobility. In fact, several work investigate the possibility of monitoring road traffic conditions by UAVs [31] and also UAVs assisting data dissemination in VANETs [32]. As in the terrestrial domain, drones are used in the maritime domain to conduct certain operations such as surveying ships, supervising offshore installations [33] and delivering goods and supplies [34]. Nevertheless, certain aspects must be addressed independently, in fact, the technological challenges and applied legislative are specific to each area. For instance, the signal propagation model on the air and over water surface are not the same. Furthermore, the types of vehicles, communication levels as well as the wireless technologies differ from one field to another.

3   C-V2X Enabling Smart Mobility

Communication technologies, standards and vehicular applications are collectively referred as Vehicle-to-Everything (V2X) communications [35]. These communication models enable the vehicles to interact with each other (vehicle to vehicle), infrastructure (vehicle to infrastructure), vulnerable road users (vehicle to pedestrian), network (vehicle to network) and devices (vehicle to device). Several communication technologies can be deployed in the different domains; (i) Dedicated Short Range Communications (DSRC) and Light Fidelity (LiFi) in the terrestrial domain [36], (ii) zigbee and WiFi in the aerial domain [37], (iii) satellite communication and WiFi in the marine domain [38]. However, none of these technologies can meet the requirements in terms of reliability, effectiveness, robustness and cost-efficiency needed in the different domains. These constraint pave the way to Cellular-V2X (C-V2X), which seems to be the only technology that enables all the aforementioned interactions in the vehicular environment [39]. In addition, it is expected to accommodate the massive growth of the mobile data demand generated by the huge number of connected vehicles [40]. In fact, C-V2X offers a unified connectivity platform for the connected vehicles of the different domains. Cellular communication bypassed the existing infrastructure and enables direct data transfer between the users. It is basically the next generation of machine-to-machine communication where an infrastructureless communication will be offered with significantly lower delay performance and higher throughput and reliability [41]. In this section, we will present the initiatives carried out to enable C-V2X in the different domains, as summarised in Table 1, paving the way to a 5G vehicular ecosystem.

3.1   Terrestrial Domain

Due to the international nature and the large scope of the 5G deployment in the vehicular environment the ETSI automotive community cooperates closely with other international standardization bodies such as 3GPP, IEEE, ITU, 5G-PPP and 5GAA, in order to achieve worldwide internationally and harmonised standards on ITS. ETSI [42] specifies 5G technologies; Network Functions Virtualization (NFV), Multi-access Edge Computing (MEC), Millimetre Wave Transmission (mWT) and Next Generation Protocols (NGP). The 3rd Generation

Table 1. Vehicular communication standardization bodies

Domain	Projects and initiatives
Terrestrial	**ETSI** [42] Network Functions Virtualization (NFV), Multi-access Edge Computing (MEC), Millimetre Wave Transmission (mWT) and Next Generation Protocols (NGP)
	3GPP [43] Radio access network, service and systems aspects, core network and terminals
	UIT [44] IMT-2020: radio regulations, operational aspects, protocols and test specifications; performance, QoS and QoE, security
	IEEE [45] Technical community: providing practical, timely technical and theoretical content, development and deployment of 5G
	5G-PPP [46] 5GCroCo Working groups: infrastructure, architecture
	5GAA [47] Mobility and transportation services: use cases and technical requirements, system architecture, standards and spectrum, business models
Aerial	**3GPP** [48] uplink/downling power control and transmission, channel Modelling, signaling and interference detection
	ETSI [49,50] Specific use cases, spectrum and bandwidth considerations, future Internet protocol suite architecture
	UIT [51] Providing a functional architecture, the service and application support layer, implementing security measures
	IEEE [52,53] Drones Working Group: taxonomy and definitions for consumer drones, requirements, systems, methods, testing and verification, privacy and security
Marine	**3GPP** [54] Study of the feasibility of maritime communication services over 3GPP system
	Korean Register [55] Testbeds and evaluation
	MIO [55] Specifying use cases for maritime communication services

Partnership Project (3GPP) [43] provides the technology specifications: radio access network, service and systems aspects, core network and terminals. Under the International Mobile Telecommunications for 2020 and Beyond (IMT-2020) working group, the International Telecommunication Union (ITU) [44] establishes radio regulations, operational aspects, protocols and test specifications, QoS and QoE requirements and security. The technical community of the Institute of Electrical and Electronics Engineers (IEEE) [45] provides practical, timely technical and theoretical content of 5G development and deployment. 5GCroCo Working groups of the 5G Public Private Partnership (5G-PPP) [46] works on 5G infrastructure and architecture in order to develop innovation at the intersection of automotive and mobile communications sectors. And finally, the

5G Automotive Association (5GAA) [47] is responsible of specifying use cases and technical requirements, system architecture, standards and business models.

3.2   Aerial Domain

Tremendous work are carried out to enable UAVs communication through cellular networks. Several standardization bodies have considered the particular characteristics of UAVs when defining the new specifications. 3GPP works on uplink/downling power control and transmission, channel modelling, signaling and interference detection [48]. The ITU works on providing a functional architecture for UAVs, the service and application support layer, as well as implementing security measures [51]. ETSI works on identifying UAV-specific use cases and specifying required spectrum and bandwidth [49]. Additionally, the specifications of UAV wireless communications have been considered for determining how the future Internet protocol suite architecture should be shaped [50]. IEEE defined the Drones Working Group in 2015, which aims to develop a standard for consumer drones, primarily with the intention of addressing privacy and security concerns. With this purpose, the standard specified; the taxonomy and definitions for consumer drones [52], along with the requirements, systems, methods, testing and verification required to preserve the privacy and security of people and properties within range of the drones [53].

3.3   Marine Domain

Divers 3GPP maritime related work have been conducted these past few years to enable maritime communication services over 5G systems [54]. In 2016, 3GPP approved stage 1 study of the feasibility of maritime communication services over 3GPP systems. 3GPP is working along with IMO (International Maritime Organization) [55] and the Korean Register [56], for the modernization of maritime safety by focusing on Global Maritime Distress and Safety System (GMDSS). Academic work have investigated the use of cellular communications for maritime communications. For instance, the work in [5], presents a study of quality of service provisions for maritime communications based on cellular networks. The authors, in [57], introduced a long-term evolution for maritime (LTE-Maritime), an ongoing research project in South Korea, with the objective of developing a maritime communication infrastructure supporting the data rates in the order of megabits per second within the communication coverage of 100 km. The feasibility of LTE-Maritime was confirmed by implementing a testbed consisting of ships equipped with LTE-Maritime routers, base stations (BSs) along the coast, and an operation center.

4   Open Research Issues and Future Trends

In addition to the specific challenges inherent to each domain separately, the proposed vision of the Smart Mobility will imply a set of new directives at different levels:

- Laws, civil legislative and jurisdictional issues for a holistic framework managing the cooperation and interactions between terrestrial, aviation and maritime operations need to be further explored.
- International and national standardization bodies, consortia and industry have to collaborate in order to provide homogenized platforms, architectures and communications technologies. The specification and the deployment of a V2X fifth generation-based ecosystem still requires considerable work.
- For cost efficient solutions, communication infrastructure must be adapted to enable access to the different vehicles. For instance, at a city scale, the infrastructure related to cellular network should provide services for both terrestrial and aerial vehicles, as illustrated in Fig. 2.
- Physical channel characteristics of land-air-sea communications should be further investigated in order to offer more reliable links with higher bandwidth for QoS-sensitive and safety applications.
- While heterogeneous-based routing protocols enabling the direct exchange of information between terrestrial and aerial vehicles were proposed [58,59], more work is needed to enable aerial-marine multi-hop communications.
- One important challenge is to preserve the confidentiality of sensitive information (e.g. location) of other vehicles and UAVs. An investigation must be conducted to identify new threats resulting from the integration of the domains. Then, security mechanisms such as the encryption algorithm or security modules such as the key management mechanism, the intrusion detection system and the trust management mechanism must be deployed.
- In order to meet specific requirements for stakeholder and end users, large scale field experiments and tests are needed to approve the integration solutions.

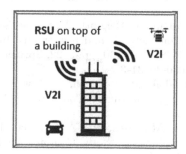

Fig. 2. Smart Mobility shared infrastructure

5   Conclusion

In this work, we proposed a wider vision of Smart Mobility ecosystem taking into account the new advances made in the field of transport. This new proposition structures SM around three domains namely terrestrial, aerial and marine and stresses out the need for a thoroughly cooperation between all transport modes. Then, we specified the different initiatives conducted by international standardization bodies for cellular communications technologies in each domain. Finally, we discuss some of the most significant future research directions for enabling a full integration of land, air and sea transport for a multi-modal mobility. In future work, we would like to investigate Smart Mobility enabling technologies such as SDN (Software Defined Network) and Edge Computing.

References

1. Electric vehicles. https://www.fueleconomy.gov/feg/evtech.shtml. Accessed Sept 2020
2. Autonomous car. https://www.synopsys.com/automotive/what-is-autonomous-car.html. Accessed Sept 2020
3. Connected car. https://connectedcars.dk/. Accessed Sept 2020
4. Bekmezci, I., Sahingoz, O.K., Temel, Ş.: Flying ad-hoc networks (FANETs): a survey. Ad Hoc Netw. **11**(3), 1254–1270 (2013)
5. Xu, Y.: Quality of service provisions for maritime communications based on cellular networks. IEEE Access **5**, 23881–23890 (2017)
6. Trasport pollution. https://www.futura-sciences.com/planete/questions-repon ses/pollution-transport-co2-part-emissions-1017/. Accessed Sept 2020
7. Mortality ratio. https://www.theguardian.com/news/datablog/2012/nov/06/ deaths-mortality-rates-cause-death-2011. Accessed Sept 2020
8. Šemanjski, I., Mandžuka, S., Gautama, S.: Smart mobility. In: 2018 International Symposium ELMAR, pp. 63–66, September 2018
9. ETSI ITS. https://www.etsi.org/images/files/etsitechnologyleaflets/intelligent transportsystems.pdf. Accessed Sept 2020
10. Liu, N.: Internet of vehicles: your next connection. Huawei WinWin **11**, 23–28 (2011)
11. Ksouri, C., Jemili, I., Mosbah, M., Belghith, A.: VANETs routing protocols survey: classifications, optimization methods and new trends. In: Jemili, I., Mosbah, M. (eds.) DiCES-N 2019. CCIS, vol. 1130, pp. 3–22. Springer, Cham (2020). https:// doi.org/10.1007/978-3-030-40131-3_1
12. Ksouri, C., Jemili, I., Mosbah, M., Belghith, A.: Towards general internet of vehicles networking: routing protocols survey. Concurrency Comput. Pract. Exp. e5994 (2020)
13. Al-Sultan, S., Al-Doori, M.M., Al-Bayatti, A.H., Zedan, H.: A comprehensive survey on vehicular ad hoc network. J. Netw. Comput. Appl. **37**, 380–392 (2014)
14. C-ITS. https://www.etsi.org/technologies/automotive-intelligent-transport. Acce ssed Sept 2020
15. Jia, D., Lu, K., Wang, J., Zhang, X., Shen, X.: A survey on platoon-based vehicular cyber-physical systems. IEEE Commun. Surv. Tutorials **18**(1), 263–284 (2016)
16. Jameel, F., Chang, Z., Huang, J., Ristaniemi, T.: Internet of autonomous vehicles: architecture, features, and socio-technological challenges. IEEE Wireless Commun. **26**(4), 21–29 (2019)
17. Anaya, J.J., Merdrignac, P., Shagdar, O., Nashashibi, F., Naranjo, J.E.: Vehicle to pedestrian communications for protection of vulnerable road users. In: 2014 IEEE Intelligent Vehicles Symposium Proceedings, pp. 1037–1042. IEEE (2014)

18. Parkinson, S., Ward, P., Wilson, K., Miller, J.: Cyber threats facing autonomous and connected vehicles: future challenges. IEEE Trans. Intell. Transp. Syst. **18**(11), 2898–2915 (2017)
19. Dubai. https://www.volocopter.com/en/urban-mobility/. Accessed Sept 2020
20. Voom. https://www.airbus.com/innovation/urban-air-mobility/voom.html. Accessed Sept 2020
21. UAM. https://www.airbus.com/innovation/urban-air-mobility.html. Accessed Sept 2020
22. UAM infrastructure. https://www.airbus.com/innovation/urban-air-mobility/infrastructure.html. Accessed Sept 2020
23. Zeng, Y., Wu, Q., Zhang, R.: Accessing from the sky: a tutorial on UAV communications for 5g and beyond. arXiv preprint arXiv:1903.05289 (2019)
24. UAM regulation. https://www.airbus.com/newsroom/stories/urban-air-mobility-the-sky-is-yours.html. Accessed Sept 2020
25. D'Andrea, R.: Guest editorial can drones deliver? IEEE Trans. Autom. Sci. Eng. **11**(3), 647–648 (2014)
26. Rolls-Royce. https://interestingengineering.com/rolls-royce-partners-with-intel-to-build-autonomous-ships. Accessed Sept 2020
27. Kim, Y., Song, Y., Lim, S.H.: Hierarchical maritime radio networks for internet of maritime things. IEEE Access **7**, 54218–54227 (2019)
28. Yau, K.A., Syed, A.R., Hashim, W., Qadir, J., Wu, C., Hassan, N.: Maritime networking: bringing internet to the sea. IEEE Access **7**, 48236–48255 (2019)
29. Cybersecurity. https://eprints.lancs.ac.uk/id/eprint/72696/1/cyber_operations_in_the_maritime_environment_v2.0.pdf. Accessed Sept 2020
30. IMO. http://www.imo.org/en/mediacentre/hottopics/pages/autonomous-shipping.aspx. Accessed Sept 2020
31. Elloumi, M., Dhaou, R., Escrig, B., Idoudi, H., Saidane, L.A.: Monitoring road traffic with a UAV-based system. In: 2018 IEEE Wireless Communications and Networking Conference (WCNC), pp. 1–6, April 2018
32. Zeng, F., Zhang, R., Cheng, X., Yang, L.: UAV-assisted data dissemination scheduling in VANETs. In: 2018 IEEE International Conference on Communications (ICC), pp. 1–6, May 2018
33. Offshore installations. https://www.offshore-mag.com/field-development/article/16755873/role-of-drones-expanding-over-offshore-installations. Accessed Sept 2020
34. Delivering goods. https://www.bairdmaritime.com/work-boat-world/tug-and-salvage-world/harbour-tugs-and-operation/kotug-tests-drones-for-safer-tug-operations. Accessed Sept 2020
35. Muhammad, M., Safdar, G.A.: Survey on existing authentication issues for cellular-assisted V2X communication. Veh. Commun. **12**, 50–65 (2018)
36. Ksouri, C., Jemili, I., Mosbah, M., Belghith, A.: Data gathering for internet of vehicles safety. In: 2018 14th International Wireless Communications & Mobile Computing Conference (IWCMC), pp. 904–909. IEEE (2018)
37. Oubbati, O.S., Atiquzzaman, M., Lorenz, P., Tareque, M.H., Hossain, M.S.: Routing in flying ad hoc networks: survey, constraints, and future challenge perspectives. IEEE Access **7**, 81057–81105 (2019)
38. Du, W., Zhengxin, M., Bai, Y., Shen, C., Chen, B., Zhou, Y.: Integrated wireless networking architecture for maritime communications. In: 2010 11th ACIS International Conference on Software Engineering, Artificial Intelligence, Networking and Parallel/Distributed Computing, pp. 134–138. IEEE (2010)

39. Molina-Masegosa, R., Gozalvez, J.: LTE-V for sidelink 5G V2X vehicular communications: a new 5G technology for short-range vehicle-to-everything communications. IEEE Veh. Technol. Mag. **12**(4), 30–39 (2017)
40. Chiti, F., Fantacci, R., Giuli, D., Paganelli, F., Rigazzi, G.: Communications protocol design for 5G vehicular networks. In: Xiang, W., Zheng, K., Shen, X.S. (eds.) 5G Mobile Communications, pp. 625–649. Springer, Cham (2017). https://doi.org/10.1007/978-3-319-34208-5_23
41. Storck, C.R., Duarte-Figueiredo, F.: A 5G V2X ecosystem providing internet of vehicles. Sensors **19**(3), 550 (2019)
42. ETSI. http://www.etsi.org/technologies-clusters/technologies/5g. Accessed Sept 2020
43. 3GPP. https://www.3gpp.org/release-15. Accessed Sept 2020
44. UIT. https://www.itu.int. Accessed Sept 2020
45. IEEE Future Networks Enabling 5G and Beyond. https://futurenetworks.ieee.org. Accessed Sept 2020
46. 5G-PPP. https://5g-ppp.eu/5gcroco/. Accessed Sept 2020
47. 5G Automotive Association. https://5gaa.org/5g-technology/paving-the-way/. Accessed Sept 2020
48. 3GPP. Technical report 36.777. Technical specification group radio access network; study on enhanced LTE support for aerial vehicles (release 15) (2017)
49. ETSI Technical Report 103 373. Use cases and spectrum considerations for UAS (unmanned aircraft systems), February 2018
50. ETSI Group Specification Next Generation Protocols 001. Next generation protocols (NGP); scenarios definitions (v1.1.1), November 2016
51. ITU-T Work Item Y.UAV.arch. Functional architecture for unmanned aerial vehicles and unmanned aerial vehicle controllers using IMT-2020 networks (2017)
52. IEEE Project P2025.1. Standard for consumer drones: taxonomy and definitions, December 2015
53. IEEE Project P2025.1. Standard for consumer drones: privacy and security, December 2015
54. 3GPP. Maritime communication services over 5G systems, December 2018
55. IMO. http://www.imo.org/fr/pages/default.aspx. Accessed Sept 2020
56. Korean Register. http://www.krs.co.kr/. Accessed Sept 2020
57. Yanli, X.: Quality of service provisions for maritime communications based on cellular networks. IEEE Access **5**, 23881–23890 (2017)
58. Oubbati, O.S., Lakas, A., Lagraa, N., Yagoubi, M.B.: CRUV: connectivity-based traffic density aware routing using UAVs for VANETs. In: 2015 International Conference on Connected Vehicles and Expo (ICCVE), pp. 68–73, October 2015
59. Sharma, V., Kumar, R., Kumar, N.: DPTR: distributed priority tree-based routing protocol for FANETs. Comput. Commun. **122**, 129–151 (2018)

Author Index

Adell, Gemma Morral   137
Adin, Iñigo   157
Ahmed, Toufik   55
Alsaba, Yamen   137
Alvarado, Unai   157
Aniss, Hasnaâ   99
Añorga, Javier   78
Arrizabalaga, Jaione   78
Aymen, Abdallah   39

Badis, Hakim   166
Belghith, Abdelfettah   203
Belmekki, Sabrine   113
Berbineau, Marion   99, 137, 166
Bindel, Sébastien   66
Bourebia, Soumia   66
Boutahala, Ramzi   25

Cassou-Mounat, Jean   3
Chalhoub, Gerard   89
Chukwuka, Ozuem   125
Cormier, Stephane   25

Dayoub, Iyad   137
de Runz, Cyril   25
Drouhin, Frédéric   66

Fernández-Berrueta, Nerea   78
Fouchal, Hacène   25
Freitas, Antonio   89

García-Albertos, Sonsoles   148
George, Laurent   166
Goya, Jon   78
Gruyer, Dominique   113
Guérin, François   181
Guinand, Frédéric   181

Hilt, Benoît   66

Imen, Jemili   39

Jarillo, Julián Martín   148
Jemili, Imen   203

Kambiré, Sidoine Juicielle   99
Karoui, Mouna   89
Khatoun, Rida   3
King, Eric   194
Krief, Francine   99
Ksouri, Chahrazed   203
Kumar, Naveen   125

Labiod, Houda   3
Lacoste, Marc   15
Leblanc, Brice   25
Łubniewski, Pawel   181

Maaloul, Sassi   99
Mamadou Mamadou, Ali   89
Masson, Emilie   137
Mendizabal, Jaizki   157
Molla, Dereje Mechal   166
Monterde, Mario   78
Moreno, Juan   148
Mosbah, Mohamed   39, 55, 203
Moso, Juliet Chebet   25
Moya, Iker   78, 157
Murrell, Ethan   194

Namuduri, Kamesh   194

Puy, Imanol   157

Ramirez, Roberto C.   157
Robert, Eric   137

Sabra, Mabrouk   39
Seetharamdoo, Divitha   125
Sondi, Patrick   113

Tabary, Dorine   66
Tatkeu, Charles   113

Wahl, Martine   113
Walker, Zach   194

Wandeto, John   25
Wonjiga, Amir Teshome   15

Yacheur, Badreddine Yacine   55

Printed in the United States
By Bookmasters